SAINT THOMAS AQUINAS

SUMMA CONTRA GENTILES

BOOK THREE: PROVIDENCE
Part II

University
of
Notre Dame Press
Notre Dame
London

Translated,
with an Introduction
and Notes,
by
VERNON J. BOURKE

Library of Congress Cataloging in Publication Data

Thomas Aquinas, Saint, 1225?-1274.
    Summa contra gentiles.

    Reprint of the ed. published by Hanover House,
Garden City, N.Y., under title: On the truth of
the Catholic faith.
    Includes bibliographies.
    CONTENTS: book 1. God, translated, with an
introd. and notes, by A. C. Pegis. —book 2. Creation, translated, with an introd. and notes, by
J. F. Anderson. [etc.]
    1. Apologetics—Middle Ages, 600-1500. I. Ti-
tle.
[BX1749.T4 1975]   239   75-19883

ISBN 0-268-01675-5
ISBN 0-268-01676-3 pbk.

Contents

Saint Thomas Aquinas

ON THE TRUTH OF THE CATHOLIC FAITH

BOOK THREE: PROVIDENCE

PART II

Chapter 84.

THAT THE CELESTIAL BODIES MAKE NO
IMPRESSION ON OUR INTELLECTS

[1] From the things set forth earlier it is immediately evident that celestial bodies cannot be causes of events which go on in the understanding. Indeed, we have already shown[1] that the order of divine providence requires the lower things to be ruled and moved by the higher ones. But the understanding surpasses all bodies in the order of nature, as is also clear from what we have said before.[2] So, it is impossible for celestial bodies to act directly on the intellect. Therefore, they cannot be the direct cause of things that pertain to understanding.

[2] Again, no body acts except through motion, as is proved in *Physics* VIII.[3] But things that are immovable are not caused by motion, for nothing is caused by the motion of an agent, unless the agent moves a passive subject during the motion. So, things that are utterly apart from motion cannot be caused by the celestial bodies. But things that are in the area of understanding are entirely apart from motion, properly speaking, as is evident from the Philosopher, in *Physics* VII.[4] On the contrary, "through being undisturbed by motions, the soul becomes prudent and knowing," as is stated in the same place. Therefore, it is impossible for celestial bodies to be the direct cause of things that pertain to understanding.

[3] Besides, if nothing is caused by a body unless the body is moved while the motion is going on, it is necessary for

1. See above, ch. 78ff.
2. SCG, II, ch. 49ff.
3. Aristotle, *Physics*, VIII, 6 (259b 7).
4. *Ibid.*, VII, 3 (247b 1).

everything that receives an impression from a body to be moved. Now, nothing is so moved except a body, as is proved in *Physics* VI.[5] So, everything that receives an impression from a body must be a body, or some power of a body. Now, we showed in Book Two[6] that the intellect is neither a body nor a bodily power. Therefore, it is impossible for the celestial bodies directly to make an impression on the intellect.

[4]   Moreover, everything that is moved by another thing is reduced by it from potency to act. But nothing is reduced by a thing from potency to act unless that thing is actual. So, every agent and mover must be in some way actual, in regard to the effects to which the passive and movable subject is in potency. Now, the celestial bodies are not actually intelligible, for they are certain individual, sensible things. And so, since our intellect is not in potency to anything except actual intelligibles, it is impossible for celestial substances directly to act on the intellect.

[5]   Furthermore, the proper operation of a thing depends on its nature, which, in things that are generated, is acquired, along with the proper operation, through the process of generation. This is clear in the case of heavy and light things, which immediately at the end of the process that generates them possess their proper motion unless there be some impediment. Because of this the generating agent is called a mover. So, that which in regard to the beginning of its nature is not subject to the actions of celestial bodies cannot be subject to them in regard to its operation. Now, man's intellectual nature is not caused by any corporeal principles, but is of completely extrinsic origin, as we proved above.[7] Therefore, the operation of the intellect does not come directly under the celestial bodies.

[6]   Again, effects caused by celestial motions are subject to time, which is "the measure of the first celestial mo-

5. *Ibid.*, VI, 4 (234b 10).
6. *SCG*, II, ch. 49ff.
7. *SCG*, II, ch. 86ff.

tion.''[8] And so, events that abstract from time entirely are not subject to celestial motions. But the intellect in its operation does abstract from time, as it does also from place; in fact, it considers the universal which is abstracted from the here and now. Therefore, intellectual operation is not subject to celestial motions.

[7] Besides, nothing acts beyond the capacity of its species. But the act of understanding transcends the species and form of every sort of bodily agent, since every corporeal form is material and individuated, whereas the act of understanding is specified by its object which is universal and immaterial. As a consequence, no body can understand through its corporeal form. Still less, then, can any body cause understanding in another being.

[8] Moreover, a being cannot be subject to its inferiors by the same part whereby it is united to its superiors. But our soul is united to the intellectual substances, which are superior to the celestial bodies in the order of nature, by virtue of the part which is the understanding. In fact, our soul cannot understand unless it receives intellectual light from those substances. Therefore, it is impossible for intellectual operation directly to be subject to the celestial motions.

[9] Furthermore, our confidence in this view will be increased if we consider the statements of the philosophers on the point. As a matter of fact, the ancient natural philosophers, like Democritus, Empedocles, and those of similar persuasion, claimed that understanding does not differ from sense perception, as is evident from *Metaphysics* IV[9] and from Book III of *On the Soul*.[10] And so, the conclusion was made that, since sensation is a bodily power depending on changes in bodies, the same thing is also true of understanding. For this reason, they said that intellectual operation results from the motion of the celestial bodies,

8. Aristotle, *Physics*, IV, 4 (223b 17).
9. Aristotle, *Metaphysics*, IV, 5 (1009b 13).
10. Aristotle, *De anima*, III, 3 (427a 21).

because change in lower bodies results from change in the higher bodies. According to a passage in Homer: "So understanding in gods and in earthly men is like the daylight which the father of men and gods brings down";[11] the reference is to the sun, or, better, to Jupiter, whom they called the highest god, understanding him to be the whole heavens, as is clear from Augustine in his *City of God*.[12]

[10]   Next came the opinion of the Stoics, who said that intellectual knowledge is caused by the fact that the images of bodies are impressed on our minds, as a sort of mirror or as a page receives the letters imprinted on it without its doing anything; as Boethius reports in Book v of the *Consolation*.[13] According to their view, it followed that intellectual notions are impressed on us chiefly by an impression from the celestial bodies. Hence, the Stoics were the ones who especially asserted that the life of man is directed by a fatal necessity.

However, this theory appeared false, as time went on, as Boethius says in the same place, for the understanding combines and separates, compares the highest things with the lowest, and knows universals and simple forms that are not found in bodies. So, it is obvious that the understanding is not simply receptive of bodily images, but has a power higher than bodies, since external sensation which is only receptive of bodily images does not encompass the actions mentioned above.

[11]   Now, all the philosophers who followed distinguished understanding from sense perception and attributed the cause of our knowledge not to bodies, but to immaterial things. Thus, Plato claimed that the cause of our knowledge is the *Ideal Forms*; while Aristotle said that it is the *agent intellect*.

[12]   From all these views we may gather that the assertion that the celestial bodies are the cause of our act of

11. Homer, *Odyssey*, XVIII, 136ff.
12. See St. Augustine, *De civitate Dei*, IV, 11 (PL, 41, col. 121).
13. Boethius, *De consolatione philosophiae*, V, verse 4 (PL, 63, col. 850).

understanding is a consequence of the opinion of those who claimed that understanding does not differ from sensation, as is clear from Aristotle in his book *On the Soul*.[14] Now, it has been shown that this opinion is false. So, it is also obvious that the opinion which asserts that celestial bodies are directly the cause of our act of understanding is false.

[13] Hence, Sacred Scripture also ascribes the cause of our understanding, not to any body but to God: "Where is God, Who made me, Who hath given songs in the night; Who teacheth us more than the beasts of the earth, and instructeth us more than the fowls of the air?" (Job 35:10–11). Again, in the Psalm (93:10): "He that teacheth man knowledge."

[14] However, we should note that, though celestial bodies cannot be directly the causes of our understanding, they may do something indirectly in regard to it. For, although the understanding is not a corporeal power, the operation of understanding cannot be accomplished in us without the operation of corporeal powers: that is, the imagination, the power of memory, and the cogitative power, as is evident from preceding explanations.[15] And as a result, if the operations of these powers are blocked by some indisposition of the body, the operation of the intellect is impeded, as is evident in demented and sleeping persons, and in others similarly affected. And that is why even the good disposition of the human body makes one able to understand well, for, as a result of this, the aforesaid powers are in a stronger condition. Thus it is stated in Book II of *On the Soul*[16] that we observe that "men with soft flesh are well endowed mentally."

Now, the condition of the human body does come under the influence of celestial motions. In fact, Augustine says, in the *City of God* v, that "it is not utterly absurd to say that certain influences of the stars are able to produce dif-

14. Aristotle, *De anima, loc. cit.*
15. *SCG*, II, ch. 68.
16. Aristotle, *De anima*, II, 9 (421a 26).

ferences in bodies only."[17] And Damascene says, in Book II, that "different planets establish in us diverse temperaments, habits and dispositions."[18] So, the celestial bodies work indirectly on the good condition of understanding. Thus, just as physicians may judge the goodness of an intellect from the condition of its body, as from a proximate disposition, so also may an astronomer judge from the celestial motions, as the remote cause of such dispositions. In this way, then, it is possible that there is some truth in what Ptolemy says in his Centiloquium: "When, at the time of a man's birth, Mercury is in conjunction with Saturn and is itself in a strong condition, it gives inwardly to things the goodness of understanding."[19]

Chapter 85.

THAT THE CELESTIAL BODIES ARE NOT THE CAUSES OF OUR ACTS OF WILL AND CHOICE

[1]   It further appears from this that the celestial bodies are not the causes of our acts of will or of our choices.

[2]   Indeed, the will belongs in the intellectual part of the soul, as is evident from the Philosopher in Book III of On the Soul.[1] So, if celestial bodies cannot directly make an impression on our intellect, as we showed,[2] then neither will they be able to make an impression directly on the will.

[3]   Again, every choice and act of will is caused immediately in us from an intelligible apprehension, for the intellectual good is the object of the will, as is clear from

17. St. Augustine, De civitate Dei, V, 6 (PL, 41, col. 146).
18. St. John Damascene, De fide orthodoxa, II, 7 (PG, 94, col. 893).
19. Claudius Ptolemaeus, Liber quattuor tractatuum cum Centiloquio (Venetiis: 1484), verbum 38.
1. Aristotle, De anima, III, 9 (432b 6).
2. See above, ch. 84.

Book III of *On the Soul*.³ For this reason, perversity cannot result in the act of choice, unless the intellectual judgment is defective in regard to the particular object of choice, as is evident from the Philosopher in *Ethics* VII.⁴ But the celestial bodies are not the cause of our act of understanding. Therefore, they cannot be the cause of our act of choice.

[4] Besides, whatever events occur in these lower bodies as a result of the influence of celestial bodies happen naturally, because these lower bodies are naturally subordinated to them. So, if our choices do occur as a result of the impression of celestial bodies, they will have to occur naturally; that is to say, a man might choose naturally to have his operations go on, just as brutes are involved in operations by natural instinct, and as inanimate bodies are moved naturally. In that case, there would not be choice and nature, as two active principles, but only one, and that is nature. The contrary of this view is evident from Aristotle, in *Physics* II.⁵ Therefore, it is not true that our choices originate from the influence of the celestial bodies.

[5] Moreover, things that are done naturally are brought to their end by determinate means, and so they always happen in the same way, for nature is determined to one result. But human choices tend to their end in various ways, both in moral actions and in artistic productions. Therefore, human choices are not accomplished by nature.

[6] Furthermore, things that are done naturally are done rightly in most cases, for nature does not fail, except in rare cases. So, if man were to choose naturally, his choices would be right in most cases. Now, this is evidently false. Therefore, man does not choose naturally. But he would have to if he chose as a result of the impulsion of celestial bodies.

[7] Again, things that belong to the same species do not differ in their natural operations which result from the na-

3. Aristotle, *De anima*, III, 10 (433a 28).
4. Aristotle, *Nicomachean Ethics*, VII, 3 (1147a 1).
5. Aristotle, *Physics*, II, 5 (196b 19).

ture of their species. Thus, every swallow builds its nest in the same way, and every man understands naturally known first principles in the same way. Now, choice is an operation resulting from the species of man. So, if man were to choose naturally, then all men would have to choose in the same way. This is clearly false, both in moral and in artistic actions.

[8]   Besides, virtues and vices are the proper principles for acts of choice, for virtues and vices differ in the fact that they choose contraries. Now, the political virtues and vices are not present in us from nature but come from custom, as the Philosopher proves, in *Ethics II*,[6] from the fact that whatever kind of operations we have become accustomed to, and especially from boyhood, we acquire habits of the same kind. And so, our acts of choice are not in us from nature. Therefore, they are not caused from the influence of celestial bodies, according to which things occur naturally.

[9]   Moreover, celestial bodies make no direct impression, except on bodies, as we showed.[7] So, if they are the cause of our acts of choice, this will be either because they influence our bodies, or because they influence external things. But in neither way can they be an adequate cause of our act of choice. In fact, it is not an adequate cause of our choice, for some corporeal things to be externally presented to us; for it is clear that on encountering some pleasurable object, say an item of food or a woman, the temperate man is not moved to choose it, but the intemperate man is moved. Likewise, whatever change might take place in our body as a result of the influence of a celestial body, it would not suffice to cause our choice, because there are no other results from this in us than certain passions, more or less strong. But passions, whatever their strength, are not an adequate cause for choice, since by the same passions an incontinent man is led to follow them by choice, while a continent man is not so induced. Therefore, it cannot

6. Aristotle, *Nicomachean Ethics*, II, 1 (1103a 19).
7. See above, ch. 84.

be said that celestial bodies are the causes of our acts of choice.

[10] Furthermore, no power is given anything unless it has a use. But man has the power of judging and deliberating on all the things that may be done by him, whether in the use of external things or in the entertaining or repelling of internal passions. Of course, this would be useless if our choice were caused by celestial bodies which do not come under our control. Therefore, celestial bodies are not the cause of our act of choice.

[11] Again, man is naturally a political animal, or a social one.[8] This is apparent, indeed, from the fact that one man is not sufficient unto himself if he lives alone, because nature provides but few things that are sufficient for man. Instead, it gives him reason whereby he may make ready all the things needed for life, such as food, clothing, and the like; one man is not sufficient to do all these things. So, to live in society is naturally implanted in man. But the order of providence does not take away from a thing what is natural to it, but provides for each thing in accord with its nature, as is evident from what we have said.[9] Therefore, man is not so ordered by the order of providence that his social life is taken away. Now, it would be removed if our acts of choice arose from impressions due to the celestial bodies, as do the natural instincts of other animals.

[12] Besides, it would be useless for laws and rules of living to be promulgated if man were not master of his own choices. Useless, too, would be the employment of punishments and rewards for good or evil deeds, in regard to which it is not in our power to choose one or the other. In fact, if these things disappear, social life is at once corrupted. Therefore, man is not so established by the order of providence that his choices originate from the motions of the celestial bodies.

8. See Aristotle, *Politics*, I, 2 (1253a 2); *Nicomachean Ethics*, I, 7 (1097b 11).
9. See above, ch. 71.

[13]   Moreover, men's choices are made in regard to goods and evils. So, if our choices originated from the motions of the stars, it would follow that the stars would be the direct cause of evil choices. But an evil thing has no cause in nature, since evil results from a defect of a cause and has no direct cause, as we showed above.[10] Therefore, it is not possible for our choices to originate directly and of themselves from celestial bodies as causes.

[14]   Now, someone might be able to oppose this argument by saying that every bad choice arises from a good that is desired, as we showed above.[11] For instance, the choice of an adulterer arises from the desire for a pleasurable good associated with sexual activity, and some star moves him toward this universal good. As a matter of fact, this is necessary for the accomplishment of the generating of animals, and this common good should not be set aside because of the particular evil of this person who makes a bad choice as a result of such prompting.

[15]   But this argument is not adequate if celestial bodies are claimed to be the direct cause of our choices, in the sense that they make direct impressions on the intellect and will. For the impression of a universal cause is received in any being according to the mode of that being. So, the influence of a star, that impels toward the pleasure associated with the generative act will be received in any being according to its own mode. Thus we observe that different animals have different times and various ways of reproducing, according to what befits their nature, as Aristotle says in his treatise on the *History of Animals*.[12] So, intellect and will are going to receive the influence of this star according to their own mode. But, when an object is desired in accordance with the mode of intellect and reason, there is no sin in the choice; in fact, a choice is bad, always because it is not in accord with right reason. Therefore, if celestial

10. See above, ch. 4ff.
11. See above, ch. 5–6.
12. Aristotle, *De historia animalium*, V, 8 (542a 1).

bodies were the cause of our choices, there would never be a bad choice for us.

[16] Moreover, no active power extends to effects that are beyond the species and nature of the agent, for every agent acts by virtue of its form. But the act of willing surpasses every bodily species, as does the act of understanding. Indeed, just as we understand universals, so also is our will attracted to the universal object; for example, "we hate every kind of thief," as the Philosopher says in his *Rhetoric*.[13] Therefore our will-act is not caused by a celestial body.

[17] Furthermore, things that are related to an end are proportioned to that end. But human choices are ordered to felicity as their ultimate end. Of course, it does not consist in any corporeal goods but in the union of the soul with divine things by way of understanding, as we showed above[14] both according to the view of faith and according to the opinions of the philosophers. Therefore, celestial bodies cannot be the cause of our acts of choice.

[18] Hence it is said: "Be not afraid of the signs of heaven which the heathens fear; for the laws of people are vain" (Jer. 10:2-3).

[19] By this conclusion the theory of the Stoics is also refuted, for they claimed that all our acts, and even our choices, are ordered by the celestial bodies.[15] This is also said to have been the position of the ancient Pharisees among the Jews.[16] The Priscillianists, too, shared this error, as is stated in the book *On Heresies*.[17]

[20] It was also the opinion of the old natural philosophers who claimed that sensation and understanding did not

13. Aristotle, *Rhetoric*, II, 4 (1382a 6).
14. See above, ch. 25ff.
15. See above, ch. 84, ¶10.
16. See Josephus, XIII, 5, 9 (trans. Thackeray and Marcus, VII, 310).
17. St. Augustine, *De haeresibus*, 70 (PL, 42, col. 44).

differ.[18] Thus, Empedocles said that "the will is increased
in men, as in other animals, in respect to what is present";
that is, according to the present instant resulting from the
celestial motion that causes time, as Aristotle reports it in
his book *On the Soul*.[19]

[21]   Yet we should note that, though celestial bodies are
not directly the cause of our choices, in the sense of directly making impressions on our wills, some occasion for
our choices may be indirectly offered by them, because they
do make an impression on bodies, and in a twofold sense.
In one way, the impressions of the celestial bodies on external bodies are for us the occasion of a certain act of
choice; for instance, when the atmosphere is disposed to
severe cold by the celestial bodies, we choose to get warmed
near a fire or to do other such acts which suit the weather.
In a second way, they make an impression on our bodies;
when a change occurs in them, certain movements of the
passions arise in us; or we are made prone by their impressions to certain passions, as the bilious are prone to anger;
or again, some bodily disposition that is an occasion for an
act of choice may be caused in us by their impression, as
when, resulting from our illness, we choose to take medicine. At times, too, a human act may be caused by the
celestial bodies, in the sense that some people become demented as a result of a bodily indisposition and are deprived
of the use of reason. Strictly speaking, there is no act of
choice for such people, but they are moved by a natural
instinct, as are brutes.

[22]   Moreover, it is plain and well known by experience
that such occasions, whether they are external or internal,
are not the necessary cause of choice, since man is able, on
the basis of reason, either to resist or obey them. But there
are many who follow natural impulses, while but few, the
wise only, do not take these occasions of acting badly and
of following their natural impulses. This is why Ptolemy

18. See above, ch. 84, ¶9.
19. Aristotle, *De anima*, III, 3 (427a 22).

says, in his *Centiloquium:* "the wise soul assists the work of the stars"; and that "the astronomer could not give a judgment based on the stars, unless he knew well the power of the soul and the natural temperament"; and that "the astronomer should not speak in detail on a matter, but in general."[20] That is to say, the impression from the stars produces its result in most people who do not resist the tendency that comes from their body, but it is not always effective, for, in one case or another a man may resist, perhaps, the natural inclination by means of reason.

Chapter 86.

THAT THE CORPOREAL EFFECTS IN THINGS HERE BELOW DO NOT NECESSARILY RESULT FROM THE CELESTIAL BODIES

[1] Not only is it impossible for the celestial bodies to impose necessity on human choice; in fact, not even corporeal effects in things here below necessarily result from them.

[2] For the impressions of universal causes are received in their effects according to the mode of the recipients. Now, these lower things are fluctuating and do not always maintain the same condition: because of matter which is in potency to many forms and because of the contrariety of forms and powers. Therefore, the impressions of celestial bodies are not received in these lower things by way of necessity.

[3] Again, an effect does not result from a remote cause unless there be also a necessary intermediate cause; just as in syllogisms, from a necessary major and a contingent minor, a necessary conclusion does not follow. But celestial

20. Claudius Ptolemaeus, *op. cit.;* the quotations are, respectively, from *verbum* 8; 7; and 1; their location in the *incunabulum* is approximately from fol. 45v to 47r.

bodies are remote causes, whereas the proximate causes of lower effects are the active and passive powers in these lower things, which are not necessary causes, but contingent, for they may fail in a few instances. So, effects in these lower bodies do not follow of necessity from the motions of the celestial bodies.

[4]   Besides, the motion of the celestial bodies always is in the same mode. So, if the effect of the celestial bodies on these lower ones came about from necessity, the events in lower bodies would always happen in the same way. Yet they do not always occur in the same way, but in most cases. So, they do not come about by necessity.

[5]   Moreover, it is not possible for one necessary thing to come to be out of many contingent things, because, just as any contingent thing of itself can fall short of its effect, so, too, all of them may together. Now, it is obvious that the individual effects that are accomplished in these lower things, as a result of the impression of celestial bodies, are contingent. Therefore, the combination of these events that occur in lower things as a result of the impression of celestial bodies is not a necessary one, for it is plain that any one of them may be prevented from happening.

[6]   Moreover, the celestial bodies are agents in the order of nature; they need matter on which to act. So, the need for matter is not removed as a result of the action of celestial bodies. Now, the matter on which the celestial bodies act consists of the lower bodies which, being corruptible in their nature, may be just as able to fail in their operations as they are able to fail in their being. Thus, their nature has this characteristic: they do not produce their effects by necessity. Therefore, the effects of the celestial bodies do not come about by necessity, even in the lower bodies.

[7]   But someone will say, perhaps, that the effects of the celestial bodies must be accomplished. Yet, possibility is not removed from the lower bodies by this fact, because each effect is in potency before it comes about. So, it is then

called possible, but when it now becomes actual, it passes from possibility to necessity. All of this comes under the control of the celestial bodies; and so, the fact that the effect is at one time possible is not removed in this way, even though it is necessary that this effect be produced at another time. Indeed, this is the way that Albumasar, in his book, *Introduction to Astronomy*, tries to defend the *possible*.[1]

[8] But one cannot defend this meaning of the *possible*. For there is a sort of possibility that depends on what is necessary. Indeed, what is necessary in regard to actual being must be possible in regard to being; and what is not possible in relation to being is impossible in regard to being; and what is impossible in regard to being is necessarily nonbeing. Therefore, what is necessary in relation to being is necessary in relation to non-being. But this is impossible. So, it is impossible for something to be necessary in relation to being, yet not possible in regard to this being. Therefore, possible being follows from necessary being.

[9] As a matter of fact, we do not have to defend this meaning of *possible* against the statement that effects are caused by necessity, but, rather, the *possible* that is *opposed to the necessary*, in the sense that the possible is called *that which can be, and also not be*. Now, a thing is not called possible, or contingent, in this way from the sole fact that it is at one time in potency and at another time in act, as the preceding answer takes it. In fact, in that preceding sense there is possibility and contingency even in celestial motions, for there is not always an actual conjunction or opposition of the sun or moon. Rather, it is sometimes actually so, sometimes potentially so; yet these events are necessary, for demonstrations of such events may be given. But the possible, or contingent, that is opposed to the necessary has this characteristic: it is not necessary for it to happen when it is not. This is indeed so, because it

1. Albumasar, *Introductorium ad artem astronomiae* (Augsburg: 1489); cited without folio ref. in the Leonine *Indices*; not seen by translator.

does not follow of necessity from its cause. Thus, we say that Socrates will sit is a contingent fact, but that he will die is necessary, because the second of these facts follows necessarily from its cause, whereas the first does not. So, if it follows necessarily from the celestial motions that their effects will occur at some time in the future, then the possible and contingent that is opposed to the necessary is thereby excluded.

[10]   Moreover, we should note that, in order to prove that the effects of the celestial bodies come about by necessity, Avicenna uses an argument like this in his *Metaphysics*.[2] If any effect of the celestial bodies is blocked, this must be due to some voluntary or natural cause. But every voluntary or natural cause is reducible to some celestial source. Therefore, even the blocking of the effects of the celestial bodies results from some celestial sources. So, if the entire order of celestial things be taken together, it is impossible for its effect ever to fail to come about. Hence he concludes that the celestial bodies produce necessarily the effects which must occur in these lower bodies, both the voluntary and the natural ones.

[11]   But this way of arguing, as Aristotle says in *Physics* II,[3] was used by some of the ancients who denied chance and fortune on the basis of the view that there is a definite cause for every effect. If the cause be granted, then the effect must be granted. Thus, since everything occurs by necessity, there is nothing fortuitous or by chance.

[12]   He answers this argument, in *Metaphysics* VI,[4] by denying two propositions which the argument uses. One of these is: "if any cause be granted, it is necessary to grant its effect." Indeed, this is not necessary in the case of all causes, for a certain cause, though it may be the direct, proper and sufficient cause of a given effect, may be hin-

2. Avicenna, *Metaphysica*, X, 1 (ed. Venetiis: 1508, fol. 108r).
3. Aristotle, *Physics*, II, 4 (195b 36).
4. Aristotle, *Metaphysics*, VI, 2–3 (1027a 5–b 16).

dered by the interference of another cause so that the effect does not result. The second proposition that he denies is: "not everything that exists in any way at all has a direct cause, but only those things that exist of themselves; on the other hand, things that exist accidentally have no cause." For instance, there is a cause within a man for the fact that he is musical, but there is no cause for the fact that he is at once white and musical. As a matter of fact, whenever plural things occur together because of some cause they are related to each other as a result of that cause, but whenever they occur by accident they are not so related to each other. So, they do not occur as a result of a cause acting directly; their occurrence is only accidental. For instance, it is an accident to the teacher of music that he teaches a white man; indeed, it is quite apart from his intention; rather, he intends to teach someone who is capable of learning the subject.

[13]   And thus, given a certain effect, we will say that it had a cause from which it did not necessarily follow, since it could have been hindered by some other accidentally conflicting cause. And even though it be possible to trace this conflicting cause back to a higher cause, it is not possible to trace this conflict, which is a hindrance, back to any cause. Thus, it cannot be said that the hindrance of this or that effect proceeds from a celestial source. Hence, we should not say that the effects of celestial bodies come about in these lower bodies as a result of necessity.

[14]   Hence, Damascene says, in Book II, that "the celestial bodies are not the cause of any process of generating things that come into being, or of the process of corrupting things that are corrupted";[5] that is to say, these effects do not come about of necessity from them.

[15]   Aristotle also says, in *On Sleep* II, that "of those signs which occur in bodies, and even of the celestial signs, such as movements of water and wind, many of their results do

5. St. John Damascene, *De fide orthodoxa*, II, 7 (*PG*, 94, col. 893).

not come about. For, if another movement occurs, stronger than the one which is a sign of the future, then the event does not happen; just as many of our well laid plans, which were suitable to be accomplished, come to no result, because of the interference of higher powers."[6]

[16]   Ptolemy, too, in his *Fourfold Work*, says: "Again, we should not think that higher events proceed inevitably, like things that happen under divine control and which can in no way be avoided, nor as things which come about truly and of necessity."[7] He also says in the *Centiloquium*: "These prognostications that I give you are midway between the necessary and the possible."[8]

Chapter 87.

THAT THE MOTION OF A CELESTIAL BODY IS NOT THE CAUSE OF OUR ACTS OF CHOICE BY THE POWER OF ITS SOUL MOVING US, AS SOME SAY

[1]   However, we should note that Avicenna maintains[1] that the motions of the celestial bodies are also the causes of our acts of choice, not simply as occasions, as was said above,[2] but directly. For he claims that the celestial bodies are animated. Hence, since celestial motion is from a soul and is the motion of a body, therefore, just as it is a bodily motion with the power of causing change in bodies, so as a motion from the soul it must have the power to make an impression on our souls. And thus, the celestial motion is the cause of our acts of will and choice. On this point also

6. Aristotle, *De divinatione per somnum*, II (463b 23).
7. Claudius Ptolemaeus, op. cit., I, 2, fol. 2r.
8. *Ibid*, verbum 1, fol. 45v.
1. Avicenna, *Metaphysica*, X, 1 (fol. 108r).
2. See above, ch. 85.

he seems to return to the theory of Albumasar, in his *Introduction* 1.[3]

[2] But this theory is not reasonable. Every effect proceeding through an instrument from an efficient cause must be proportionate to the instrument, as also to the agent, for we cannot use just any instrument for any effect. Hence, a result cannot be accomplished by means of an instrument if the action of the instrument in no way covers the result. Now, the action of a body in no way extends to the production of a change of understanding and will, as we showed,[4] unless, perchance, by accident, through a change in the body, as we said before.[5] So, it is impossible for the soul of a celestial body, if it be animated, to make an impression on the intellect and will by means of the motion of a celestial body.

[3] Again, a particular agent cause, when acting, bears a likeness to the universal agent cause and is patterned on it. But, if a human soul were to impress another human soul through a corporeal operation, as when it reveals its thought by means of meaningful speech, the bodily action initiated by one soul does not reach the other soul without the mediation of its body. In fact, the spoken word moves the auditory organ, and then, having been so perceived by the sense power, it extends its message to the understanding. So, if the celestial soul makes an impression on our souls through bodily movement, that action will not reach our soul without making a change in our body. Now, this is not a cause of our acts of choice, but simply an occasion, as is clear from the foregoing.[6] Therefore, celestial motion will not be a cause of our act of choice, except as a mere occasion.

[4] Besides, since the mover and the thing moved must be simultaneous, as is proved in *Physics* VII,[7] the motion must

3. See above, ch. 86, ¶7. See also P. Duhem, *Le système du monde* (Paris: 1913–17), II, pp. 374–376.
4. See above, ch. 84ff.
5. *Ibid.*
6. *Ibid.*
7. Aristotle, *Physics*, VII, 2 (243a 3).

extend in a definite order, from the first mover to the last thing that is moved; that is, such that the mover moves what is far away from it by means of what is near to it. Now, our body is nearer than our soul is to the celestial body which is asserted to be moved by a soul joined to it, for our soul has no relation to a celestial body except through our body. This is evident from the fact that separate intelligences have no relation to a celestial body, unless, perhaps, that of a mover to a thing moved. So, a change in a celestial body, initiated by its soul, does not reach our soul except through the mediation of our body. But our soul is not moved when our body is moved, except accidentally; nor does choice result from a change in our body, except by way of occasion, as we said. Therefore, celestial motion, by virtue of the fact that it is from a soul, cannot be the cause of our act of choice.

[5]   Moreover, according to the theory of Avicenna and some other philosophers, the agent intellect is a separate substance that acts on our souls by making potentially understood things to be actually understood.[8] Now, this is done by abstraction from all material conditions, as is evident from our explanations in Book Two.[9] So, that which acts directly on the soul does not act on it through corporeal motion, but, rather, through abstraction from everything corporeal. Therefore, the soul of the heavens, if it be animated, cannot be the cause of our acts of choice or understanding through the motion of the heavens.

[6]   It is also possible to prove by the same arguments that the motion of the heavens is not the cause of our acts of choice by means of separate substances, if someone claims that the heavens are not animated, but moved by a separate substance.

8. SCG, II, ch. 76.
9. SCG, II, ch. 50 and 59.

Chapter 88.

THAT SEPARATE CREATED SUBSTANCES CANNOT BE DIRECTLY THE CAUSE OF OUR ACTS OF CHOICE AND WILL, BUT ONLY GOD

[1] Now, we must not think that the souls of the heavens, if there be such,[1] or any other created, separate, intellectual substances can directly insert a will-act into us or cause our act of choice to occur.

[2] For the actions of all creatures are embraced under the order of divine providence, so they cannot operate outside its laws. But it is the law of providence that everything be moved immediately by its proximate cause. So, unless such an order were obeyed, a superior created cause could neither move nor do anything. Now, the proximate mover of the will is the good as apprehended, which is its object, and it is moved by it, just as sight is by color. So, no created substance can move the will except by means of a good which is understood. Now, this is done by showing it that something is a good thing to do: this is the act of *persuading*. Therefore, no created substance can act on the will, or be the cause of our act of choice, except in the way of a persuading agent.

[3] Again, a thing is by nature capable of being moved by, and of undergoing a passion from, an agent with a form by which the thing can be reduced to act, for every agent acts through its form. But the will is reduced to act by the desirable object which gives rest to its desire. Now, the will's desire finds rest in the divine good only, as in its ultimate end, as is evident from what we said above.[2] Therefore, God alone can move the will in the fashion of an agent.

1. *SCG*, II, ch. 70.
2. See above, ch. 37 and 50.

[4]   Besides, as natural inclination in an inanimate thing, which is also called natural appetite, is related to its proper end, so also is the will, which is also called intellectual appetite, in an intellectual substance. Now, to give natural inclinations is the sole prerogative of Him Who has established the nature. So also, to incline the will to anything, is the sole prerogative of Him Who is the cause of the intellectual nature. Now, this is proper to God alone, as is evident from our earlier explanations.[3] Therefore, He alone can incline our will to something.

[5]   Moreover, the violent, as is said in *Ethics* iii, is "that whose principle is outside; the patient making no contribution of force."[4] So, if the will is moved by some external principle, the motion will be violent. Now, I am talking about being moved by some external principle which moves *in the way of an agent*, and not *in the way of an end*. But the violent is incompatible with the voluntary. So, it is impossible for the will to be moved by an extrinsic principle as by an agent; rather, every movement of the will must proceed from within. Now, no created substance is joined to the intellectual soul in regard to its inner parts, but only God, Who is alone the cause of its being and Who sustains it in being. Therefore, by God alone can voluntary movement be caused.

[6]   Furthermore, violent movement is opposed to natural and voluntary movement, because both of the latter must arise from an intrinsic source. The only way in which an external agent moves a thing naturally is by causing an intrinsic principle of motion within the movable thing. Thus, a generating agent, which gives the form of weight to a heavy generated body, moves it downward in a natural way. No other extrinsic being can move a natural body without violence, except perhaps accidentally, by removing an impediment, and this uses a natural motion, or action, rather than causes it. So, the only agent that can cause a move-

3. *SCG*, II, ch. 87.
4. Aristotle, *Nicomachean Ethics*, III, 1 (1110b 1).

ment of the will, without violence, is that which causes an intrinsic principle of this movement, and such a principle is the very power of the will. Now, this agent is God, Who alone creates a soul, as we showed in Book Two.[5] Therefore, God alone can move the will in the fashion of an agent, without violence.

[7] Hence it is said in Proverbs (21:1): "The heart of the king is in the hand of the Lord; whithersoever He will, He shall turn it." And again in Philippians (2:13; Douay modified): "It is God Who worketh in us, both to will and to accomplish, according to His good will."

Chapter 89.

THAT THE MOVEMENT OF THE WILL IS CAUSED BY GOD AND NOT ONLY THE POWER OF THE WILL

[1] Some people, as a matter of fact, not understanding how God could cause a movement of the will in us without prejudice to freedom of will, have tried to explain these texts[1] in a wrong way. That is, they would say that God causes *willing and accomplishing* within us in the sense that He causes in us the power of willing, but not in such a way that He makes us will this or that. Thus does Origen, in his *Principles*,[2] explain free choice, defending it against the texts above.

[2] So, it seems that there developed from this view the opinion of certain people who said that providence does not apply to things subject to free choice, that is, to acts of choice, but, instead, that providence is applied to external events. For he who chooses to attain or accomplish some-

---

5. *SCG*, II, ch. 87.
1. See above, ch. 88, ¶7.
2. Origen, *Peri Archon*, III, 1 (*PG*, 11, col. 293); on this theory see Gilson, *History of Christian Philosophy*, pp. 41–43.

thing, such as to make a building or to become rich, is not always able to reach this end; thus, the results of our actions are not subject to free choice, but are controlled by providence.

[3]   To these people, of course, opposition is offered quite plainly by the texts from Sacred Scripture. For it is stated in Isaias (26:2): "O Lord, Thou hast wrought all our works in us." So, we receive not only the power of willing from God, but also the operation.

[4]   Again, this statement of Solomon, "whithersoever He will, He shall turn it,"³ shows that divine causality is not only extended to the power of the will but also to its act.

[5]   Besides, God not only gives powers to things but, beyond that, no thing can act by its own power unless it acts through His power, as we showed above.⁴ So, man cannot use the power of will that has been given him except in so far as he acts through the power of God. Now, the being through whose power the agent acts is the cause not only of the power, but also of the act. This is apparent in the case of an artist through whose power an instrument works, even though it does not get its own form from this artist, but is merely applied to action by this man. Therefore, God is for us the cause not only of our will, but also of our act of willing.

[6]   Moreover, a more perfect order is found in spiritual things than in corporeal ones. Among bodies, however, every motion is caused by the first motion. Therefore, among spiritual things, also, every movement of the will must be caused by the first will, which is the will of God.

[7]   Furthermore, we showed somewhat earlier⁵ that God is the cause of every action and that He operates in every agent. Therefore, He is the cause of the movements of the will.

3. See above, ch. 88, ¶7.
4. See above, ch. 67 and 70.
5. Ibid.

[8] Besides, an argument that is pertinent is offered by Aristotle, in Book viii of the *Eudemian Ethics*, as follows.[6] There must be a cause for the fact that a person understands, deliberates, chooses, and wills, for every new event must have some cause. But, if its cause is another act of deliberation, and another act of will preceding it, then, since one cannot go on to infinity in these acts, one must reach something that is first. Now, a first of this type must be something that is better than reason. But nothing is better than intellect and reason except God. Therefore, God is the first principle of our acts of counsel and of will.

Chapter 90.

THAT HUMAN ACTS OF CHOICE AND OF WILL ARE SUBJECT TO DIVINE PROVIDENCE

[1] It is clear, next, that even acts of human willing and choosing must be subject to divine providence.

[2] For, everything that God does He does as a result of the order of His providence. So, since He is the cause of our act of choice and volition, our choices and will-acts are subject to divine providence.

[3] Again, all corporeal things are governed through spiritual beings, as we showed above.[1] But spiritual beings act on corporeal things through the will. Therefore, if choices and movements of the wills of intellectual substances do not belong to God's providence, it follows that even corporeal things are withdrawn from His providence. And thus, there will be no providence at all.

[4] Besides, the more noble things are in the universe, the more must they participate in the order in which the good of the universe consists. So, in *Physics* ii,[2] Aristotle accuses

6. Aristotle, *Eudemicae Ethicae*, VII, 14 (1248a 18).
1. See above, ch. 78.
2. Aristotle, *Physics*, II, 4 (196a 25).

the ancient philosophers of putting chance and fortune in the make-up of the celestial bodies, but not in things below. Now, the intellectual substances are more noble than bodily substances. Therefore, if bodily substances, in their substances and actions, fall under the order of providence, so do intellectual substances, for a greater reason.

[5]   Moreover, things that are nearer the end fall more definitely under the order which is for the end, for by their mediation other things also are ordered to the end. But the actions of intellectual substances are more closely ordered to God as end than are the actions of other things, as we showed above.[3] So, the actions of intellectual substances, by which God orders all things to Himself, more definitely fall under the order of providence than the actions of other things.

[6]   Furthermore, the governance of providence stems from the divine love whereby God loves the things created by Him; in fact, love consists especially in this, "that the lover wills the good for his loved one."[4] So, the more that God loves things, the more do they fall under His providence. Moreover, Sacred Scripture also teaches this in the Psalm (144:20) when it states: "The Lord keepeth all them that love Him." And the Philosopher, also, supports this view, in Ethics x,[5] when he says that God takes greatest care of those who love understanding, as He does of His friends. It may, then, be gathered from this, that He loves intellectual substances best. Therefore, their acts of will and choice fall under His providence.

[7]   Again, man's internal goods, which are dependent on will and action, are more proper to man than things that are outside him, like the acquisition of wealth or anything else of that kind. Hence, man is deemed good by virtue of the former and not of the latter. So, if acts of human choice and movements of will do not fall under divine provi-

3. See above, ch. 25 and 78.
4. Aristotle, Rhetoric, II, 4 (1380b 35).
5. Aristotle, Nicomachean Ethics, X, 8 (1179a 29).

dence, but only their external results, it will be truer that human affairs are outside providence than that they come under providence. But this view is suggested by the words of blasphemers: "He walketh about the poles of heaven, and He doth not consider our things" (Job 22:14); and again: "The Lord hath forsaken the earth, and the Lord seeth not" (Ezech. 9:9); and also: "Who is he that hath commanded a thing to be done, when the Lord commandeth it not?" (Lam. 3:37).

[8] However, certain passages in Sacred Scripture appear to be consonant with the aforementioned view. It is said in fact (Ecclus. 15:14): "God made man from the beginning, and left him in the hand of his own counsel"; and later: "He hath set water and fire before thee; stretch forth thy hand to which thou wilt. Before man is life and death, good and evil; that which he shall choose shall be given him" (Ecclus. 15:14, 17-18). And also: "Consider that I have set before thee this day life and good, and on the other hand death and evil" (Deut. 30:15).—But these words are brought forward to show that man is possessed of free choice, not that his choices are placed outside divine providence.

[9] Likewise, Gregory of Nyssa states in his book *On Man:* "Providence is concerned with the things that are not in our power, but not with those that are in our power";[6] and, following him, Damascene states in Book II, that "God foreknows the things that are within our power, but He does not predetermine them."[7] These texts should be explained as meaning that things in our power are not subject to determination by divine providence in the sense that they receive necessity from it.

6. Nemesius, *De natura hominis*, 44 (*PG*, 40, col. 813).
7. St. John Damascene, *De fide orthodoxa*, II, 30 (*PG*, 94, col. 972).

Chapter 91.

HOW HUMAN EVENTS MAY BE TRACED
BACK TO HIGHER CAUSES

[1] From the things shown above we can gather how human actions may be traced back to higher causes and are not performed fortuitously.

[2] Of course, acts of choice and movements of the will are controlled immediately by God.[1] And human intellectual knowledge is ordered by God through the mediation of the angels.[2] Whereas matters pertinent to bodily things, whether they are internal or external, when they come within the use of man, are governed by God by means of the angels and the celestial bodies.[3]

[3] Now, in general, there is one reason for this. Everything that is multiform, mutable, and capable of defect must be reducible to a source in something that is uniform, immutable, and capable of no defect. But all things that are within our power are found to be multiple, variable, and defectible.

[4] It is clear that our acts of choice have the character of multiplicity, since choices are made of different things, by different people, in different ways. They are also mutable, both because of the instability of the mind, which is not firmly fixed on the ultimate end, and also because of the fluctuating character of the things which provide our circumstantial environment. That they are defectible, of course the sins of men testify. But the divine will is uniform, because by willing one object it wills all else, and it is immutable and without defect, as we showed in Book

1. See above, ch. 85ff.
2. See above, ch. 79.
3. See above, ch. 78 and 82.

One.[4] So, the movement of all wills and choices must be traced back to the divine will, and not to any other cause, for God alone is the cause of our acts of will and choice.

[5]   Likewise, our understanding has the quality of multiplicity, since we gather, as it were, intelligible truth from many sense objects. It is also mutable, for it advances by discursive movement from one thing to another, proceeding from known things to unknown ones. It is, moreover, defectible, because of the admixture of imagination with sensation, as the errors of mankind show. On the other hand, the cognitive acts of the angels are uniform: for they receive the knowledge of truth from one fount of truth; namely, God.[5] Their cognition is also immutable, because they see directly the pure truth about things by a simple intuition, not by a discursive movement from effects to their causes or the reverse.[6] It is even incapable of defect, since they directly intuit the very natures, or quiddities, of things, and understanding cannot err in regard to such objects, just as sense cannot err in regard to proper sensibles. We, however, make guesses as to the quiddities of things from their accidents and effects. Therefore, our intellectual knowledge must be regulated by means of the angels' knowledge.

[6]   Again, in regard to human bodies and the external things that men use, it is obvious that there is in them a multiplicity of admixture and contrariety; and that they are not moved uniformly, since their motions cannot be continuous; and that they are defectible through alteration and corruption. In contrast, the celestial bodies are uniform, in the way of simple beings with no contrariety in their constitution. Their motions are also uniform, continuous, and always in the same condition. Nor can there be corruption or alteration in them. Hence, it is necessary for our bodies, and the others which come under our use, to be regulated by means of the motions of the celestial bodies.

4. *SCG*, I, ch. 13 and 75.
5. See above, ch. 80.
6. *SCG*, II, 96ff.

Chapter 92.

HOW A PERSON IS FAVORED BY FORTUNE AND HOW MAN IS ASSISTED BY HIGHER CAUSES

[1] Next, we can show how a person might be said to be favored by fortune.

[2] In fact, we say that some good fortune has befallen a man "when something good happens to him, without his having intended it."[1] For example, a man digging in a field may find a treasure for which he was not looking. Now, something may happen to a certain agent which is not intended by him as he is doing his job, but which is not unintended by the superior under whom he is working. Suppose, for instance, a master orders a servant to go to a certain place to which the master has already sent another servant, unknown to the first one; the encounter with his fellow servant is not intended by the servant who has been sent, but it is not unintended by the master who sent him. And so, though the meeting is fortuitous and a matter of chance to this servant, it is not so to the master, but has been a planned event. So, since man is ordered in regard to his body under the celestial bodies, in regard to his intellect under the angels, and in regard to his will under God— it is quite possible for something apart from man's intention to happen, which is, however, in accord with the ordering of the celestial bodies, or with the control of the angels, or even of God. For, though God alone directly works on the choice made by man, the action of an angel does have some effect on man's choice by way of persuasion, and the action of a celestial body by way of disposition, in the sense that the corporeal impressions of celestial bodies on our bodies give a disposition to certain choices. So, when as a result of the influence of higher

1. Aristotle, *Magna Moralia*, II, 8 (1207a 28).

causes in the foregoing way a man is inclined toward certain choices that are beneficial to him, but whose benefit he does not know by his own reasoning, and when besides this his intellect is illuminated by the light of intellectual substances so that he may do these things, and when his will is inclined by divine working to choose something beneficial to him while he is ignorant of its nature, he is said to be *favored by fortune*. And, on the contrary, he is said to be subject to *misfortune* when his choice is inclined to contrary results by higher causes, as is said of a certain man: "Write this man barren, a man that shall not prosper in his days" (Jer. 22:30).

[3] But, on this point, a difference is to be noted. The impressions of celestial bodies on our bodies cause natural dispositions of our bodies within us. Thus, as a result of a disposition left by a celestial body in our body, a man is called not merely fortunate or unfortunate, but also well or ill favored by nature, and it is in this way that the Philosopher says, in his *Magna Moralia*,[2] that a man favored by fortune is also favored by nature. Indeed, this fact, that one man chooses things beneficial to him, whereas another man chooses things harmful to him, apart from their proper reasoning, cannot be understood as resulting from differences of intellectual nature, because the nature of intellect and will is one in all men. In fact, a formal diversity would lead to a difference according to species, whereas a material diversity leads to a numerical difference. Hence, in so far as man's intellect is enlightened for the performance of some action, or as his will is prompted by God, the man is not said to be favored by birth, but, rather, well guarded or well governed.

[4] Again, another difference on this matter is to be observed. As a matter of fact, the operation of an angel and of a celestial body is merely like something *disposing* toward choice; while God's operation is like something *perfecting*. Now, since a disposition which results from a quality of the

2. *Ibid.,* II, 9 (1207a 35).

body, or from an intellectual persuasion, does not bring necessity to the act of choice, a man does not always choose what his guardian angel intends, or that toward which a celestial body gives inclination. But a man does choose in all cases the object in accord with God's operation within his will. Consequently, the guardianship of the angels is sometimes frustrated, according to this text: "We would have cured Babylon, but she is not healed" (Jer. 51:9); and still more is this true of the inclination of the celestial bodies, but divine providence is always steadfast.

[5] Moreover, there is still another difference to be considered. Since a celestial body does not dispose to a choice, unless it makes an impression on our body by which man is stimulated to choose in the way that passions induce one to choose, every disposition to choice which results from the celestial bodies works by means of some passion, as when a person is led to choose something by means of hatred, or love, or anger, or some similar passion. But a person is disposed to an act of choice by an angel, by means of an intellectual consideration, without passion. In fact, this happens in two ways. Sometimes, a man's understanding is enlightened by an angel to know only that something is a good thing to be done, but it is not instructed as to the reason why it is a good, since this reason is derived from the end. Thus, at times, a man thinks that something is a good thing to be done, "but, if he be asked why, he would answer that he does not know."[3] Hence, when he reaches a beneficial end, to which he has given no thought before, it will be fortuitous for him. But sometimes he is instructed by angelic illumination, both that this act is good and as to the reason why it is good, which depends on the end. And if this be so, when he reaches the end which he has thought about before, it will not be fortuitous. We should also note that, just as the active power of a spiritual nature is higher than a corporeal one, so also is it more universal. Consequently, the disposition resulting from a celestial body does not extend to all the objects which human choice covers.

3. *Ibid.*, (1207b 1).

[6]   Still another point: the power of the human soul, or also of an angel, is particularized in comparison with divine power which, in fact, is universal in regard to all beings. Thus, then, some good thing may happen to a man which is apart from his own intention, and apart from the inclination given by celestial bodies, and apart from the enlightenment coming from the angels—but not apart from divine providence, which is regulative, just as it is productive, of being as such, and, consequently, which must include all things under it. Thus, some good or evil may happen to man that is fortuitous in relation to himself, and in relation to the celestial bodies, and in relation to the angels, but not in relation to God. Indeed, in relation to Him, nothing can be a matter of chance and unforeseen, either in the sphere of human affairs or in any matter.

[7]   But, since fortuitous events are those apart from intention, and since moral goods cannot be apart from intention, because they are based on choice, in their case no one can be called well or ill favored by fortune. However, in regard to them, a person can be called well or ill favored by *birth*; when, as a result of the natural disposition of his body, he is prone to virtuous, or vicious, acts of choice. But in regard to external goods, which can accrue to a man apart from his intention, a man may be said to be both favored by *birth* and by *fortune*, and also *governed* by God and *guarded* by the angels.

[8]   Moreover, man may obtain from higher causes still another help in regard to the outcome of his actions. For, since a man has both the ability to choose and to carry out what he chooses, he may at times be assisted by higher causes in regard to both or he may also be hindered. In regard to choice, of course, as we said, man is either disposed by the celestial bodies to choose something, or he is enlightened by the guardianship of the angels, or even he is inclined by divine operation. But in regard to the carrying out of the choice man may obtain from a higher cause the strength and efficacy needed to accomplish what he has chosen. Now, this can come not only from God and the

angels, but also from the celestial bodies, to the extent that
such efficacy is located in his body. For it is obvious that
inanimate bodies also obtain certain powers and abilities
from the celestial bodies, even beyond those which go along
with the active and passive qualities of the elements, which,
doubtless, are also subject to the celestial bodies. Thus, the
fact that a magnet attracts iron is due to the power of a
celestial body, and so have certain stones and herbs other
hidden powers. So, nothing prevents a man, too, from
getting, as a result of the influence of a celestial body, a
certain special efficiency in doing some bodily actions,
which another man does not possess: for instance, a physician in regard to healing, a farmer in regard to planting, and
a soldier in regard to fighting.

[9] Now, in a much more perfect way, God lavishes on
man this special efficiency in the carrying out of His works
efficaciously. So, in regard to the first kind of help, which
applies to the act of choosing, God is said to direct man,
whereas in regard to the second kind of help He is said to
strengthen man. And these two forms of help are touched
on together in the Psalms (26:1), where it is said in regard
to the first: "The Lord is my light and my salvation, whom
shall I fear?" and in regard to the second: "The Lord is the
protector of my life, of whom shall I be afraid?"

[10] But there are two differences between these two
helps. First, man is assisted by the first kind of help, both
in regard to things subject to the power of man, and also
in regard to other things. But the second sort of help extends only to things of which man's power is capable. Indeed, the fact that a man digging a grave discovers a
treasure results from no power of man; so, in regard to such
an outcome, man may be helped by the fact that he is
prompted to look in the place where the treasure is, not,
however, in the sense that he is given any power to find
treasure. But, in the case of the physician healing, or the
soldier winning a fight, he may be helped in regard to the
end, and also in the sense that he may carry out the choice
efficaciously, by means of a power acquired from a higher

cause. Hence, the first kind of help is more universal. The second difference is that the second help is given to carry out efficaciously what he intends. Consequently, since fortuitous events are apart from one's intention, man cannot, properly speaking, be called fortunate as a result of such help, as he can be from the first, as we showed above.

[11] Now, it is possible for a man to be well or ill favored by fortune, in some cases, when he is the sole agent, as for instance, when he is digging in the earth, he finds a treasure lying there. In other cases, it may result from the action of another concurrent cause, as when the man going to market to buy something encounters a debtor whom he did not think he would find. Now, in the first case, the man is helped so that something good happens to him, only in the fact that he is directed to the choosing of an object to which something advantageous is attached, and this comes about apart from his intention. But in the second case, both agents must be directed to choose the action, or movement, which is the occasion for their meeting.

[12] We must consider another thing in regard to what was said above. For we said that, in order for something favorable or unfavorable to happen to a man on the basis of fortune, the help can come from God, and it can also come from a celestial body: in so far as a man is inclined by God to choose something with which there is combined an advantageous, or disadvantageous, result which the chooser has not thought of before, and in so far as he is disposed by a celestial body to choose such an object. Now, this advantage, or disadvantage, is fortuitous in regard to man's choice; in regard to God, it loses the character of the fortuitous, but not in regard to the celestial body.

This becomes evident, as follows. In fact, an event does not lose its fortuitous character unless it may be referred back to a direct cause. But the power of a celestial body is an agent cause, not by way of understanding and choice, but as a nature. Now, it is proper for a nature to tend to one objective. So, if an effect is not simply one result, then its direct cause cannot be a natural power. But, when two things are combined with each other accidentally, they are not truly one, but only accidentally so. Hence, there can be no direct, natural cause for this union. Let us suppose, then, that a certain man is prompted to dig a grave by the influence of a celestial body, working by way of a passion as we said. Now, the grave and the location of the treasure are one only accidentally, for they have no relation to each other. Hence, the power of the celestial body cannot directly give an inclination toward this entire result: that this man should dig this grave and that it should be done at the place where the treasure is. But an agent working through understanding can be the cause of an inclination to this entire result, for it is proper to an intelligent being to order many things into one. It is clear, indeed, that even a man who knew where the treasure was might send another man who did not know to dig a grave in that same place and thus to find a treasure unintentionally. So, in this way, fortuitous events of this kind, when referred to their ·divine cause, lose their fortuitous character, but when referred to a celestial cause, they do not.

[13]   It is also apparent by the same reasoning that a man cannot be universally favored by fortune through the power of a celestial body, but only in regard to this or that incident. I say *universally*, meaning that a man might have the ability in his nature, resulting from the influence of a celestial body, to choose always, or in most cases, objects to which certain advantages or disadvantages are accidentally connected. For nature is ordered to one result only. But these factors, in terms of which good or bad fortune befalls a man, are not reducible to any one thing; rather, they are indeterminate and indefinite, as the Philosopher teaches in *Physics* II,[4] and as is clear to our senses. So, it is not possible for a man to have the ability in his nature to choose always those objects from which advantageous results accidentally follow. But it is possible that, by celestial influence, he may be inclined to choose one thing to which an advantage is accidentally attached; then, from another

4. Aristotle, *Physics*, II, 5 (196b 28).

inclination to another advantage; and from a third to a third advantage; but not in such a way that all such advantages would follow from one inclination. However, from one divine disposition a man can be directed to all results.

Chapter 93.

ON FATE: WHETHER AND WHAT IT IS

[1]   It is evident from the points set forth above what view we should take regarding fate.

[2]   Indeed, men observe that many things happen by accident in this world if their particular causes be considered, and some men have maintained that they are not even ordered by higher causes. To these people it has appeared that there is no fate at all.

[3]   But others have attempted to reduce these events to certain higher causes from which they result in an orderly way, in accord with a definite plan. These people have asserted that there is *fate* in the sense that things observed to happen by chance are "pre-fated," that is, *foretold* and pre-ordained to happen.

[4]   Some of these people, then, have tried to reduce all contingent events which occur by chance, here below, to causes among the celestial bodies, and even human acts of choice to the controlling power of the stars; to which power all things are subject, they claimed, with a certain necessity which they called *fate*. Of course, this theory is impossible and foreign to the faith, as is clear from our preceding considerations.[1]

[5]   On the other hand, some men have desired to reduce to the control of divine providence all things whatsoever that appear to happen by chance in these lower beings. Hence, they said that all things are done by *fate*, meaning

1. See above, ch. 84ff.

by *fate* the ordering which is found in things as a result of divine providence. Thus, Boethius says: "fate is a disposition inherent in mutable things, whereby providence connects each thing with His orders."[2] In this description of fate, "disposition" is used for *ordering*; while the phrase "inherent in things" is used to distinguish fate from providence; since the ordering, as present in the divine mind and not yet impressed on things, is *providence*, but, as already unfolded in things, it is called *fate*. Moreover, he speaks of "mutable things" to show that the order of providence does not take away contingency and mobility from things, as some men have claimed.

[6]   So, according to this meaning, to deny fate is to deny providence. But, since we should not even have names in common with unbelievers, lest occasion for error could be taken from the association of names, the name *fate* is not to be used by the faithful lest we appear to agree with those who have held a wrong opinion about fate, by subjecting all things to the necessitation of the stars. Consequently, Augustine says, in Book v of the *City of God*: "If any man calls the will, or power, of God by the name, fate, let him hold his view, but correct his way of speaking."[3] And also Gregory, in accord with the same understanding of it, says: "Far be it from the minds of the faithful to say that there is any fate."[4]

Chapter 94.

ON THE CERTAINTY OF DIVINE PROVIDENCE

[1]   Now, there is a difficulty that arises out of the foregoing. If all things that are done here below, even contingent events, are subject to divine providence, then, seem-

2. Boethius, *De consolatione philosophiae*, IV, prose 6 (*PL*, 63, col. 815).

3. St. Augustine, *De civitate Dei*, V, 1 (*PL*, 41, col. 141).

4. St. Gregory, *In Evangelium*, homil. 10 (*PL*, 76, col. 1112).

ingly, either providence cannot be certain or else all things happen by necessity.

[2]   In fact, the Philosopher shows in the *Metaphysics*[1] that, if we assert that every effect has a direct cause, and again that, given any direct cause we must necessarily grant its effect, it follows that all future events come about by necessity. For, if each effect has a direct cause, then any future effect will be reducible to a present or past cause. Thus, if we ask whether a certain man is to be killed by robbers, the cause preceding this effect is his encounter with the robbers; and, in turn, another cause precedes this effect, namely, the fact that he went out of his home; still another precedes this, that he wished to look for water; and a cause precedes this, namely, his thirst; and this was caused by the eating of salted foods; and this eating is going on now, or was done in the past. Therefore, if it be so, that, granted the cause, the effect must be granted, then necessarily, if he eats salt foods, he must get thirsty; and if he is thirsty, he must desire to get water; and if he desires to get water, he must go out of his home; and if he leaves his home, the robbers must encounter him; and if they encounter him, he must be killed. So, from the first to the last, it is necessary for this eater of salty foods to be killed by robbers. Therefore, the Philosopher concludes that it is not true that, granted the cause, the effect must be granted; since there are some causes which can fail. Again, it is not true that every effect has a direct cause, for something that comes about accidentally, for instance, that this man who wishes to look for water encounters the robbers, has no cause.

[3]   Now, by this reasoning it appears that all effects that may be reduced to some direct cause, present or past, which when granted requires that the effect be granted must of necessity happen. Either, then, we must say that not all effects are subject to divine providence and, thus, that providence does not apply to all—but we showed

1. Aristotle, *Metaphysics*, V, 3 (1027a 29).

earlier that it does;[2] or else it is not necessarily so, that, granted providence, its effect must be granted, and thus providence is not certain; or, finally, it is necessary for all things to happen by necessity. For providence is not only in present or past time, but in eternity, since nothing can be in God that is not eternal.

[4]   Again, if divine providence is certain, then this conditional proposition must be true: *If God foresees this, then this will happen.* Now, the antecedent of this conditional proposition is necessary, for He is eternal. Therefore, the consequent is necessary, for every consequent in a conditional proposition must be necessary when the antecedent is necessary. So, the consequent is like the conclusion of the antecedent, and whatever follows from a necessary proposition must be necessary. Therefore, it follows that, if divine providence is certain, all things must occur by necessity.

[5]   Besides, suppose that something is foreseen by God; for example, that a certain man will become a ruler. Now, it is either possible that he will not rule, or it is not. But, if it is not possible that he will not rule, then it is impossible for him not to rule; therefore, it is necessary for him to rule. However, if it is possible that he will not rule, and if, given the possible something impossible does not follow, then it does follow that divine providence will fail; hence, it is not impossible for divine providence to fail. Therefore, it is either necessary, if all things are foreseen by God, that divine providence be not certain or else that all things happen by necessity.

[6]   Moreover, Tully argues as follows, in his book *On Divination:*[3] if all things are foreseen by God, the order of causes is certain. But, if this is true, all things are done by fate. And if all things are done by fate, nothing is within our power; there is no volitional choice. Therefore, it follows that free choice is taken away if divine providence be

2. See above, ch. 64.
3. Cicero, *De divinatione,* II, 7 (Teubner ed., 1938, p. 71b).

certain. And in the same way it will follow that all contingent causes are taken away.

[7]   Furthermore, divine providence does not exclude intermediate causes, as we showed above.[4] But, among causes, some are contingent and capable of failing. So, it is possible for an effect of providence to fail. Therefore, God's providence is not certain.

[8]   However, for the purpose of answering these arguments, we must repeat some of the observations put down before, so that it may be made clear that nothing escapes divine providence; also, that the order of divine providence cannot possibly be changed; and yet that it is not necessary for all things to happen of necessity simply because they come about as a result of divine providence.

[9]   First, then, we must consider the fact that, since God is the cause of all existing things, giving being to all, the order of His providence must embrace all things. Indeed, on the things on which He has lavished being He must also lavish preservation and guide them toward perfection in their ultimate end.[5]

[10]   Now, two things must be considered in the case of any provident agent[6]—namely, premeditation of the order, and the establishment of the premeditated order—in the things that are subject to providence. The first of these pertains to the cognitive power, while the second belongs to the operative. Between the two there is this difference: in the act of premeditating the order, the more perfect that providence is, the more can the order of providence be extended to the smallest details. The fact that we are not able to think out, ahead of time, the order of all particular events in regard to matters to be arranged by us stems from the deficiency of our knowledge, which cannot embrace all singular things. However, the more a person is able to think

4. See above, ch. 77.
5. See above, ch. 64ff.
6. See above, ch. 77.

ahead about a plurality of singular things, the more adroit does he become in his foresight; while the man whose foresight is restricted to universals only participates but little in prudence. Now, a similar consideration can be made in regard to all the operative arts. But, in regard to imposing the premeditated order on things, the providence of a governing agent is more noble and perfect the more universal it is and the more it accomplished his premeditated plan by means of a plurality of ministers, because this controlling of ministers occupies an important place in the order that pertains to foresight.

Moreover, divine providence must consist in the highest perfection, since He is absolutely and universally perfect, as we showed in Book One.[7] So, in the function of providential foresight, by means of the sempiternal meditative act of His wisdom, He orders all things, no matter how detailed they may appear; and whatever things perform any action, they act instrumentally, as moved by Him.[8] And they obediently serve as His ministers in order to unfold in things the order of providence, which has been thought out, as I might say, from eternity. But, if all things able to act must serve as ministers to Him in their actions, it is impossible for any agent to block the execution of divine providence by acting in opposition to it. Nor is it possible for divine providence to be hindered by the defect of any agent or patient, since every active and passive power is caused in things in accord with divine disposition.[9] It is also impossible for the execution of divine providence to be impeded by a change in the provident Agent, since God is altogether immutable, as we showed above.[10] The conclusion remains, then, that divine foresight is utterly incapable of being frustrated.

[11]   Next, we must consider that every agent intends the good and the better, in so far as he can, as we showed

7. SCG, I, ch. 28.
8. See above, ch. 67.
9. See above, ch. 70.
10. SCG, I, ch. 13.

above.[11] But the good and the better are not considered in the same way, in the whole and in the parts.[12] For, in the whole, the good is integrity, which is the result of the order and composition of its parts. Consequently, it is better for there to be an inequality among the parts of the whole, without which the order and perfection of the whole cannot be, than for all its parts to be equal, even if each of them were to exist on the level of the most important part. However, if the parts are considered in themselves, each part of a lower grade would be better if it were on the level of the higher part. This is exemplified in the human body: in fact, the foot would be a more worthy part if it possessed the beauty and power of the eye, but the whole body would be more imperfect if it lacked the functioning of the foot.

Therefore, the intention of a particular agent tends toward a different objective from that of the universal agent. Indeed, the particular agent tends to the good of the part without qualification, and makes it the best that it can, but the universal agent tends to the good of the whole. As a result, a defect which is in accord with the intention of the universal agent may be apart from the intention of the particular agent. Thus, it is clear that the generation of a female is apart from the intention of a particular nature, that is, of the power which is in this semen which, as much as possible, tends to a perfect result of conception; but it is in accord with the intention of the universal nature, that is, of the power of the universal agent for the generation of inferior beings, that a female be generated; for without a female the generation of a number of animals could not be accomplished. Similarly, corruption, decrease, and every defect pertain to the intention of the universal nature, but not of the particular nature, for each thing avoids defect, and tends to perfection, to the extent that it can. So, it is evident that the intention of the particular agent is that its effect become as perfect as is possible in its kind, but the intention of the universal nature is that this individual effect become perfect in a certain type of perfection, say in

11. See above, ch. 3.
12. See above, ch. 71.

male perfection, while another would become so in female perfection.

Now the primary perfection among the parts of the whole universe appears on the basis of the contingent and the necessary.[13] For the higher beings are necessary and incorruptible and immobile, and the more they fall short of this condition, the lower the level on which they are established. Thus, the lowest things may be corrupted even in regard to their being, whereas they are changed in regard to their dispositions, and they produce their effects not necessarily but contingently. So, any agent that is a part of the universe intends as much as possible to persevere in its actual being and natural disposition, and to make its effect stable. However, God, Who is the governor of the universe, intends some of His effects to be established by way of necessity, and others contingently. On this basis, He adapts different causes to them; for one group of effects there are necessary causes, but for another, contingent causes. So, it falls under the order of divine providence not only that this effect is to be, but also that this effect is to be contingently, while another is to be necessarily. Because of this, some of the things that are subject to providence are necessary, whereas others are contingent and not at all necessary.

[12] So, it is obvious that, though divine providence is the direct cause of an individual future effect, and though it is so in the present, or in the past, indeed from eternity, it does not follow, as the first argument[14] implies, that this individual effect will come about of necessity. For divine providence is the direct cause why this effect occurs contingently. And this cannot be prevented.

[13] From this it is also evident that this conditional proposition is true: *If God foresees that this event will be, it will happen,* just as the *second* argument[15] suggested. But

13. See above, ch. 72.
14. Above, ¶2.
15. Above, ¶4.

it will occur in the way that God foresaw that it would be. Now, He foresaw that it would occur contingently. So, it follows that, without fail, it will occur contingently and not necessarily.

[14]   It is also clear that, if this thing which, we grant, is foreseen by God as to occur in the future belongs in the genus of contingent beings, it will be possible for it, considered in itself, not to be; for thus is it foreseen, as something that is contingent, as able not to be. Yet it is not possible for the order of providence to fail in regard to its coming into being contingently. Thus the *third* argument[16] is answered. Consequently, it can be maintained that this man may not become a ruler if he be considered in himself, but not if he be considered as an object of divine foresight.

[15]   Also, the objection that Tully offers[17] seems frivolous, in view of the foregoing. Indeed, since not only effects are subject to divine providence, but also causes and ways of being, as is obvious from what we have asserted before, it does not follow that, if everything be done by divine providence, nothing is within our power. For the effects are foreseen by God, as they are freely produced by us.

[16]   Nor can the possibility of failure on the part of secondary causes, by means of which the effects of providence are produced, take away the certainty of divine providence, as the *fifth* argument[18] implied. For God Himself operates in all things, and in accord with the decision of His will, as we showed above.[19] Hence, it is appropriate to His providence sometimes to permit defectible causes to fail, and at other times to preserve them from failure.

[17]   Finally, those arguments in favor of the necessity of effects foreseen by God, which might be drawn from the

16. Above, ¶5.
17. Above, ¶6.
18. Above, ¶7.
19. *SCG*, II, ch. 23; III, ch. 67.

certainty of knowledge, are solved above, where we treated of God's knowledge.[20]

Chapter 95.

THAT THE IMMUTABILITY OF DIVINE PROVIDENCE DOES NOT SUPPRESS THE VALUE OF PRAYER

[1]   We should also keep in mind the fact that, just as the immutability of providence does not impose necessity on things that are foreseen, so also it does not suppress the value of prayer. For prayer is not established for the purpose of changing the eternal disposition of providence, since this is impossible, but so that a person may obtain from God the object which he desires.

[2]   Indeed, it is appropriate for God to consent to the holy desires of a rational creature, not in the sense that our desires may move the immutable God, but that He, in His goodness, takes steps to accomplish these desired effects in a fitting way. For, since all things naturally desire the good, as we proved above,[1] and since it pertains to the supereminence of divine goodness to assign being, and well-being, to all in accord with a definite order, the result is that, in accord with His goodness, He fulfills the holy desires which are brought to completion by means of prayer.

[3]   Again, it is proper for a mover to bring the object that is moved to its end; hence, a thing is moved toward its end, and attains its end, and finds rest in it, by means of the same nature. Now, every desire is a certain movement toward the good, and indeed it cannot be present in things unless it be from God, Who is good essentially and the source of goodness. In fact, every mover moves toward something like itself. So, it is proper for God, in accord

20. SCG, I, ch. 63ff.
1. See above, ch. 3.

with His goodness, to bring to a fitting conclusion the proper desires that are expressed by our prayers.

[4]   Besides, the nearer certain things are to the mover, the more efficaciously do they follow the influence of the mover; for instance, things that are nearer to a fire become hotter from it. Now, intellectual substances are nearer to God than are inanimate natural substances. Therefore, the influence of divine motion is more efficacious on intellectual substances than on other natural substances. But natural bodies participate in divine motion to the extent that they receive from Him a natural appetite for the good, and even in the appetite for fulfillment which is realized when they attain their appropriate ends. Therefore, there is much more reason for intellectual substances attaining the fulfillment of their desires which are presented to God by prayer.

[5]   Moreover, it pertains to the essential meaning of friendship for the lover to will the fulfillment of the desire of the beloved, because he wishes the good and the perfect for the beloved. This is the reason for the statement that "it is characteristic of friends that they will the same thing."[2] Now, we showed above[3] that God loves His creature, and the more that any one of them participates in His goodness which is the first and chief object of His love, the more does He love it.[4] So, He wills the desires of a rational creature to be satisfied, for, compared to other creatures, it participates most perfectly in divine providence. But His will is perfective in regard to things; indeed, He is the cause of things through His will, as we showed above.[5] Therefore, it is appropriate to divine providence for Him to fulfill the desires of a rational creature when they are presented to Him through prayer.

[6]   Furthermore, a creature's good is transmitted by the divine goodness in accord with a certain likeness. But this

2. Sallust, *Catiline*, XX (Teubner ed., 1919, p. 16).
3. *SCG*, I, ch. 75.
4. *SCG*, I, ch. 74.
5. *SCG*, II, ch. 23ff.

characteristic seems most approvable among men: that they should not refuse consent to those who ask for favors in a just manner. Because of this, men are called liberal, clement, merciful, and upright. Therefore, this characteristic, of granting upright prayers, especially belongs to divine goodness.

[7]   Hence, it is said in the Psalm (144:19): "He will do the will of them that fear Him, and He will hear their prayers and save them"; and again the Lord says: "Everyone that asketh receiveth, and he that seeketh findeth, and to him that knocketh it shall be opened" (Matt. 7:8).

Chapter 96.

THAT SOME PRAYERS ARE NOT GRANTED BY GOD[1]

[1]   Now, it is not inappropriate if also, at times, the requests of some who pray are not granted by God.

[2]   For we showed by reasoning that God fulfills the desires of a rational creature, to the extent that he desires the good.[2] Now, it sometimes happens that what is sought in prayer is not a true, but an apparent, good; speaking absolutely, it is an evil. Therefore, such a prayer is not capable of being granted by God. Hence, it is said in James (4:3): "You ask and you receive not, because you ask amiss."

[3]   Likewise, because God moves us to the act of desiring, we showed that it is appropriate for Him to fulfill our desires.[3] Now, the thing that is moved is not brought to its end by the mover unless the motion be continued. So, if the movement of desire is not continued by constant prayer, it is not inappropriate for the prayer to fail to receive its

1. Title supplied by translator.
2. See above, ch. 95, ¶2.
3. Ibid., ¶3.

expected result. Hence, the Lord says in Luke (18:1) "that we ought always to pray and not to faint"; also, the Apostle says, in I Thessalonians (5:17): "Pray without ceasing."

[4] Again, we showed that God fulfills in a suitable way the desire of a rational creature, depending on its nearness to Him.[4] But one becomes near to Him through contemplation, devout affection, and humble but firm intention. So, the prayer which does not approach God in this way is not capable of being heard by God. Hence, it is said in the Psalm (101:18): "He hath had regard to the prayer of the humble"; and in James (1:6): "Let him ask in faith, nothing wavering."

[5] Besides, we showed that on the basis of friendship God grants the wishes of those who are holy.[5] Therefore, he who turns away from God's friendship is not worthy of having his prayer granted. Hence, it is said in Proverbs (28:9): "He that turneth away his ears from hearing the law, his prayer shall be an abomination." And again in Isaias (1:15): "When you multiply prayer, I will not hear, for your hands are full of blood."

[6] For the same reason it happens sometimes that a friend of God is not heard when he prays for those who are not God's friends, according to the passage in Jeremias (7:16): "Therefore, do not thou pray for this people, nor take to thee praise and supplication for them, and do not withstand me: for I will not hear thee."

[7] However, it happens at times that a person is refused because of friendship a petition which he asks of a friend, since he knows that it is harmful to him, or that the opposite is more helpful to him. Thus, a physician may deny sometimes the request of a sick person, having in mind that it is not beneficial to him in the recovery of his health. Consequently, since we showed that God, because of the love which He has for the rational creature, satisfies his desires

4. *Ibid.*, ¶4.
5. *Ibid.*, ¶5.

when they are presented to Him through prayer, it is no cause for astonishment if at times He does not grant the petition, even of those whom He especially loves, in order to provide something that is more helpful for the salvation of the petitioner. For this reason, He did not withdraw the sting of the the flesh from Paul, though he asked it thrice, for God foresaw that it was helpful to him for the preservation of humility, as is related in II Corinthians (12:7–9). Hence, the Lord says to certain people, in Matthew (20:22): "You know not what you ask"; and it is said in Romans (8:26): "For we know not what we should pray for as we ought." For this reason, Augustine says in his letter to Paulinus and Therasia: "The Lord is good, for He often does not grant what we desire, so that He may give us what we desire even more."[6]

[8]   It is apparent, then, from the foregoing that the cause of some things that are done by God is prayers and holy desires. But we showed above[7] that divine providence does not exclude other causes; rather, it orders them so that the order which providence has determined within itself may be imposed on things. And thus, secondary causes are not incompatible with providence; instead, they carry out the effect of providence. In this way, then, prayers are efficacious before God, yet they do not destroy the immutable order of divine providence, because this individual request that is granted to a certain petitioner falls under the order of divine providence. So, it is the same thing to say that we should not pray in order to obtain something from God, because the order of His providence is immutable, as to say that we should not walk in order to get to a place, or eat in order to be nourished; all of which are clearly absurd.

[9]   So, a double error concerning prayer is set aside as a result of the foregoing. Some people have said that prayer is not fruitful. In fact, this has been stated both by those

6. St. Augustine, *Epistola*, XXXI, 1 (PL, 33, col. 121).
7. See above, ch. 77.

who denied divine providence altogether, like the Epicureans, and by those who set human affairs apart from divine providence, as some Peripatetics do,[8] and also by those who thought that all things subject to providence occur of necessity, as the Stoics did.[9] From all these views, it follows that prayer is fruitless and, consequently, that all worship of the Deity is offered in vain. Indeed, this error is mentioned in Malachias (3:14), where it states: "You have said: He laboreth in vain that serveth God. And what profit is it that we have kept His ordinances, and that we have walked sorrowful before the Lord of hosts?"

[10] Contrariwise, others have in fact said that the divine disposition is capable of being changed by prayers; thus, the Egyptians said that fate was subject to change by prayers and by means of certain idols, incensings, or incantations.

[11] Indeed, certain statements in the divine Scriptures seem, according to their superficial appearance, to favor this view. For it is said that Isaias, at the command of the Lord, said to King Ezechias: "Thus saith the Lord: Take order with thy house, for thou shalt die, and shalt not live"; and that, after the prayer of Ezechias, "the word of the Lord came to Isaias, saying: Go and say to Ezechias . . . I have heard thy prayer . . . behold I will add to thy days fifteen years" (Isa. 38:1–5). And again, it is said in the name of the Lord: "I will suddenly speak against a nation and against a kingdom to root out and to pull down and to destroy it. If that nation against which I have spoken shall repent of their evil, I will also repent of the evil that I have thought to do to them" (Jer. 18:7–8). And in Joel (2:13–14; Douay modified): "Turn to the Lord your God, for He is gracious and merciful . . . Who knoweth whether God will return and forgive?"

[12] Now, these texts, if understood superficially, lead to an unsuitable conclusion. For it follows, first of all, that God's will is mutable; also, that something accrues to God

8. See above, ch. 75, ¶16.
9. See above, ch. 73, ¶7.

in the course of time; and further, that certain things that occur in time to creatures are the cause of something occurring in God. Obviously, these things are impossible, as is evident from earlier explanations.[10]

[13]   They are opposed, too, by texts of Sacred Scripture which contain the infallible truth clearly expressed. Indeed, it is said in Numbers (23:19): "God is not as a man that He should lie, nor as the son of man that He should be changed. Hath He said then, and will He not do? Hath he spoken, and Will He not fulfill?" And in I Kings (15:29): "The triumpher in Israel will not spare, and will not be moved to repentance; for He is not a man that He should repent." And in Malachias (3:6): "I am the Lord and I change not."

[14]   Now, if a person carefully considers these statements, he will find that every error that occurs on these points arises from the fact that thought is not given to the difference between universal and particular order. For, since all effects are mutually ordered, in the sense that they come together in one cause, it must be that, the more universal the cause is, the more general is the order. Hence, the order stemming from the universal cause which is God must embrace all things. So, nothing prevents some particular order from being changed, either by prayer, or by some other means, for there is something outside that order which could change it. For this reason, it is not astonishing for the Egyptians, who reduce the order of human affairs to the celestial bodies, to claim that fate, which depends on the stars, can be changed by certain prayers and ceremonies. Indeed, apart from the celestial bodies and above them is God, Who is able to impede the celestial bodies' effect which was supposed to follow in things here below as a result of their influence.

But, outside the order that embraces all things, it is not possible for anything to be indicated by means of which the order depending on a universal cause might be changed.

10. *SCG*, I, ch. 13ff.

That is why the Stoics, who considered the reduction of the order of things to God to be to a universal cause of all things, claimed that the order established by God could not be changed for any reason. But, again on this point, they departed from the consideration of a universal order, because they claimed that prayers were of no use, as if they thought that the wills of men and their desires, from which prayers arise, are not included under that universal order. For, when they say that, whether prayers are offered or not, in any case the same effect in things follows from the universal order of things, they clearly isolate from that universal order the wishes of those who pray. For, if these prayers be included under that order, then certain effects will result by divine ordination by means of these prayers, just as they do by means of other causes. So, it will be the same thing to exclude the effect of prayer as to exclude the effect of all other causes. Because, if the immutability of the divine order does not take away their effects from other causes, neither does it remove the efficacy of prayers. Therefore, prayers retain their power; not that they can change the order of eternal control, but rather as they themselves exist under such order.

[15] But nothing prevents some particular order, due to an inferior cause, from being changed through the efficacy of prayers, under the operation of God Who transcends all causes, and thus is not confined under the necessity of any order of cause; on the contrary, all the necessity of the order of an inferior cause is confined under Him as being brought into being by Him. So, in so far as something in the order of inferior causes established by God is changed through prayer, God is said *to turn* or *to repent*; not in the sense that His eternal disposition is changed, but that some effect of His is changed. Hence, Gregory says that "God does not change His plan, though at times He may change His judgment";[11] not, I say, the judgment which expresses His eternal disposition, but the judgment which expresses the order of inferior causes, in accord with

11. St. Gregory, *Moralia*, XVI, 10 (*PL*, 76, col. 1127).

which Ezechias was to have died, or a certain people were
to have been punished for their sins.[12] Now, such a change
of judgment is called God's *repentance*, using a metaphor-
ical way of speaking, in the sense that God is disposed
like one who repents, for whom it is proper to change
what he had been doing. In the same way, He is also said,
metaphorically, *to become angry*, in the sense that, by
punishing, He produces the same effect as an angry person.[13]

Chapter 97.

HOW THE DISPOSITION OF PROVIDENCE HAS
A RATIONAL PLAN

[1]   From the points set forth above it may be seen
clearly that the things which are disposed by divine
providence follow a rational plan.

[2]   Indeed, we showed that God, through His providence,
orders all things to the divine goodness, as to an end;[1] not,
of course, in such a way that something adds to His goodness by means of things that are made, but, rather, that the
likeness of His goodness, as much as possible, is impressed
on things.[2] However, since every created substance must
fall short of the perfection of divine goodness, in order
that the likeness of divine goodness might be more perfectly communicated to things, it was necessary for there to
be a diversity of things, so that what could not be perfectly
represented by one thing might be, in more perfect fashion,
represented by a variety of things in different ways. For
instance, when a man sees that his mental conception cannot be expressed adequately by one spoken word, he multi-
plies his words in various ways, to express his mental conception through a variety of means. And the eminence of

12. Above, ¶11.
13. SCG, I, ch. 91.
1. See above, ch. 64.
2. See above, ch. 18ff.

divine perfection may be observed in this fact, that perfect goodness which is present in God in a unified and simple manner cannot be in creatures except in a diversified manner and through a plurality of things. Now, things are differentiated by their possession of different forms from which they receive their species. And thus, the reason for the diversity of forms in things is derived from this end.

[3] Moreover, the reason for the order of things is derived from the diversity of forms. Indeed, since it is in accord with its form that a thing has being, and since anything, in so far as it has being, approaches the likeness of God Who is His own simple being, it must be that form is nothing else than a divine likeness that is participated in things. Hence, Aristotle, where he speaks about form in *Physics* I, quite appropriately says that it is "something godlike and desirable."³ But a likeness that is viewed in relation to one simple thing cannot be diversified unless by virtue of the likeness being more or less close or remote. Now, the nearer a thing comes to divine likeness, the more perfect it is. Consequently, there cannot be a difference among forms unless because one thing exists more perfectly than another. That is why Aristotle, in *Metaphysics* VIII,⁴ likens definitions, through which the natures of things and forms are signified, to numbers, in which species are varied by the addition or subtraction of unity; so, from this, we are made to understand that the diversity of forms requires different grades of perfection.

This is quite clear to one who observes the natures of things. He will find, in fact, if he makes a careful consideration, that the diversity of things is accomplished by means of gradations. Indeed, he will find plants above inanimate bodies, and above plants irrational animals, and above these intellectual substances. And among individuals of these types he will find a diversity based on the fact that some are more perfect than others, inasmuch as the highest members of a lower genus seem quite close to the

3. Aristotle, *Physics*, I, 9 (192a 17).
4. Aristotle, *Metaphysics*, VIII, 3 (1043b 34).

next higher genus; and the converse is also true; thus, immovable animals are like plants. Consequently, Dionysius says "Divine wisdom draws together the last members of things in a first class, with the first members of things in a second class."[5] Hence, it is apparent that the diversity of things requires that not all be equal, but that there be an order and gradation among things.

[4]   Now, from the diversity of forms by which the species of things are differentiated there also results a difference of operations. For, since everything acts in so far as it is actual (because things that are potential are found by that very fact to be devoid of action), and since every being is actual through form, it is necessary for the operation of a thing to follow its form. Therefore, if there are different forms, they must have different operations.

[5]   But, since each thing attains its proper end through its own action, various proper ends must be distinguished in things, even though the ultimate end is common to all.

[6]   From the diversity of forms there also follows a diverse relationship of matter to things. In fact, since forms differ because some are more perfect than others, there are some of them so perfect that they are self-subsistent and self-complete, requiring no sub-structure of matter. But other forms cannot perfectly subsist by themselves, and do require matter as a foundation, so that what does subsist is not simply form, nor yet merely matter, but a thing composed of both.

[7]   Now, matter and form could not combine to make up one thing unless there were some proportion between them. But, if they must be proportionally related, then different matters must correspond to different forms. Hence, it develops that some forms need simple matter, while others need composite matter; and also, depending on the various forms, there must be a different composition of parts, adapted to the species of the form and to its operation.

5. Pseudo-Dionysius, De divinis nominibus, VII, 3 (PG, 3, col. 872).

[8] Moreover, as a result of the diversified relationship to matter, there follows a diversity of agents and patients. For, since each thing acts by reason of its form, but suffers passion and is moved by reason of its matter, those things whose forms are more perfect and less material must act on those that are more material and whose forms are more imperfect.

[9] Again, from the diversity of forms and matters and agents there follows a diversity of properties and accidents. Indeed, since substance is the cause of accident, as the perfect is of the imperfect, different proper accidents must result from different substantial principles. In turn, since from different agents there result different impressions on the patients, there must be, depending on the different agents, different accidents that are impressed by agents.

[10] So, it is evident from what we have said that, when various accidents, actions, passions, and arrangements are allotted things by divine providence, this distribution does not come about without a rational plan. Hence, Sacred Scripture ascribes the production and governance of things to divine wisdom and prudence. Indeed, it is stated in Proverbs (3:19-20): "The Lord by wisdom hath founded the earth; He hath established the heavens by prudence. By His wisdom the depths have broken out, and the clouds grow thick with dew." And in Wisdom (8:1) it is said of the wisdom of God that "it reacheth from end to end mightily, and ordereth all things sweetly." Again, it is said in the same book: "Thou hast ordered all things in measure, and number, and weight" (Wisd. 11:21). Thus, we may understand by *measure*: the amount, or the mode, or degree, of perfection pertaining to each thing; but by *number*: the plurality and diversity of species resulting from the different degrees of perfection; and by *weight*: the different inclinations to proper ends and operations, and also the agents, patients, and accidents which result from the distinction of species.

[11] Now, in the aforesaid order, in which the rational plan of divine providence is observed, we have said that first place is occupied by divine goodness as the ultimate end, which is the first principle in matters of action. Next comes the numerical plurality of things, for the constitution of which there must be different degrees in forms and matters, and in agents and patients, and in actions and accidents. Therefore, just as the first rational principle of divine providence is simply the divine goodness, so the first rational principle in creatures is their numerical plurality, to the establishment and conservation of which all other things seem to be ordered. Thus, on this basis it seems to have been reasonably stated by Boethius, at the beginning of his *Arithmetic*, that: "All things whatsover that have been established, at the original coming into being of things, seem to have been formed in dependence on the rational character of numbers."[6]

[12] Moreover, we should consider the fact that operative and speculative reason partly agree and partly disagree. They agree, indeed, on this point: just as speculative reason starts from some principle and proceeds through intermediaries to the intended conclusion, so does operative reason start from something that is first, and go through certain intermediaries to the operation, or to the product of the operation, which is intended. But the principle in speculative matters is the form and *that which is*; while in operative matters it is the end, which at times is the form, at other times something else. Also, the principle in speculative matters must always be necessary, but in operative matters it is sometimes necessary and sometimes not. Indeed, it is necessary for a man to will felicity as his end, but it is not necessary to will to build a house. Likewise, in matters of demonstration the posterior propositions always follow of necessity from the prior ones, but it is not always so in operative reasoning; rather, it is only so when there can be only this single way of reaching the end. For instance, it is necessary for a man who wishes to build

6. Boethius, *Arithmeticae*, I, 2 (PL, 63, col. 1083).

a house to get some lumber, but the fact that he tries to get lumber made of fir depends solely on his own will, and not at all on the reason for building the house.

[13] And so, the fact that God loves His goodness is necessary, but the fact that it is represented by means of creatures is not necessary, because divine goodness is perfect without them. Hence, the fact that creatures are brought into existence, though it takes its origin from the rational character of divine goodness, nevertheless depends solely on God's will. But, if it be granted that God wills to communicate, in so far as is possible, His goodness to creatures by way of likeness, then one finds in this the reason why there are different creatures, but it does not necessarily follow that they are differentiated on the basis of this or that measure of perfection, or according to this or that number of things. On the other hand, if we grant that, as a result of an act of divine will, He wills to establish this particular number of things, and this definite measure of perfection for each thing, then as a result one finds the reason why each thing has a certain form and a certain kind of matter. And the same conclusion is obvious in regard to the things that follow.

[14] So, it becomes apparent that providence disposes things according to a rational plan; yet this plan is taken as something based on the divine will.

[15] Thus, a double error is set aside by the foregoing points. There is the mistake of those who believe that all things follow, without any rational plan, from God's pure will. This is the error of the exponents of the Law of the Moors, as Rabbi Moses says;[7] according to them, it makes no difference whether fire heats or cools, unless God wills it so. Also refuted is the error of those who say that the order of causes comes forth from divine providence

7. Moses Maimonides, *Guide for the Perplexed*, III, 25 (trans. Friedländer, p. 308). On these Moslem theologians, see above, ch. 69.

by way of necessity.[8] It is evident from what we have said that both of these views are false.

[16]   However, there are some texts of Scripture that seem to attribute all things to the pure divine will. These are not expressed in order that reason may be removed from the dispensation of providence, but to show that the will of God is the first principle of all things, as we have already said above. Such a text is that of the Psalm (134:6): "All things whatsoever the Lord hath willed, He hath done";[9] again in Job (9:12): "Who can say to Him: Why dost Thou so?" Also in Romans (9:19): "Who resisteth His will?" And Augustine says: "Nothing but the will of God is the first cause of health and sickness, of rewards and punishments, of graces and retributions."[10]

[17]   And so, when we ask the reason why,[11] in regard to a natural effect, we can give a reason based on a proximate cause; provided, of course, that we trace back all things to the divine will as a first cause. Thus, if the question is asked: "Why is wood heated in the presence of fire?" it is answered: "Because heating is the natural action of fire"; and this is so "because heat is its proper accident." But this is the result of its proper form, and so on, until we come to the divine will. Hence, if a person answers someone who asks why wood is heated: "Because God willed it," he is answering it appropriately, provided he intends to take the question back to a first cause; but not appropriately, if he means to exclude all other causes.[12]

8. See above, ch. 72ff. and ch. 94.
9. Douay modified; it has "pleased" instead of "willed," and omits "All"; in the text from Job Douay does not have "to Him." The present translation follows the Latin texts as cited by St. Thomas.
10. St. Augustine, *De Trinitate*, III, 3–4 (*PL*, 42, col. 872–873).
11. That is, "cum quaeritur *propter quid.*"
12. These lines are very important in determining the relation of St. Thomas' view of causality to that of St. Augustine.

Chapter 98.

HOW GOD CAN ACT APART FROM THE ORDER OF HIS PROVIDENCE, AND HOW NOT

[1]   Moreover, from the foregoing, consideration can be made of a twofold order: one depends on the first cause of all, and consequently takes in all things; while the other is particular, since it depends on a created cause and includes the things that are subject to it. The second is also of many types, depending on the diversity of causes that are found among creatures. Yet, one order is included under another, just as one cause stands under another. Consequently, all particular orders are contained under the universal order, and they come down from that order which is present in things by virtue of their dependence on the first cause. An illustration of this may be observed in the political area. As a matter of fact, all the members of a family, with one male head of the household, have a definite order to each other, depending on their being subject to him. Then, in turn, both this head of the family and all other fathers who belong to his state have a certain order in regard to each other, and to the governor of the state; and again, the latter, together with all other governors who belong in the kingdom, have an order in relation to the king.

[2]   However, we can consider the universal order in two ways, in accord with which all things are ordered by divine providence: that is to say, in regard to the things subject to the order, and in regard to the plan of the order which depends on the principle of order. Now, we showed in Book Two[1] that these things which are subordinated to God do not come forth from Him, as from one who acts by natural necessity, or any other kind of necessity, but from His simple will, especially as regards the original establishment

1. *SCG*, II, ch. 23ff.

of things. The conclusion remains, then, that apart from the things that fall under the order of divine providence God can make other things, for His power is not tied down to these things.

[3]   But, if we were to consider the foregoing order in relation to the rational plan which depends on the principle, then God cannot do what is apart from that order. For that order derives, as we showed,[2] from the knowledge and will of God, ordering all things to His goodness as an end. Of course, it is not possible for God to do anything that is not willed by Him, since creatures do not come forth from Him by nature but by will, as has been shown.[3] Nor, again, is it possible that something be done by Him which is not comprehended in His knowledge, since it is impossible for anything to be willed unless it be known. Nor, further, is it possible for Him to do anything in regard to creatures which is not ordered to His goodness as an end, since His goodness is the proper object of His will. In the same way, since God is utterly immutable, it is impossible for Him to will something which He has previously rejected with His will; or for Him to begin to know something new; or to order it to His goodness in a new way. Therefore, God can do nothing that does not fall under the order of His providence, just as He can do nothing that is not subject to His operation. Nevertheless, *if His power be considered without qualification*, He can do other things than those which are subject to His providence or operation, but, *because of the fact that He cannot be mutable*, He cannot do things that have not been eternally under the order of His providence.

[4]   Now, certain people who have not kept this distinction in mind have fallen into various errors. Thus, some have tried to stretch the immutability of divine order to the things themselves that are subject to the order, asserting that all things must be as they are, with the result that some

2. See above, ch. 97.
3. Above, ¶2.

have said that God can do no things other than what He does.[4] Against this view is what is found in Matthew (26:53): "Cannot I ask my Father, and He will give me more than twelve legions of angels?"

[5]   Certain others, conversely, have transferred the mutability of things subject to divine providence to a mutability of divine providence, thinking in their carnal wisdom that God, in the fashion of a carnal man, is mutable in His will. Against this it is stated in Numbers (23:19): "God is not as a man that He should lie, nor as the son of man that He should be changed."

[6]   Others still have removed contingent events from divine providence. Against them it is said in Lamentations (3:37): "Who is he that commandeth a thing to be done, when the Lord commandeth it not?"

Chapter 99.

THAT GOD CAN WORK APART FROM THE ORDER IMPLANTED IN THINGS, BY PRODUCING EFFECTS WITHOUT PROXIMATE CAUSES

[1]   It remains to show now that He can act apart from the order implanted by Him in things.

[2]   Indeed, there is an order divinely instituted in things to the effect that lower things are moved through higher ones by God, as we said above.[1] Now, God can act apart from this order; for instance, He may Himself produce an effect in lower things, with nothing being done, in this case, by a higher agent. In fact, there is a difference on this point between an agent that acts by natural necessity and one that acts according to will; an effect cannot result from

4. See St. Thomas, *De potentia Dei*, q. I, art. 5.
1. See above, ch. 83 and 88.

one that acts by natural necessity except according to the mode of the active power—so, an agent that has very great power cannot directly produce a small effect, but it produces an effect in proportion to its power. But, in this effect, there is sometimes less power than in the cause, and so, by means of many intermediaries, there finally comes to be a small effect from the highest cause. However, the situation is not the same in the case of an agent working through will. For one who acts through will is able at once to produce without an intermediary any effect that does not exceed its power. For instance, the very perfect artisan can produce any kind of work that the less perfect artisan could make. Now, God operates through will, and not through natural necessity, as we showed above.[2] Therefore, He can produce immediately, without special causes, the smaller effects that are produced by lower causes.

[3]   Again, the divine power is related to all active powers as a universal power in regard to particular powers, as is evident from our earlier statements.[3] Now, universal active power can be limited in two ways for the purpose of producing a particular effect. One way is by means of a particular intermediate cause: thus, the active power of a celestial body is limited to the effect of generating human beings, by the particular power which is in the semen; so, too, in syllogisms, the force of the universal proposition is limited to a particular conclusion, by the inclusion of a particular premise. Another way is by means of understanding, which apprehends a definite form and produces it in the effect. But the divine understanding is capable of knowing not only the divine essence which is like a universal active power, and also not only of knowing universal and first causes, but all particular ones, as is clear from the things said above.[4] Therefore, it is able to produce immediately every effect that any particular agent can bring about.

2. *SCG*, ch. 23ff.
3. See above, ch. 67.
4. *SCG*, I, ch. 50.

[4] Besides, since accidents result from the substantial principles of a thing, the agent who immediately produces the substance of a thing must be able immediately to cause, in relation to this thing, anything whatever that results from the thing's substance. For instance, the generating agent, because it gives the form, gives all the properties and resultant motions. Now, we showed above[5] that God, at the first establishment of things, brought all things immediately into being by creation. Therefore, He is able immediately to move anything to any effect without intermediate causes.

[5] Moreover, the order of things flows forth from God into things, according as it is foreknown in His intellect. We observe, for example, in human affairs that the head of a state imposes on the citizens an order that is preconceived within himself. But the divine understanding is not determined by necessity to this particular order, in the sense that He can understand no other order; because even we can apprehend intellectually another order. For instance, it can be understood by us that God may form a man from the earth without the use of semen. Therefore, God can bring about the proper effect of these causes without lower causes.

[6] Furthermore, although the order implanted in things by divine providence represents in its own way divine goodness, it does not represent it perfectly, because the goodness of a creature does not attain to equality with divine goodness. But that which is not perfectly represented by a given copy may again be represented in another way besides this one. Now, the representation in things of the divine goodness is the end for the production of things by God, as we showed above.[6] Therefore, the divine will is not limited to this particular order of causes and effects in such a manner that it is unable to will to produce im-

5. *SCG*, II, ch. 21.
6. See above, ch. 19.

mediately an effect in things here below without using any other causes.

[7]   Again, the whole of creation is more subject to God than the human body is to its soul, for the soul is in proportion to its body, as its form, but God surpasses all proportion to creation. Now, as a result of the soul imagining something and being moved by strong emotion in regard to it, there follows at times a change in the body toward good health or sickness, independent of the action of the bodily principles that are present from birth in the body, in order to affect sickness or health. Therefore, by all the greater reason, as a result of divine will, an effect can be produced in creatures without using the causes that are naturally brought into being for the purpose of producing such an effect.

[8]   Besides, according to the order of nature, the active powers of the elements are subordinated to the active powers of the celestial bodies. But, at times, celestial power brings about the proper effect of the elemental powers without the action of the element. An example is the sun heating, independently of the action of fire. Therefore, the divine power, for a much greater reason, can produce the proper effects of created causes without the action of these causes.

[9]   Now, if someone says that, since God did implant this order in things, the production in things of an effect independently of its proper causes, and apart from the order established by Him, could not be done without a change in this order, this objection can be refuted by the very nature of things. For the order imposed on things by God is based on what usually occurs, *in most cases*, in things, but not on what is always so. In fact, many natural causes produce their effects in the same way, but not always. Sometimes, indeed, though rarely, an event occurs in a different way, either due to a defect in the power of an agent, or to the unsuitable condition of the matter, or to an agent with greater strength—as when nature gives rise to a sixth finger on a man. But the order of providence

does not fail, or suffer change, because of such an event. Indeed, the very fact that the natural order, which is based on things that happen in most cases, does fail at times is subject to divine providence. So, if by means of a created power it can happen that the natural order is changed from what is usually so to what occurs rarely—without any change of divine providence—then it is more certain that divine power can sometimes produce an effect, without prejudice to its providence, apart from the order implanted in natural things by God. In fact, He does this at times to manifest His power. For it can be manifested in no better way, that the whole of nature is subject to the divine will, than by the fact that sometimes He does something outside the order of nature. Indeed, this makes it evident that the order of things has proceeded from Him, not by natural necessity, but by free will.

[10] Nor should this argument, that God does a thing in nature in order to manifest Himself to the minds of men, be regarded as of slight importance, because we showed above[7] that all corporeal creatures are, in a sense, ordered to intellectual nature as an end; moreover, the end of this intellectual nature is divine knowledge, as we showed in earlier remarks.[8] So, it is not astonishing that some change is made in corporeal substance in order to make provision for the knowing of God by intellectual nature.

Chapter 100.

THAT THINGS WHICH GOD DOES APART FROM THE ORDER OF NATURE ARE NOT CONTRARY TO NATURE

[1] However, it seems that we should keep in mind that, though God at times does something apart from the order implanted in things, He does nothing contrary to nature.

7. See above, ch. 22.
8. See above, ch. 25.

[2]   In fact, since God is pure act, whereas all other things have some admixture of potency, God must be related to all else as a mover is to what is moved, and as the active is to what is in potency. Now, considering a thing that is in potency in the natural order to a certain agent, if some impression is made on it by that agent, this is not contrary to nature in an absolute sense, though it may be at times contrary to the particular form which is corrupted by this action. Thus, when fire is generated and air is corrupted by the fiery agent, natural generation and corruption take place. So, whatever is done by God in created things is not contrary to nature, even though it may seem to be opposed to the proper order of a particular nature.

[3]   Again, since God is the primary agent, as we showed above,[1] all things that come after Him are like instruments for Him. But instruments are made for the purpose of subserving the action of the principal agent, while being moved by him. Consequently, the matter and form of an instrument should be such that they are suitable for the action which the principal agent intends. This is why it is not contrary to the nature of an instrument for it to be moved by a principal agent, but, rather, is most fitting for it. Therefore, it is not contrary to nature when created things are moved in any way by God; indeed, they were so made that they might serve Him.

[4]   Besides, even among corporeal agents it may be observed that the motions that go on in lower bodies, as a result of the action of higher ones, are not violent or contrary to nature, though they may not seem to be in agreement with the natural motion which the lower body has in accord with the particular character of its form. For instance, we do not say that the tidal ebb and flow of the sea is a violent motion, because it results from the influence of a celestial body; even though the natural motion of water is only in one direction, toward the center. Therefore, it is much more impossible to say that whatever is done in any creature by God is violent or contrary to nature.

1. SCG, I, ch. 13.

[5]   Moreover, the primary measure of the essence and nature of each thing is God; just as He is the first being, which is the cause of being in all things. Now, since a judgment concerning anything is based on its measure, what is natural for anything must be deemed what is in conformity with its measure. So, what is implanted by God in a thing will be natural to it. Therefore, even if something else is impressed on the same thing by God, that is not contrary to nature.

[6]   Furthermore, all creatures are related to God as art products are to an artist, as is clear from the foregoing.[2] Consequently, the whole of nature is like an artifact of the divine artistic mind. But it is not contrary to the essential character of an artist if he should work in a different way on his product, even after he has given it its first form. Neither, then, is it against nature if God does something to natural things in a different way from that to which the course of nature is accustomed.

[7]   Hence, Augustine says: "God, the creator and founder of all natures, does nothing contrary to nature; for what the source of all measure, number and order in nature does, is natural to each thing."[3]

Chapter 101.

ON MIRACLES

[1]   Things that are at times divinely accomplished, apart from the generally established order in things, are customarily called *miracles*; for we admire with some astonishment a certain event when we observe the effect but do not know its cause. And since one and the same cause is at times known to some people and unknown to others, the result is that, of several who see an effect at the same time,

2. *SCG*, II, ch. 24.
3. St. Augustine, *Contra Faustum*, XXVI, 3 (*PL*, 42, col. 480).

some are moved to admiring astonishment, while others are not. For instance, the astronomer is not astonished when he sees an eclipse of the sun, for he knows its cause, but the person who is ignorant of this science must be amazed, for he ignores the cause. And so, a certain event is wondrous to one person, but not so to another. So, a thing that has a completely hidden cause is wondrous in an unqualified way, and this the name, *miracle*, suggests; namely, *what is of itself filled with admirable wonder*, not simply in relation to one person or another. Now, absolutely speaking, the cause hidden from every man is God. In fact, we proved above[1] that no man in the present state of life can grasp His essence intellectually. Therefore, those things must properly be called miraculous which are done by divine power apart from the order generally followed in things.

[2] Now, there are various degrees and orders of these miracles. Indeed, the highest rank among miracles is held by those events in which something is done by God which nature never could do. For example, that two bodies should be coincident; that the sun reverse its course, or stand still; that the sea open up and offer a way through which people may pass. And even among these an order may be observed. For the greater the things that God does are, and the more they are removed from the capacity of nature, the greater the miracle is. Thus, it is more miraculous for the sun to reverse its course than for the sea to be divided.

[3] Then, the second degree among miracles is held by those events in which God does something which nature can do, but not in this order. It is a work of nature for an animal to live, to see, and to walk; but for it to live after death, to see after becoming blind, to walk after paralysis of the limbs, this nature cannot do—but God at times does such works miraculously. Even among this degree of miracles a gradation is evident, according as what is done is more removed from the capacity of nature.

[4] Now, the third degree of miracles occurs when God does what is usually done by the working of nature, but

1. See above, ch. 47.

without the operation of the principles of nature. For example, a person may be cured by divine power from a fever which could be cured naturally, and it may rain independently of the working of the principles of nature.

Chapter 102.

THAT GOD ALONE WORKS MIRACLES

[1] It can be shown from the foregoing that God alone can work miracles.

[2] In fact, whatever is completely confined under a certain order cannot work above that order. But every creature is established under the order which God has put in things. So, no creature can operate above this order; but that is what it means to work miracles.

[3] Again, when any finite power produces the proper effect to which it is determined, this is not a miracle, though it may be a matter of wonder for some person who does not understand that power. For example, it may seem astonishing to ignorant people that a magnet attracts iron or that some little fish might hold back a ship. But the potency of every creature is limited to some definite effect or to certain effects. So, whatever is done by the power of any creature cannot be called a miracle properly, even though it may be astonishing to one who does not comprehend the power of this creature. But what is done by divine power, which, being infinite, is incomprehensible in itself, is truly miraculous.

[4] Besides, every creature needs for its action some subject on which to act, for it is the prerogative of God alone to make something out of nothing, as we showed above.[1] Now, nothing that requires a subject for its action can do anything other than that to which the subject is in potency, for the agent acts on the subject in order to bring it from

1. *SCG*, II, ch. 16 and 21.

potency to act. So, just as no creature can create, so no creature can produce any effect in a thing except what is within the potency of that thing. But many miracles are divinely accomplished, when something is done in a thing, which is not within the potency of that thing; for instance, that a dead person be revived, that the sun move backwards, that two bodies be coincident. Therefore, these miracles cannot be done by any created power.

[5] Moreover, the subject in which an action goes on has a relation both to the agent that reduces it from potency to act and to the act to which it is reduced. Hence, just as a certain subject is in potency to some definite act, and not to merely any act, so also is it impossible for it to be reduced from potency to some definite act except by means of some definite agent. Indeed, a different kind of agent is required to reduce to different types of act. For instance, since air is potentially either fire or water, it is actually made into fire by one agent and into water by a different one. Likewise, it is clear that corporeal matter is not brought to the condition of perfect actuality by the sole power of a universal agent; rather, there must be a particular agent by which the influence of the universal power is limited to a definite effect. Of course, corporeal matter may be brought to less perfect actuality by universal power alone, without a particular agent. For example, perfect animals are not generated by celestial power alone, but require a definite kind of semen; however, for the generation of certain imperfect animals, celestial power by itself is enough, without semen. So, if the effects that are accomplished in these lower bodies are naturally capable of being done by superior universal causes without the working of particular lower causes, such accomplishment is not miraculous. Thus, it is not miraculous for animals to be originated from putrefaction, independently of semen. But, if they do not naturally come about through superior causes alone, then particular lower causes are needed for their development. Now, when some effect is produced by a higher cause through the mediation of proper principles, there is no miracle. Therefore, no

miracles can be worked in any way by the power of the higher creatures.

[6] Furthermore, it seems to pertain to the same rational principle for a thing to be produced from a subject; for that to which the subject is in potency to be produced; and for an orderly action to be produced through definite intermediate stages. Indeed, a subject is not advanced to proximate potency unless it has become actual in regard to the intermediate stages; thus, food is not immediately potential flesh, but only when it has been changed into blood. Now, every creature must have a subject, in order to make something, nor can it make anything to which the subject is not in potency, as we showed. So, it cannot make anything unless the subject is brought to actuality through definite intermediate stages. Miracles, then, which result from the fact that an effect is produced, but not according to the order in which it can be accomplished naturally, cannot be worked by the power of a creature.

[7] Again, a certain order may be observed in the types of motion. The primary motion is local movement, and so it is the cause of the other kinds, since the first in any genus is the cause of the subsequent items in that genus. Now, every effect that is produced in these lower things must be produced by some generation or alteration. So, this must occur by means of something that is moved locally if it be accomplished by an incorporeal agent, which, strictly speaking, cannot be moved locally. Now, the effects that are produced by incorporeal substances through corporeal instruments are not miraculous, since bodies only work naturally. Therefore, created incorporeal substances cannot work any miracles by their own power, and much less can corporeal substances whose every action is natural.

[8] So, it is the prerogative of God alone to work miracles. Indeed, He is superior to the order in which the whole of things are contained, just as from His providence this entire order flows. Moreover, His power, being utterly infinite, is

not limited to any special effect or to the production of a particular effect in any limited way, or order.

[9]   Hence it is said about God in the Psalm (135:4): "Who alone doth great wonders."

Chapter 103.

HOW SPIRITUAL SUBSTANCES DO CERTAIN WONDERFUL THINGS WHICH, HOWEVER, ARE NOT TRULY MIRACLES

[1]   It was Avicenna's position that matter is much more obedient to separate substances, in the production of a certain effect, than it is to the contrary agencies within matter. Consequently, he claimed that, when there is an act of apprehension in the aforesaid substances, there results at times an effect in these things here below—for instance, rain, or the healing of a sick person—without the mediation of a corporeal agent.

[2]   He took an indication of this from our soul.[1] For, when it is possessed of a strong imagination, its body may be changed by an act of cognition alone. For example, when a man is walking over a beam placed at some height, he falls quite easily because, through fear, he imagines his fall. But he would not fall if the beam were placed on the earth, where there would be no possibility of fearing a fall. It is also obvious that, simply as a result of the cognitive act of the soul, the body becomes hot, as happens in those who are prone to concupiscence, or anger; or it may also grow cold, as happens in those subject to fear. Sometimes, too, it is moved by a strong cognitive act toward some illness, such as fever, or even leprosy. And on this basis, he says that, if the soul be pure, not subject to bodily passions, and strong in its cognitive functioning, then not only its own body, but even external bodies, obey its act of appre-

1. Avicenna, De anima, IV, 4, fol. 20v.

hension. So much so, that on the occurrence of its act of apprehension a sick person may be cured, or some similar result may occur. And he claims that this is the explanation of the casting of a spell by fascination;[2] namely, that the soul of a person strongly moved by malevolence has the power to inflict an injury on someone, particularly a child, who is quite susceptible to impressions, because of the tender condition of his body. Consequently, Avicenna favored the notion that it is much more likely that the cognitive functions of separate substances, which he regarded as the souls or movers of the spheres, result in certain effects in lower bodies, without the action of any corporeal agent.

[3] Now, this theory is in agreement with his other views.[3] For he asserts that all substantial forms flow down to these lower bodies from separate substances, and that corporeal agents are merely to prepare matter to receive the impression of a separate agent. Of course, this is not true, according to the teaching of Aristotle, who proves, in the *Metaphysics*,[4] that the forms which are in matter do not come from separate forms, but from forms which are in matter; in this way, in fact, the likeness between the maker and the thing made is discovered.

[4] Moreover, the example that he takes from the influence of the soul on the body does not help his contention much. For no change in the body results from an act of apprehension unless there be attached to the apprehension some sort of emotion, such as joy or fear, or lust, or some other passion. Now, passions of this kind occur along with a definite motion of the heart, from which there results later a change of the whole body, either in the way of local motion or of alteration. Consequently, it still remains true that the act of apprehension in a spiritual substance does not alter the body except through the mediation of local motion.

2. See St. Thomas, *Summa Theologiae*, I, 117, 3, ad 2, for a further discussion of "fascination" or the "evil eye."
3. See Avicenna, *Metaphysica*, IX, 5, fol. 105rv.
4. Aristotle, *Metaphysics*, VI, 8 (1033b 26).

[5]   Again, what he suggests in regard to fascination does not happen as a result of the apprehension of one person immediately changing the body of another, but because, by means of the motion of the heart, it causes a change in the body that is united with the soul; and its change reaches the eye, from which it is possible to affect something external, particularly if it is easily changed. Thus, for instance, the eye of a menstruating woman may affect a mirror.[5]

[6]   So, with the exception of the use of the local motion of some body, a created spiritual substance cannot by its own power produce any form in bodily matter, in the sense that matter would be directly subject to it in order to become actual in terms of a form. Of course, there is this capacity within the power of a spiritual substance: a body is obedient to it in regard to local motion. But, to move any body locally, it makes use of any naturally active power in order to produce its effects, just as the art of metal working makes use of fire in order to soften the metal. Now, this is not miraculous, properly speaking. So, the conclusion stands, that created spiritual substances do not work miracles by their own power.

[7]   Now, I say by their own power, since nothing prevents these substances from working miracles provided they act through divine power. This may be seen from the fact that one order of angels is specially assigned, as Gregory says,[6] to the working of miracles. He even says that some of the saints "work miracles by their power," and not merely through intercession.[7]

[8]   However, we should bear in mind the fact that, when either angels or demons make use of natural things in order to produce definite effects, they use them as instruments, just as a physician uses certain herbs as instruments of healing. Now, there proceeds from an instrument not merely an effect corresponding to the power of the instrument, but

5. See Aristotle, De somniis, II (459b 29).
6. See above, ch. 80.
7. St. Gregory, Dialogus, II, 31 (PL, 66, col. 190).

also an effect beyond its power, in so far as it acts through the power of the principal agent. For instance, a saw or an axe could not make a bed unless they worked as things moved by the art adapted to such a product. Nor could natural heat generate flesh without the power of the vegetative soul which uses it as a sort of instrument. So, it is appropriate that certain higher effects result from these natural things, due to the fact that spiritual substances use them as instruments.

[9] So, then, although such effects cannot be called miracles without qualification, since they do result from natural causes, they remain wonderful to us, in two senses. In one way, this is because such causes are applied by spiritual substances to the production of their effects, in a fashion that is strange to us. As a consequence, the works of clever artisans appear wondrous because it is not evident to other people how they are produced. In a second way, this is due to the fact that natural causes which are applied to the production of certain effects receive a particular power as a result of their being instruments of spiritual substances. This latter way comes rather close to the notion of a miracle.

Chapter 104.

THAT THE WORKS OF MAGICIANS ARE NOT SOLELY DUE TO THE INFLUENCE OF CELESTIAL BODIES

[1] There have been some who say that works of this kind, which are astonishing to us when accomplished by the arts of magic, are not performed by spiritual substances but by the power of celestial bodies.[1] And indication of this is seen

1. In his Introduction (pp. xxxviii and xlvi) to Giles of Rome, *Errores Philosophorum*, trans. J. Riedl (Milwaukee: 1944), Joseph Koch indicates the importance of the treatise of Alkindi, *Theorica artium magicarum*, in the background of this and the next chapter.

in the fact that the precise position of the stars is carefully noted by those who perform these works. Moreover, they make use of certain herbs, and other corporeal things, as aids in the preparation, as it were, of low-grade matter for the reception of the influence of celestial power.

[2] But this view is clearly opposed by the apparitions. Indeed, since it is not possible for understanding to be caused by corporeal principles, as we proved above,[2] it is impossible for effects peculiar to intellectual nature to be caused by the power of a celestial body. Now, among these workings of the magicians some events appear which are the proper functions of a rational nature. For instance, answers are given concerning things removed by theft, and concerning other such matters, and this could be done only through understanding. So, it is not true that all effects of this kind are caused solely by the power of celestial bodies.

[3] Again, speech is itself an act peculiar to a rational nature. Now, certain agents that speak to men appear in these performances, and they reason discursively about various matters. Therefore, it is not possible for things like this to be done solely by the power of celestial bodies.

[4] Now, if someone says that apparitions of this kind do not work through external sensation, but only through the imagination, then, first of all, this does not seem true. In fact, imaginary forms do not look like true things to an observer unless there be a loss of discriminatory power in the external senses. For it is impossible for a person to be made to regard images as things unless the natural power of sense discrimination has been overcome. But these vocal messages and apparitions are made to men who exercise their external senses freely. So, it is not possible for these visions and auditory responses to be solely a matter of imagination.

[5] Then, too, from imaginary forms it is not possible for intellectual knowledge beyond the natural or acquired

2. See above, ch. 84.

ability of the intellect to come to a person. This is clear even in the case of dreams, in which, though there may be some premonition of future events, not everyone who experiences dreams is able to understand their meaning. But, through these visions or auditory messages which appear in the performances of magicians, intellectual knowledge of things which surpass the capacity of his understanding often comes to a person. Examples are the revealing of hidden treasures, the showing of future events, and sometimes true answers are given concerning scientific demonstrations. So, it must be that either these apparitions and vocal messages are not grasped through the imagination only, or, at least, that this case of a man being brought to a knowledge of such matters through imaginary presentations of this kind is done by the power of a higher understanding, and is not done solely by the power of celestial bodies.

[6] Again, what is done by the power of celestial bodies is a natural effect, for the forms that are caused in lower bodies by the power of celestial bodies are natural. So, that which cannot be natural for anything cannot be done by the power of celestial bodies. But some such things are said to be done during the aforementioned performances; for instance, in the presence of a certain man, the bolt of any door is opened for him, a certain person can become invisible, and many other such things are reported. Therefore, it is not possible for this to be done by the power of celestial bodies.

[7] Besides, whenever a subsequent perfection is conferred on a subject by the power of the celestial bodies, what is prior to this perfection is also conferred. Now, the power of self-movement is subsequent to the possession of a soul, for it is proper to animated beings for them to move themselves. So, it is impossible for something inanimate to be made able to move itself by the power of celestial bodies. But it is said that this can be done by the arts of magic; that a statue, for instance, can move itself, or even speak. So, it is not possible for the effect of the arts of magic to be done by celestial power.

[8]   Now, if it is suggested that this statue receives a principle of life from the power of celestial bodies, this is impossible. In fact, the principle of life in all living things is the substantial form, "for living beings, to live is to be," as the Philosopher says in Book II of *On the Soul*.[3] But it is impossible for a thing to receive a new substantial form without losing the form which it previously possessed, "for the generation of one thing is the corruption of another thing."[4] Now, in the process of making a statue no substanial form is ejected; rather, what is accomplished is a change of shape only, and this is accidental; the form of copper, or other material, remains. So, it is not possible for these statues to receive a principle of life.

[9]   Again, if anything is moved by a principle of life, it must have sense power: the mover is, in fact, sense or understanding. Now, understanding is not present in things subject to generation and corruption, without sensation. But sensation cannot be present where there is no touch, nor can touch be without an organ that has a balanced mixture of sensory qualities. Now, such a balanced mixture is not found in stone, or wax, or metal, from which a statue is made. Therefore, it is not possible for these statues to be moved by a principle of life.

[10]   Besides, perfect living things are not generated by the celestial power alone, but also from semen, "for man, together with the sun, generates a man."[5] On the other hand, things generated without semen, by the celestial power alone, are animals generated from putrefaction, and they are the lower type of animals. So, if these statues receive a principle of life, whereby to move themselves, through the celestial power alone, they must be the lowest grade of animals. Yet this would be false if they work through an internal principle of life, for noble operations appear among their activities, since they give answers about hidden things.

3. Aristotle, *De anima*, II, 4 (415b 13).
4. Aristotle, *Physics*, III, 8 (208a 10).
5. *Ibid.*, II, 2 (194b 14).

Therefore, it is not possible that they are worked, or moved, by a principle of life.

[11]   Moreover, it is possible for a natural effect produced by the power of celestial bodies to be accomplished without the operation of an art. For, though a man might work by means of some artful device for the purpose of generating frogs, yet it happens that frogs are generated without any artificial device. So, if these statues that are made by the art of necromancy receive their principle of life from the power of celestial bodies, there should be a possibility of finding a case of the generation of such statues apart from art of this kind. But such a case is not found. It is obvious, then, that these statues do not have a principle of life, nor are they moved by the power of a celestial body.

[12]   The position of Hermes is disposed of by these considerations, for he spoke as follows, as Augustine reports it in the *City of God*: "Just as God is the maker of the celestial gods, so man is the maker of the gods who are in the temples, content in their nearness to man. I mean the animated statues, endowed with sense and spirit, that do such great and unusual things; statues that foresee future events, predicting them from dreams and from many other things, that cause weaknesses in men and also cure them, that give sorrow and joy, in accord with one's merits."[6]

[13]   This view is also refuted by divine authority, for it is said in the Psalm (134:15–17): "The idols of the Gentiles are silver and gold, the works of men's hands. They have a mouth and they speak not . . . neither is there any breath in their mouths."

[14]   However, it does not seem necessary to deny altogether that some power may be present in the aforementioned objects, resulting from the power of the celestial bodies—only it will be for those effects, of course, which any lower bodies are able to produce by the power of celestial bodies.

6. St. Augustine, *De civitate Dei*, VIII, 23 (PL, 41, col. 247).

Chapter 105.

WHERE THE PERFORMANCES OF THE MAGICIANS GET THEIR EFFICACY

[1]   Now, it remains to investigate where the arts of magic get their efficacy. Indeed, this can easily be thought out if attention is paid to their method of operation.

[2]   As a matter of fact, in their performances they use certain significant words in order to produce given effects. But a word, as endowed with meaning, has no force except as derived from some understanding: either from the understanding of the speaker or from the understanding of the one to whom it is spoken. As an example of such dependence on the understanding of the speaker, suppose an intellect is of such great power that a thing can be caused by its act of conception, and that the function of the spoken word is to present, in some way, this conception to the effects that are produced. As an example of dependence on the understanding of the person to whom the speech is directed, take the case of a listener who is induced to do something, through the reception in his intellect of the meaning of the word. Now, it cannot be claimed that these meaningful words spoken by magicians get their efficacy from the understanding of the speaker. Indeed, since power results from essence, a diversity of power manifests a diversity of essential principles. But the intellect of men in general is so disposed that its knowledge is caused by things, instead of it being able to cause things by its act of conception. So, if there be any men who, by their own power, can change things by the words which express their intellectual thought, they will belong to a different species and will be called men in an equivocal sense.

[3]   Moreover, the power to do something is not acquired by study, but only the knowledge of what to do. Now, some

men acquire through study the ability to produce these magical performances. So, there is no special power in them to produce effects of this kind, but only knowledge.

[4] Now, if someone says that men like this, in distinction from other men, receive the aforesaid power from birth, due to the power of the stars, so that, no matter how much instruction is given to other men, if they do not possess this from birth, they cannot be successful in works of this kind, our first answer must be that the celestial bodies are not able to make an impression on the understanding, as we showed above.[1] Therefore, no intellect can receive from the power of the stars such a power that the expression of its thought through speech is capable of producing something.

[5] But, if it be said that even the imagination produces something when it utters meaningful words, and that the celestial bodies can make an impression on this utterance since this action is performed by means of a bodily organ, this cannot be true in regard to all the effects produced by these arts. It has been shown that not all of these effects can be produced by the power of the stars.[2] Neither, then, can a man receive from the power of the stars this power to produce such effects.

[6] So, we are left with the conclusion that effects of this kind are accomplished by some understanding to which the speech of the person uttering these words is addressed. An indication of this fact is that meaningful words such as the magicians use are called *invocations, supplications, adjurations,* or even *commands,* implying that one person is speaking to another.

[7] Again, in the practices of this art they use certain symbols and specially shaped figures. Now, shape is the principle of neither action nor passion; if it were, mathematical bodies would be active and passive. Hence, it is not

1. See above, ch. 84.
2. See above, ch. 104.

possible to dispose matter by special figures so that it will be receptive to a natural effect. So, the magicians do not use figures as dispositions. The conclusion remains, then, that they may use them only as signs, for there is no third possibility. Now, we do not use signs except in regard to other intelligent beings. Therefore, the arts of magic get their efficacy from another intelligent being to whom the speech of the magician is addressed.

[8]   Now, if someone says that some figures are proper to certain celestial bodies, and so lower bodies are marked by certain figures for the reception of the influences of the celestial bodies, this does not seem a reasonable answer. In fact, a patient is not ordered to the reception of the influence of an agent, unless it be because it is in potency. So, only those things whereby a thing becomes potential, in some way, determine it to receive a special impression. But matter is not disposed by figures so that it is in potency to any form, because figure, according to its rational meaning, abstracts from all sensible matter and form, for it is a mathematical object. Therefore, a body is not determined by figures or symbols for the reception of any influence from a celestial body.

[9]   Moreover, certain figures are assigned as proper to celestial bodies, as their effects; for the shapes of lower bodies are caused by the celestial bodies. But the aforesaid arts do not use characters or figures like the effects of celestial bodies. Rather, they are the productions of man, working by means of art. So, the assigning of certain figures as proper to celestial bodies seems to contribute nothing to the discussion.

[10]   Furthermore, as we have shown, natural matter is not in any way disposed toward form by figures. So, the bodies on which these figures are put have the same readiness to receive the celestial influence as any other bodies of the same species. Now, the fact that a thing acts on one of a group of things equally disposed, because of something specially assigned to that agent which is to be found on

that object and not on another, is not indicative of an agent which acts by natural necessity, but, rather, of one which acts through will. It is clear, then, that arts of this sort which use figures to produce certain effects do not get their efficacy from a natural agent, but from some intellectual substance that acts through understanding.

[11]   Indeed, the very name that they give to such figures demonstrates this point, for they call them *characters*. As a matter of fact, a character is a sign. By this usage we are given to understand that they do not use these figures except as signs addressed to some intellectual nature.

[12]   However, since figures are like specific forms for art objects, some person could say that nothing prevents the construction of a figure, which specifies an image, as a result of some power due to celestial influence, not as a figure, but as it specifies the artifact which obtains its power from the stars. However, concerning the letters with which something is written on an image, and the other characters, nothing else can be said than that they are signs. Hence, they are directed only to some intellect. This is also shown by the offerings, prostrations, and other similar practices which they use, for they can be nothing but signs of reverence addressed to some intellectual nature.

Chapter 106.

THAT THE INTELLECTUAL SUBSTANCE WHICH PROVIDES THE EFFICACY FOR MAGIC WORKS IS NOT MORALLY GOOD

[1]   We must further inquire what this intellectual nature is, by whose power such operations are done.

[2]   First of all, it appears not to be good and praiseworthy. To offer patronage to things that are contrary to virtue is not the act of a well-disposed understanding. But

this is done in these arts, for they are often used for purposes of adultery, theft, homicide, and other kinds of
wrongdoing. As a result, the practitioners of these arts are
called *malefics*. So, the intellectual nature on whose assistance these arts depend is not well disposed in relation to
virtue.

[3]   Again, a morally well-disposed intellect should not be
the associate of, and provide protection for, scoundrels,
while having nothing to do with the best men. Now, evil
men often make use of these arts. Therefore, the intellectual nature from whose help these arts get their efficacy
is not well disposed in relation to virtue.

[4]   Besides, it pertains to a well-disposed intellect to
bring men back to things that are proper goods for men,
namely, the goods of reason. Consequently, to lead them
away from these goods, by diverting them to the least important goods, is the mark of an improperly disposed intellect. Men do not make any progress by means of these arts
in the goods of reason which are the sciences and the virtues, but, rather, in certain least important things, such as
the finding of stolen goods and the catching of thieves, and
such things. Therefore, the intellectual substances with
whose aid these arts are exercised are not well disposed in
relation to virtue.

[5]   Moreover, some deception and irrationality are observable in the practices of these arts. In fact, arts of this kind
need a man who is not engrossed in sexual matters, yet they
often are used to arrange illicit affairs. But, in the workings
of a well-disposed intellect nothing unreasonable or out of
keeping with its nature is apparent. Therefore, these arts
do not employ the patronage of an intellect that is well
disposed in relation to virtue.

[6]   Furthermore, he who feels called upon to help another by the committing of a crime is not well disposed in
his intellect. But this is done in these arts, for we read
about some people who, in their practice, have killed inno-

cent children. Therefore, those by whose help such things are done are not good intellects.

[7] Again, the proper good of an intellect is truth. So, since to attract to the good is proper to a good being, it seems to be the function of every well-disposed intellect to bring others to the truth. But in the practices of the magicians many things are done whereby men are made sport of and are deceived. So, the intellect whose help they use is not well disposed morally.

[8] Besides, a well-disposed intellect is attracted by truth, takes pleasure in it and not in lies. But the magicians use certain lies in their invocations, by which they entice those whose help they employ. They also make certain impossible threats, such as, unless he who is being invoked provides help, the magician who is asking it will shatter the sky, or displace the stars, as Porphyry relates in his *Letter to Anebontes*.[1] Therefore, these intellectual substances with whose help the works of the magicians are accomplished do not seem to be well disposed in their intellect.

[9] Moreover, it does not seem the attribute of a possessor of a well-disposed intellect for it, if it be superior, to submit like an inferior to the one who commands it, or, if it is inferior, to permit itself to be invoked as if it were a superior. But the magicians humbly invoke as their superiors those whose assistance they employ, but when they appear the magicians command them like inferiors. So, in no way do they seem well disposed in relation to intellect.

[10] By these considerations the error of the pagans is set aside, for they attributed such works to the gods.

1. See St. Augustine, *De civitate Dei*, X, 11 (*PL*, 41, col. 290).

Chapter 107.

THAT THE INTELLECTUAL SUBSTANCE WHOSE HELP THE ARTS OF MAGIC USE IS NOT EVIL IN ITS OWN NATURE

[1]   Now, it is not possible for there to be natural malice in the intelligent substances with whose help the arts of magic work.[1]

[2]   A thing does not tend accidentally, but essentially, to the objective to which it inclines by its nature, as, for instance, a heavy body tends downward. But, if intellectual substances of this kind are evil in their nature, they tend to evil naturally. Therefore, they do not tend accidentally, but essentially, to evil. But this is impossible, for we showed above[2] that all things essentially tend to the good, and that nothing tends to evil, except accidentally. Therefore, these intellectual substances are not evil in their nature.

[3]   Again, whatever is present in things must be either a cause or a thing caused; otherwise, it would have no relation to other things. So, these substances are either causes only or they are also caused. Now, if they are causes, and if evil cannot be the cause of anything, except accidentally, as we showed above,[3] but if everything that is accidental must be traced back to what is essential, then there must be something in them prior to their malice, something by which they may be causes. Now, first in each thing is its nature and essence. Therefore, substances of this kind are not evil in their nature.

[4]   Moreover, the same thing follows, if they are caused. For no agent acts unless it intends the good. So, evil cannot

1. Compare this and the following chapters on demons with St. Thomas, *Quaestiones disputatae de malo*, q. XVI, art. 1–12.
2. See above, ch. 3ff.
3. See above, ch. 14.

be the effect of any cause, except accidentally. Now, that which is only caused accidentally cannot be according to nature, since every nature has a definite way of coming into being. Therefore, it is impossible for substances of this kind to be evil in their nature.

[5] Furthermore, each thing has its proper act of being in accord with the mode of its nature. Now, to be, as such, is good: the mark of this is that all things desire to be. Therefore, if substances of this kind were evil in their nature, they would have no act of being.

[6] Again, we showed above[4] that nothing can be unless it gets its act of being from the first being, and that the first being is the highest good.[5] Now, since every agent, as such, produces something like itself, the things that come from the first being must be good. Therefore, the aforesaid substances, in so far as they exist and have a nature, cannot be evil.

[7] Besides, it is impossible for anything to be which is wholly deprived of participation in the good. For, since the desirable and the good are the same thing, if something were utterly devoid of goodness it would have nothing desirable in it; but to each thing its own being is desirable. Therefore, it is necessary that, if anything is called evil in its nature, then this is not evil in the absolute sense, but evil in relation to a particular thing or in some particular way. Thus, poison is not an unqualified evil, but only to this individual for whom it is harmful. Hence, "what is one man's poison is another man's meat."[6] Now, this happens because the particular good that is proper to this individual is contrary to the particular good that is proper to another individual. Thus, heat, which is good for fire, is the contrary to and is destructive of cold, which is good for water. Now, something which is by its nature ordered to the good that is not particular, but absolute, cannot be called evil

4. *SCG*, II, ch. 15.
5. *SCG*, I, ch. 41.
6. Lucretius, *De rerum natura*, IV, 637.

naturally, even in this sense. But every intellect is such, for its good is found in its proper operation, which is concerned with universals and with things that exist without qualification. So, it is impossible for any intellect to be evil in its own nature, either absolutely or relatively so.

[8]   Moreover, in each thing that possesses understanding the intellect moves the appetite according to the natural order, for the proper object of the will is the good that is understood. But the good of the will consists in the fact that it follows the understanding; in our case, for instance, the good is what is in accord with reason, but what is apart from reason is evil. So, in the natural order, an intellectual substance wills the good. It is impossible, then, for these intellectual substances, whose help the arts of magic use, to be naturally evil.

[9]   Furthermore, since the will tends naturally toward the good that is understood as to its proper object and end, it is impossible for an intellectual substance to have a will evil in its nature unless its intellect naturally errs in regard to the judgment of the good. But no intellect can be like that, for false judgments in the area of intellectual operations are like monsters among natural things; they are not in accord with nature, but apart from nature. In fact, the good of the intellect, and its natural end, is the knowledge of truth. Therefore, it is impossible for any intellect to exist which is naturally deceived in its judgment of the true. And so, neither is it possible for there to be an intellectual substance naturally possessing a bad will.

[10]   Again, no cognitive potency fails in the knowing of its object unless because of some defect or corruption in itself, since it is ordered according to its own rational character to the knowledge of this object. Thus, sight does not fail in the knowing of color unless there be some corruption present in sight itself. But all defect and corruption are apart from nature, because nature intends the being and perfection of the thing. So, it is impossible that there be any cognitive power which naturally falls short of the right

judgment of its object. But the proper object of the intellect is the true. It is impossible, then, for there to be an intellect naturally tending to err in regard to the knowledge of the true. Therefore, neither can any will naturally fall short of the good.

[11] This is also solidly supported by the text of Scripture. Indeed, it is said in I Timothy (4:4): "Every creature of God is good"; and in Genesis (1:31): "God saw all things that He had made, and they were very good."

[12] By this, then, we refute the error of the Manicheans, who asserted that intellectual substances of this kind, whom we call by the customary name of *demons* or *devils*, are naturally evil.

[13] Also disposed of is the view which Porphyry reports, in his *Letter to Anebontes*, where he says: "Some people are of the opinion that there is a kind of spirits whose function is to hear the requests of the magicians, spirits who are false by nature, having every form, taking on the appearance of gods and demons and the souls of the dead. And this is the kind that produces all these apparitions, whether good or bad. Moreover, as regards the things that are truly good, no help is given by them; or, better, they do not even know them. Instead, they advise evil things, and blame and frequently hinder zealous followers of virtue; and they are full of boldness and pride; they take pleasure in frothy exhalations and are overcome by false praises."[7] Indeed, these words of Porphyry quite plainly express the evil character of the demons whose help the magic arts employ. The only point in which his words are objectionable is his statement that this evil is naturally present in them.

7. See St. Augustine, *De civitate Dei*, X, 11 (*PL*, 41, col. 289).

Chapter 108.

ARGUMENTS WHEREBY IT SEEMS TO BE PROVED THAT THERE CAN BE NO SIN IN DEMONS

[1] Now, if malice[1] is not natural in the demons, and if it has been shown that they are evil,[2] it must follow that they are bad voluntarily. So, we must ask how this can be, for it seems to be altogether impossible.

[2] Indeed, it was shown in Book Two[3] that no intellectual substance is naturally united to a body except the human soul, or also, according to some thinkers, the souls of celestial bodies.[4] But, in regard to the latter, it is not appropriate to think that they are evil, since the motion of the celestial bodies is most orderly, and in a way is the source of the entire order of nature. Now, every other cognitive potency besides the intellect uses animated bodily organs. So, it is not possible for there to be in substances of this kind any cognitive power other than understanding. Hence, whatever they know, they understand. Now, one does not err in regard to the object which one understands, since all error arises from a failure to understand. Therefore, there can be no error in such substances' knowledge. Moreover, no sin can occur in the will without error, since the will always tends toward the good as apprehended. Consequently, unless there is an error in the apprehension of the good, there cannot be a sin in the will. Therefore, it seems that there can be no sin in the will of these substances.

1. Note that "malice" (*malitia*) means that which is essentially evil; it is the contrary of "goodness" (*bonitas*).
2. See above, ch. 106. St. Thomas' replies to the arguments which follow are to be found later, in ch. 110.
3. *SCG*, II, ch. 90.
4. *SCG*, II, ch. 70.

[3]   Again, in our case, as regards the things of which we possess universal knowledge, sin occurs in our will because the judgment of reason is impeded on a particular point by some passion which shackles the reason. But these passions cannot occur in demons, because such passions belong to the sensitive part of the soul, which cannot operate without a bodily organ. So, if separate substances of this kind have right knowledge on the universal level, it is impossible for their will to incline to evil because of a defect of knowledge on the particular level.

[4]   Besides, no cognitive power is deceived in regard to its proper object, but only in regard to something foreign to it. For instance, sight is not deceived in judging color, but, when a man judges by sight concerning the taste or species of a thing, deception may occur in that case. But the proper object of understanding is the quiddity of a thing. Hence, in the cognitive act of an intellect, provided it apprehend pure quiddities, deception cannot occur. Rather, all intellectual deception seems to happen because it apprehends the forms of things mixed together with phantasms, as happens in our case. But such a mode of knowing is not found in intellectual substances that are not united with a body, since phantasms cannot be without a body. Therefore, it is not possible for cognitive error to occur in separate substances; neither, then, can sin be in their will.

[5]   Moreover, falsity occurs in our case in the intellectual operation of composing and dividing, as a result of the fact that it does not apprehend the quiddity of a thing simply, but, rather, combines something with the thing that is apprehended. Of course, in the operation of the intellect, whereby it apprehends *that which is*, no falsity occurs except accidentally, by virtue of mixing, even in this operation, some part of the operation of the intellect composing and dividing. Indeed, this happens because our intellect does not immediately attain the knowledge of the quiddity of a thing, but with a certain order in the process of inquiry. For example, we first apprehend animal, then we divide it into the opposed differences, and, leaving one

aside, we put the other with the genus, until we come to the definition of the species. Now, falsity may occur in this process if something is taken as a difference in the genus which is not a difference in the genus. Of course, to proceed in this way to the quidditative knowledge of something pertains to an intellect reasoning discursively from one thing to another. This is not proper to separate intellectual substances, as we showed above.[5] Hence, it does not seem that any error can occur in the knowledge of these substances. Consequently, neither can sin occur in their will.

[6]   Furthermore, since in no case does the appetite of a thing tend to anything other than its proper good, it seems impossible for that for which there is uniquely but one sole good to err in its appetite. For this reason, though something wrong may happen in natural things because of a contingent defect in the working of the appetite, such wrong never occurs in natural appetite; thus, a stone always tends downward, whether it achieves its goal or is stopped. But sin does occur in our act of appetition, because, since our nature is composed of the spiritual and the corporeal, there are several goods for us. Our good in regard to understanding is indeed different from what it is according to sensation, or even according to the body. Now, there is a certain order of these various things that are man's goods, based on the fact that what is less primary is subordinated to what is more primary. Hence, a sin occurs in our will when, failing to observe this order, we desire what is only relatively good for us, in opposition to what is absolutely good. However, such a complexity and diversity of goods is not found in the separate substances; on the contrary, every good for them is according to the understanding. Therefore, it is not possible for there to be a sin in the will for them, as it would seem.

[7]   Again, in us sin occurs in the will, as a result of excess or defect, and virtue consists in the mean between these.

5. SCG, II, ch. 101.

So, in things which do not admit of excess or defect, but only of the mean, it is not possible for the will to sin. For instance, no one can sin by desiring justice, for justice is itself a certain mean. Now, separate intellectual substances cannot desire anything except intellectual goods; indeed, it is ridiculous to say that those who are incorporeal in their nature desire corporeal goods, or that those without sense power desire sensible goods. But among intellectual goods one can find no excess, for these goods are in themselves means between excess and defect; just as the true is a mean between two errors, one of which goes too far, the other not far enough. Consequently, both sensible and corporeal goods achieve the mean, to the extent that they are in accord with reason. So, it does not seem that separate intellectual substances can sin by their will.

[8]   Besides, incorporeal substance seems farther removed from defects than is corporeal substance. But, in the case of corporeal substances that are without contrariety, no defect can occur; for instance, in the celestial bodies. Much less possible, then, is it for any sin to occur in separate substances, which are removed both from contrariety, from matter, and from motion, from which sources any possible defect would seem to come.

Chapter 109.

THAT SIN CAN OCCUR IN DEMONS, AND IN WHAT WAY

[1]   However, that there is sin of the will in demons is obvious from the text of Sacred Scripture. In fact, it is said in I John (3:8) that "the devil sinneth from the beginning"; and in John (8:44) it is said that "the devil is a liar and the father of lies" and that "he was a murderer from the beginning." And in Wisdom (2:24) it is said that "by the envy of the devil, death came into the world."

[2] Moreover, if anyone wished to follow the views of
the Platonists,[1] that would be an easy way to answer the
arguments stated above. For they say that demons are
animals with an aerial body; and so, since they have bodies
united to them, there can also be in them a sensitive part.
Hence, they also attribute passions to them, which are for
us a cause of sin; namely, anger, hate, and others of like
kind. This is why Apuleius says that they are *passive in their
mind.*[2]

[3] Also, apart from this contention that they are united
to bodies according to the views of Plato, it might perhaps
be possible to claim another kind of knowledge in them,
other than that of the intellect. For, according to Plato,
the sensitive soul is also incorruptible.[3] Hence, it must have
an operation in which the body does not share. Thus, nothing is to prevent the operation of the sensitive soul and,
consequently, passions from taking place in any intellectual
substance, even though it is not united with a body. And so,
there remains in them the same source of sinful action that
is found in us.

[4] However, both of these foregoing views are impossible. As a matter of fact, we showed above[4] that there are
no other intellectual substances united to bodies besides
human souls. Moreover, that the operations of the sensitive
soul cannot go on without the body is apparent from the
fact that, with the corruption of any organ of sensation, the
operation of one sense is corrupted. For instance, if the eye
be destroyed, vision fails. For this reason, when the organ
of touch is corrupted, without which an animal cannot
exist,[5] the animal must die.

1. See St. Augustine, *De civitate Dei,* VIII, 14 (*PL,* 41, col.
    239).
2. *Ibid.,* 16 (*PL,* 41, col. 241).
3. *SCG,* II, ch. 82.
4. *SCG,* II, ch. 90.
5. See Aristotle, *De anima,* II, 2 (413b 4).

[5] So, for the clarification of the aforesaid difficulty,[6] we must give some consideration to the fact that, as there is an order in agent causes, so also is there one in final causes, so that, for instance, a secondary end depends on a principal one, just as a secondary agent depends on a principal one. Now, something wrong happens in the case of agent causes when a secondary agent departs from the order of the principal agent. For example, when the leg bone fails because of its crookedness in the carrying out of the motion which the appetitive power has commanded, limping ensues. So, too, in the case of final causes, when a secondary end is not included under the order of the principal end, there results a sin of the will, whose object is the *good* and the *end*.

[6] Now, every will naturally wishes what is a proper good for the volitional agent, namely, perfect being itself, and it cannot will the contrary of this. So, in the case of a volitional agent whose proper good is the ultimate end, no sin of the will can occur, for the ultimate end is not included under the order of another end; instead, all other ends are contained under its order. Now, this kind of volitional agent is God, Whose being is the highest goodness, which is the ultimate end. Hence, in God there can be no sin of the will.

[7] But in any other kind of volitional agent, whose proper good must be included under the order of another good, it is possible for sin of the will to occur, if it be considered in its own nature. Indeed, although natural inclination of the will is present in every volitional agent to will and to love its own perfection so that it cannot will the contrary of this, yet it is not so naturally implanted in the agent to so order its perfection to another end, that it cannot fail in regard to it, for the higher end is not proper to its nature, but to a higher nature. It is left, then, to the agent's choice, to order his own proper perfection to a higher end. In fact,

6. See above, ch. 108, the general difficulty of which is now treated.

this is the difference between those agents who have a will, and those things which are devoid of will: the possessors of will order themselves and their actions to the end, and so they are said to be free in their choice; whereas those devoid of will do not order themselves to their end, but are ordered by a higher agent, being moved by another being to the end, not by themselves.

[8]   Therefore, it was possible for sin to occur in the will of a separate substance, because it did not order its proper good and perfection to its ultimate end, but stuck to its own good as an end. And because the rules of action must be derived from the end, the consequence is that this separate substance tried to arrange for the regulation of other beings from himself wherein he had established his end, and thus his will was not regulated by another, higher one. But this function belongs to God alone. In terms of this, we should understand that "he desired to be equal to God" (Isa. 14:14). Not, indeed, that his good would be equal to the divine good, for this thought could not have occurred in his understanding, and in desiring such a thing he would have desired not to exist, since the distinction of species arises from the different grades of things, as is clear from previous statements.[7]

However, to will to rule others, and not to have his will ruled by a higher one, is to will to take first place and, in a sense, not to be submissive; this is the sin of pride. Hence, it may appropriately be said that the first sin of the demon was pride. But since a diversified and pluralized error results from one error concerning the starting point, multiple sin followed in his will as a result of the first disorder of the will which took place in the demon: sins both of hatred toward God, as One Who resists his pride and punishes his fault most justly, and of envy toward man, and many other similar sins.

[9]   We should also consider that, when an agent's proper good is related to several higher goods, the volitional agent

7. SCG, II, ch. 95; III, ch. 97.

is free to depart from the order of one superior and free not to abandon the order of another, whether it be higher or lower. Thus, a soldier who is subordinate to the king and to the leader of the army can order his will to the leader's good and not to the king's, or vice versa. But, if the leader departs from the order of the king, the will of the soldier who abandons the will of the leader and directs his will to the king is going to be good, whereas the will of the soldier who follows the will of the leader against the will of the king is going to be bad, for the order of a lower principle depends on the order of a higher one. Now, separate substances are not only subordinated to God, but one of them is subordinated to another, from the first to the last, as we showed in Book Two.[8] And since in each volitional agent under God there can be a sin of the will, if he were considered in his own nature, it was possible for some of the higher ones, or even the highest of all, to sin in his will. And, in fact, this is probably what happened, for he would not have been satisfied with his own good as an end unless his good were quite perfect. So, it possibly happened in this way: some of the lower ones, through their own will, ordered their good to his, and departing from the divine order they sinned in like fashion; others, however, observing in the movement of their will the divine order, rightly departed from the order of the sinful one, even though he was a superior in the order of nature. But how the will of both kinds perseveres immutably in goodness, or in evil, will be shown in Book Four,[9] for this has to do with the punishments and rewards of the good and the evil.

[10] But there is this difference between man and a separate substance: in one man there are several appetitive powers, one subordinated to the other. Now, this is not the case in separate substances, though one of these substances stands under another. Now, sin occurs in the will when in any way the lower appetite rebels. So, just as sin could occur in the separate substances, either by being

8. *SCG*, II, ch. 95.
9. *SCG*, IV, ch. 92ff.

turned away from the divine order, or by one of the lower
ones being turned aside from the order of a superior one
which continues under the divine order; so also, in one
man, sin may occur in two ways. One way is due to the fact
that the human will does not order its proper good to God;
in fact, this kind of sin is common both to man himself
and to the separate substance. Another way is due to the
good of the lower appetite not being ruled in accord with
the higher appetite; for example, we may desire the pleasures of the flesh to which the concupiscible appetite inclines, in discord with the order of reason. Now, this latter
kind of sin cannot occur in separate substances.

Chapter 110.

ANSWER TO THE PREVIOUS ARGUMENTS

[1]   So, then, it is not difficult to answer the arguments
that have been presented.[1]

[2]   As a matter of fact, we are not forced to say that there
was error in the understanding of a separate substance, in
judging a good not to be a good. Instead, it was in not considering the higher good to which its proper good should
have been directed. Now, the reason for this lack of consideration could have been that the will was vehemently
turned toward its own good, for to turn to this or that
object is a characteristic of free will.[2]

[3]   It is evident, also, that he desired only one good, that
is, his own; but there was sin in this, because he set aside
the higher good to which he should have been ordered. Just
as sin in us is due to the fact that we desire lower goods,
that is, those of the body, in discord with the order of
reason, so in the devil there was sin, because he did not
relate his own good to the divine good.[3]

1. See above, ch. 108.
2. See above, ch. 108, ¶2–5.
3. Ibid., ¶6.

[4]   Moreover, it is clear that he overlooked the mean of virtue, in so far as he did not subject himself to the order of a superior; thus, he gave himself more importance than was proper, while giving less to God than was due Him to Whom all should be subject as to the Orderer of the primary rule. So, it is evident that, in this sin, the mean was not abandoned because of an excess of passion, but simply because of inequity under justice, which is concerned with actions. In fact, actions are possible in the case of separate substances, but passions are in no way possible.[4]

[5]   Nor, indeed, is it a necessary conclusion that, if no defect can be present in higher bodies, for this reason sin cannot occur in separate substances. For bodies and all things devoid of reason are only moved to action; they do not act of themselves, for they do not have control over their acts. Consequently, they cannot depart from the primary rule which actuates and moves them, except in the sense that they cannot adequately receive the regulation of the primary rule. Of course, this is so due to the indisposition of matter. For this reason, the higher bodies, in which this indisposition of matter has no place, never can fall short of the rightness of the primary rule. But rational substances, or intellectual ones, are not merely acted upon; rather, they also move themselves to their proper acts. Indeed, the more perfect their nature is, the more evident is this characteristic in them, for, the more perfect their nature is, the more perfect is their power to act. Consequently, perfection of nature does not preclude the possibility of sin occurring in them in the aforesaid way: namely, because they fasten upon themselves, and pay no attention to the order of a higher agent.[5]

4. *Ibid.*, ¶7.
5. *Ibid.*, ¶8.

Chapter 111.

THAT RATIONAL CREATURES ARE SUBJECT TO DIVINE PROVIDENCE IN A SPECIAL WAY

[1]   From the points which have been determined above,[1] it is manifest that divine providence extends to all things. Yet we must note that there is a special meaning for providence in reference to intellectual and rational creatures, over and above its meaning for other creatures.

For they do stand out above other creatures, both in natural perfection and in the dignity of their end. In the order of natural perfection, only the rational creature holds dominion over his acts, moving himself freely in order to perform his actions. Other creatures, in fact, are moved to their proper workings rather than being the active agents of these operations, as is clear from what has been said.[2] And in the dignity of their end, for only the intellectual creature reaches the very ultimate end of the whole of things through his own operation, which is the knowing and loving of God; whereas other creatures cannot attain the ultimate end except by a participation in its likeness. Now, the formal character of every work differs according to the diversity of the end and of the things which are subject to the operation; thus, the method of working in art differs according to the diversity of the end and of the subject matter. For instance, a physician works in one way to get rid of illness and in another way to maintain health, and he uses different methods for bodies differently constituted. Likewise, in the government of a state, a different plan of ordering must be followed, depending on the varying conditions of the persons subject to this government and on the different purposes to which they are directed. For soldiers

---

1. See above, ch. 64ff. With the present chapter, the third and final section of Book Three begins.
2. See above, ch. 47.

are controlled in one way, so that they may be ready to fight; while artisans will be managed in another way, so that they may successfully carry out their activities. So, also, there is one orderly plan in accord with which rational creatures are subjected to divine providence, and another by means of which the rest of creatures are ordered.

Chapter 112.

THAT RATIONAL CREATURES ARE GOVERNED FOR THEIR OWN SAKES, WHILE OTHERS ARE GOVERNED IN SUBORDINATION TO THEM

[1] First of all, then, the very way in which the intellectual creature was made, according as it is master of its acts, demands providential care whereby this creature may provide for itself, on its own behalf; while the way in which other things were created, things which have no dominion over their acts, shows this fact, that they are cared for, not for their own sake, but as subordinated to others. That which is moved only by another being has the formal character of an instrument, but that which acts of itself has the essential character of a principal agent. Now, an instrument is not valued for its own sake, but as useful to a principal agent. Hence it must be that all the careful work that is devoted to instruments is actually done for the sake of the agent, as for an end, but what is done for the principal agent, either by himself or by another, is for his own sake, because he is the principal agent. Therefore, intellectual creatures are so controlled by God, as objects of care for their own sakes; while other creatures are subordinated, as it were, to the rational creatures.

[2] Again, one who holds dominion over his own acts is free in his activity, "for the free man is he who acts for his own sake."[1] But one who is acted upon by another, under necessity, is subject to slavery. So, every other creature is

1. Aristotle, *Metaphysics*, I, 2 (982b 26).

naturally subject to slavery; only the intellectual creature is by nature free. Now, under every sort of government, provision is made for free men for their own sakes, but for slaves in such a way that they may be at the disposal of free men. And so, through divine providence provision is made for intellectual creatures on their own account, but for the remaining creatures for the sake of the intellectual ones.

[3]   Besides, whenever things are ordered to any end, and some of these things cannot attain the end through their own efforts, they must be subordinated to things which do achieve the end and which are ordered to the end for their own sakes. Thus, for instance, the end of an army is victory, and this the soldiers may achieve through their own act of fighting; that is why only soldiers are needed for their own sake in an army. All others, who are assigned to different tasks—for instance, caring for the horses and supplying the weapons—are needed for the sake of the soldiers in the army. Now, from what has been seen earlier,[2] it is established that God is the ultimate end of the whole of things; that an intellectual nature alone attains to Him in Himself, that is, by knowing and loving Him, as is evident from what has been said.[3] Therefore, the intellectual nature is the only one that is required in the universe, for its own sake, while all others are for its sake.

[4]   Moreover, in any whole the principal parts are needed in themselves in order to constitute the whole, but the other parts are for the preservation or for some betterment of the principal ones. Now, of all the parts of the universe the more noble are intellectual creatures, since they come closer to the divine likeness. Therefore, intellectual creatures are governed by divine providence for their own sakes, while all others are for the intellectual ones.

[5]   Furthermore, it is evident that all parts are ordered to the perfection of the whole, since a whole does not exist for the sake of its parts, but, rather, the parts are for the whole.

2. See above, ch. 17.
3. See above, ch. 25ff.

Now, intellectual natures have a closer relationship to a whole than do other natures; indeed, each intellectual substance is, in a way, all things. For it may comprehend the entirety of being through its intellect; on the other hand, every other substance has only a particular share in being. Therefore, other substances may fittingly be providentially cared for by God for the sake of intellectual substances.

[6] Again, as a thing is acted upon in the course of nature, so is it disposed to action by its natural origin. Now, we see that things do go on in the course of nature in such a way that intellectual substance uses all others for itself: either for the perfecting of its understanding, since it contemplates the truth in them; or for the exercise of its power and the development of its knowledge, in the fashion of an artist who develops his artistic conception in bodily matter; or even for the support of his body which is united with the intellectual soul, as we see in the case of men. Therefore, it is clear that all things are divinely ruled by providence for the sake of intellectual substances.

[7] Besides, what a man desires for its own sake is something which he always desires, for that which is, because of itself, always is. On the other hand, what a man desires for the sake of something else is not necessarily always desired; rather, the duration of the desire depends on that for which it is sought. Now, the being of things flows forth from the divine will, as is shown in our earlier considerations.[4] Therefore, those things which always exist among beings are willed by God for their own sake, while things which do not always exist are not for their own sake, but for the sake of something else. Now, intellectual substances come closest to existing always, for they are incorruptible. They are also immutable, excepting only their act of choice. Therefore, intellectual substances are governed for their own sake, in a sense, while others are for them.

[8] Nor is what was shown in earlier arguments opposed to this, namely, that all parts of the universe are ordered to

4. *SCG*, II, ch. 23.

the perfection of the whole. For all parts are ordered to the perfection of the whole, inasmuch as one is made to serve another. Thus, in the human body it is apparent that the lungs contribute to the perfection of the body by rendering service to the heart; hence, it is not contradictory for the lungs to be for the sake of the heart, and also for the sake of the whole organism. Likewise, it is not contradictory for some natures to be for the sake of the intellectual ones, and also for the sake of the perfection of the universe. For, in fact, if the things needed for the perfection of intellectual substance were lacking, the universe would not be complete.

[9] Similarly, too, the foregoing is not opposed by the fact that individuals are for the sake of their proper species. Because they are ordered to their species, they possess a further ordination to intellectual nature. For a corruptible thing is not ordered to man for the sake of one individual man only, but for the sake of the whole human species. A corruptible thing could not be of use to the whole human species except by virtue of the thing's entire species. Therefore, the order whereby corruptible things are ordered to man requires the subordination of individuals to their species.

[10] However, we do not understand this statement, that intellectual substances are ordered for their own sake by divine providence, to mean that they are not more ultimately referred to God and to the perfection of the universe. In fact, they are said to be providentially managed for their own sake, and other things for their sake, in the sense that the goods which they receive through divine goodness are not given them for the advantage of another being, but the things given to other beings must be turned over to the use of intellectual substances in accord with divine providence.

[11] Hence it is said in Deuteronomy (4:19): "Lest thou see the sun and the moon and the other stars, and being deceived by error, thou adore and serve them, which the Lord thy God created for the service of all the nations that are under heaven"; and again in the Psalm (8:8): "Thou

hast subjected all things under his feet, all sheep and oxen, moreover the beasts of the field"; and in Wisdom (12:18) it is said: "Thou, being Master of power, judgest with tranquillity, and with great favor disposest of us."

[12] Through these considerations we refute the error of those who claim that it is a sin for man to kill brute animals.[5] For animals are ordered to man's use in the natural course of things, according to divine providence. Consequently, man uses them without any injustice, either by killing them or by employing them in any other way. For this reason, God said to Noe: "As the green herbs, I have delivered all flesh to you" (Gen. 9:3).

[13] Indeed, if any statements are found in Sacred Scripture prohibiting the commission of an act of cruelty against brute animals, for instance, that one should not kill a bird accompanied by her young (Deut. 22:6), this is said either to turn the mind of man away from cruelty which might be used on other men, lest a person through practicing cruelty on brutes might go on to do the same to men; or because an injurious act committed on animals may lead to a temporal loss for some man, either for the agent or for another man; or there may be another interpretation of the text, as the Apostle (I Cor. 9:9) explains it, in terms of "not muzzling the ox that treadeth the corn" (Deut. 25:4).

5. For this Manichean view, see St. Augustine, *De moribus Manichaeorum*, 17, 5 (PL, 32, col. 1368); for the same view among the Albigensians in the thirteenth century, see A. J. Denomy, "An Enquiry into the Origins of Courtly Love," *Mediaeval Studies*, 6 (1944), 221–228.

Chapter 113.

THAT THE RATIONAL CREATURE IS DIRECTED BY GOD TO HIS ACTIONS NOT ONLY BY AN ORDERING OF THE SPECIES, BUT ALSO ACCORDING TO WHAT BEFITS THE INDIVIDUAL

[1]   It is evident, as a result, that only the rational creature is directed by God to his actions, not only in accord with what is suitable to the species, but also in accord with what is suitable to the individual. Each thing appears to exist for the sake of its operation; indeed, operation is the ultimate perfection of a thing. Therefore, each thing is ordered to its action by God according to the way in which it is subordinated to divine providence. Now, a rational creature exists under divine providence as a being governed and provided for in himself, and not simply for the sake of his species, as is the case with other corruptible creatures. For the individual that is governed only for the sake of the species is not governed for its own sake, but the rational creature is governed for his own sake, as is clear from what we have said.[1] And so, only rational creatures receive direction from God in their acts, not only for the species, but for the individual.

[2]   Again, whenever beings are directed in their acts, solely on the basis of what pertains to the species, the capacity to act or not to act is not present in them. For things that are associated with the species are common and natural to all individuals contained in the species. Now, natural functions are not within our power to control. So, if man were able to direct his acts only in accord with what is suitable to the species, he would not have within him the capacity to act or not to act. Rather, he would have to fol-

1. See above, ch. 112.

low the natural inclination common to the whole species, as is the case with all irrational creatures. Therefore, it is obvious that a rational creature has the ability to direct his acts, not only in accord with the species, but also in accord with the individual.

[3]   Besides, as we showed above,[2] divine providence extends to all singular things, even to the least. In the case of those beings, then, whose actions take place apart from the inclination appropriate to their species, it is necessary for them to be regulated in their acts by divine providence, over and above the direction which pertains to the species. But many actions are evident, in the case of the rational creature, for which the inclination of the species is not enough. The mark of this is that such actions are not alike in all, but differ in various cases. Therefore, the rational creature must be directed by God in his acts, not only specifically, but also individually.

[4]   Moreover, God takes care of each nature according to its capacity; indeed, He created singular creatures of such kinds that He knew were suited to achieving the end under His governance. Now, only the rational creature is capable of this direction, whereby his actions are guided, not only specifically, but also individually. For he possesses understanding and reason, and consequently he can grasp in what different ways a thing may be good or bad, depending on its suitability for various individuals, times, and places. Therefore, only the rational creature is directed in his acts by God, individually as well as specifically.

[5]   Furthermore, the rational creature is subject to divine providence in such a way that he is not only governed thereby, but is also able to know the rational plan of providence in some way. Hence, it is appropriate for him to exercise providence and government over other things. This is not the case with other creatures, for they participate in providence only to the extent of being subordinated to it. Through this possession of the capacity to exercise provi-

2. See above, ch. 75ff.

dence[3] one may also direct and govern his own acts. So, the rational creature participates in divine providence, not only by being governed passively, but also by governing actively, for he governs himself in his personal acts, and even others. Now, all lower types of providence are subordinated, as it were, to divine providence. Therefore, the governing of the acts of a rational creature, in so far as they are personal acts, pertains to divine providence.

[6]   Again, the personal acts of a rational creature are properly the acts that stem from the rational soul. Now, the rational soul is capable of perpetual existence, not only in function of the species, as is the case with other creatures, but also in an individual sense. Therefore, the acts of a rational creature are directed by divine providence not only for the reason that they are important to the species, but also inasmuch as they are personal acts.

[7]   This is why, though all things are subject to divine providence, the care of man is especially attributed to it in Sacred Scripture, in the text of the Psalm (8:5): "What is man that Thou art mindful of him?" and of I Corinthians (9:9): "Doth God take care of oxen?" Indeed, these statements have been so expressed because God takes care of human acts, not only as they pertain to the species, but also inasmuch as they are personal acts.

Chapter 114.

THAT LAWS ARE DIVINELY GIVEN TO MAN

[1]   It is apparent, next, that it was necessary for law to be divinely given to man. Just as the acts of irrational creatures are directed by God through a rational plan which per-

---

3. The literal meaning of providence is foresight, which is one of the component parts of the virtue of prudence. See St. Thomas, Summa Theologiae, II-II, 49, 6 c.

tains to their species, so are the acts of men directed by God inasmuch as they pertain to the individual, as we have shown.[1] But the acts of irrational creatures, as pertaining to the species, are directed by God through natural inclination, which goes along with the nature of the species. Therefore, over and above this, something must be given to men whereby they may be directed in their own personal acts. And this we call law.

[2] Again, the rational creature, as we have said,[2] is so subjected to divine providence that he even participates in a certain likeness of divine providence, in so far as he is able to govern himself in his own acts, and also others. Now, that whereby the acts of such agents are governed is called law. Quite appropriately, then, law was given to men by God.

[3] Besides, since law is simply a certain rational plan and rule of operation,[3] it is fitting that law be given only to those beings who know the rational character of their work. Now, this is proper only to a rational creature. Therefore, it was appropriate that law was given to the rational creature only.

[4] Moreover, law should be given to those having the ability to act and not to act. Now, this is true of the rational creature only. Therefore, only the rational creature is capable of receiving law.

[5] Furthermore, since law is nothing but a rational plan of operation, and since the rational plan of any kind of work is derived from the end, anyone capable of receiving the law receives it from him who shows the way to the end. Thus does the lower artisan depend on the architect, and the soldier on the leader of the army. But the rational crea-

1. See above, ch. 113.
2. *Ibid.*
3. See St. Thomas, *Summa Theologiae*, I-II, 90, 1 (in *Basic Writings of St. Thomas*, II, 742–744).

ture attains his ultimate end in God, and from God, as we have seen in the foregoing.[4] Therefore, it is appropriate for law to be given men by God.

[6]   Hence it is said in Jeremias (31:33): "I will give my law in their bowels"; and in Osee (8:12; Douay modified): "I shall write my manifold laws for them."

Chapter 115.

THAT THE DIVINE LAW PRINCIPALLY ORDERS MAN TOWARD GOD

[1]   From this conclusion we may gather what it is to which the divinely given law principally tends.

[2]   It is evident that every lawmaker intends to direct men by means of laws toward his own end, principally. Thus, the leader of an army intends victory and the ruler of a state intends peace. But the end which God intends is God Himself. Therefore, the divine law principally looks to the ordering of man toward God.

[3]   Again, as we have said,[1] law is a rational plan of divine providence, in its governing capacity, proposed to the rational creature. But the governance of God, as providence, conducts individual beings to their own ends. Therefore, man is chiefly ordered to his end by the divinely given law. Now, the end for the human creature is to cling to God, for his felicity consists in this, as we have shown above.[2] So, the divine law primarily directs man to this end: that he may cling to God.

[4]   Besides, the intention of every legislator is to make those to whom he gives the law good; as a consequence,

4. See above, ch. 37 and 52.
1. See above, ch. 114.
2. See above, ch. 37.

the precepts of law should be concerned with acts of virtue.[3] So, those acts which are best are chiefly intended by divine law. But of all human acts, those whereby man clings to God are best, in the sense that they are nearer to the end. Therefore, the divine law primarily orders men in regard to those acts.

[5] Moreover, that from which the law derives its efficacy should be the most important thing in the law. But the divinely given law derives its efficacy among men from the fact that man is subject to God, for no one is bound by the law of a ruler if he is not subject to him. Therefore, this should be of primary importance in divine law: that the human mind must cling to God.

[6] Hence it is said in Deuteronomy (10:12): "And now, Israel, what doth the Lord thy God require of thee: but that thou fear the Lord thy God, and walk in His ways, and love Him, and serve the Lord thy God, with all thy heart and with all thy soul?"

Chapter 116.

THAT THE END OF DIVINE LAW IS THE LOVE OF GOD

[1] Since the intention of divine law is primarily to this purpose, that man may cling to God, and since man is best able to cling to God through love, it must be that the intention of divine law is primarily ordered to an act of love.

[2] Now, it is quite clear that man chiefly clings to God through love. For there are two things in man by which he is enabled to cling to God, namely, intellect and will. For by means of the lower parts of his soul he cannot cling to God, but only to inferior things. Now, the union which is effected through the intellect is completed by the union

3. See Aristotle, *Nicomachean Ethics*, I, 13 (1102a 8).

which pertains to the will, because through his will man in some way rests in that which the intellect apprehends. But the will adheres to a thing, either because of love or because of fear, but not in the same way. For, if one clings to something because of fear, he clings because of something else, for instance, to avoid an evil which threatens unless he clings to that thing. But, if one clings to a thing because of love, he does so for the sake of that thing. Now, what is valued for its own sake is of greater importance than what is for the sake of something else. Therefore, the adherence to God in love is the best possible way of clinging to Him. So, this is what is chiefly intended in the divine law.

[3]   Again, the end of every law, and above all of divine law, is to make men good. But a man is deemed good from his possession of a good will, through which he may put into act whatever good there is in him. Now, the will is good because it wills a good object, and especially the greatest good, which is the end. So, the more the will desires such a good, the more does a man advance in goodness. But a man has more desire for what he wills because of love than for what he wills because of fear only, for what he loves only from a motive of fear is called an object of mixed involuntariness. Such is the case of the man who wills to throw his merchandise into the sea because of fear.[1] Therefore, the love of the highest good, namely, God, above all else makes men good, and is chiefly intended in the divine law.

[4]   Besides, man's goodness stems from virtue, "for virtue is what makes its possessor good."[2] Hence, law also intends to make men virtuous, and the precepts of law are concerned with acts of the virtues. But it is a condition of virtue that the virtuous man must act with firmness and joy. But love is the chief producer of this result, for we do a thing firmly, and with joy, as a result of love. Therefore, love of the good is the ultimate object intended in divine law.

1. See Aristotle, *Nicomachean Ethics*, III, 1 (1110a 11).
2. *Ibid.*, II, 6 (1106a 23).

[5]   Moreover, legislators move those to whom the law is given by means of a command pertaining to the law as it is promulgated. In the case of all who are moved by a first mover, any one of them is moved more perfectly when he participates more fully in the motion of the prime mover, and in his likeness. Now, God, Who is the giver of divine law, makes all things because of His love. So, he who tends toward God in this way, namely, by loving Him, is most perfectly moved toward Him. Now, every agent intends perfection in the object of his action. Therefore, this is the end of all legislation: to make man love God.

[6]   Hence it is said in I Timothy (1:5): "The end of the commandment is charity"; and in Matthew (22:37–38) it is said that "the first and greatest commandment of the law is: Love the Lord thy God."

[7]   As a further consequence, the New Law, as the more perfect, is called the *law of love;* while the Old Law, as less perfect, is the *law of fear.*

Chapter 117.

THAT WE ARE ORDERED BY DIVINE LAW TO THE LOVE OF NEIGHBOR

[1]   The next point after this is that divine law intends the love of neighbor.

[2]   For there should be a union in affection among those for whom there is one common end. Now, men share in common the one ultimate end which is happiness, to which they are divinely ordered. So, men should be united with each other by a mutual love.

[3]   Again, whoever loves a person must, as a consequence, also love those loved by that person and those related to him. Now, men are loved by God, for He has prearranged for them, as an ultimate end, the enjoyment of Himself.

Therefore, it should be that, as a person becomes a lover of God, he also becomes a lover of his neighbor.

[4]   Besides, since "man is naturally a social animal,"[1] he needs to be helped by other men in order to attain his own end. This is most fittingly accomplished by mutual love which obtains among men. Therefore, by the law of God, which directs men to their ultimate end, mutual love is prescribed for us.

[5]   Moreover, so that man may devote his time to divine matters, he needs tranquillity and peace. Now, things that are potential disturbances to peace are removed principally by mutual love. So, since the divine law orders men in order that they may devote themselves to divine matters, it is necessary for mutual love to be engendered among men by divine law.

[6]   Furthermore, divine law is offered to man as an aid to natural law. Now, it is natural to all men to love each other. The mark of this is the fact that a man, by some natural prompting, comes to the aid of any man in need, even if he does not know him. For instance, he may call him back from the wrong road, help him up from a fall, and other actions like that: "as if every man were naturally the familiar and friend of every man."[2] Therefore, mutual love is prescribed for men by the divine law.

[7]   Hence it is said in John (15:12): "This is my commandment: that you love one another"; and in I John (4:21): "This commandment we have from God, that he who loveth God love also his brother"; and in Matthew (22:39) it is said that the second commandment is: "Love thy neighbor."

1. Aristotle, *Politics*, I, 2 (1253a 2).
2. Aristotle, *Nicomachean Ethics*, VIII, 1 (1155a 21).

Chapter 118.

THAT THROUGH DIVINE LAW MEN ARE BOUND TO THE RIGHT FAITH

[1]   From this it becomes clear that men are bound to the right faith through divine law.

[2]   Indeed, just as the origin of bodily love lies in the vision accomplished through the bodily eye, so also the beginning of spiritual love ought to lie in the intellectual vision of an object of spiritual love. Now, we cannot possess the vision of God, as an object of spiritual vision, in this life except through faith, because it exceeds the power of natural reason, and particularly because our happiness consists in the enjoyment of Him. Therefore, we must be led to the right faith by the divine law.

[3]   Again, the divine law orders man for this purpose, that he may be entirely subject to God.[1] But, just as man is subject to God as far as will is concerned, through loving, so is he subject to God as far as intellect is concerned, through believing; not, of course, by believing anything that is false, for no falsity can be proposed to man by God Who is truth. Consequently, he who believes something false does not believe in God. Therefore, men are ordered to the right faith by the divine law.

[4]   Besides, whoever is in error regarding something that is of the essence of a thing does not know that thing. Thus, if someone understood irrational animal with the notion that it is a man, he would not know man. Now, it would be a different matter if he erred concerning one of man's accidents. However, in the case of composite beings, the person who is in error concerning one of their essential principles does know the thing, in a relative way, though he does not know it in an unqualified sense. For instance, he

1. See above, ch. 115.

who thinks that man is an irrational animal knows him according to his genus. But this cannot happen in reference to simple beings; instead, any error at all completely excludes knowledge of the being. Now, God is most simple. So, whoever is in error concerning God does not know God, just as the man who thinks that God is a body does not know God at all, but grasps something else in place of God. However, the way in which a thing is known determines the way in which it is loved and desired. Therefore, he who is in error about God can neither love God nor desire Him as an end. So, since the divine law intends this result, that man love and desire God,[2] man must be bound by divine law to hold a right faith concerning God.

[5]   Moreover, false opinion holds the same place in regard to objects of the intellect that vice opposed to virtue has in regard to moral matters, "for truth is the good of the intellect."[3] But it is the function of divine law to prohibit vices. Therefore, it also pertains to it to exclude false opinions about God and matters concerned with God.

[6]   Thus it is said in Hebrews (11:6): "Without faith it is impossible to please God." And in Exodus (20:2) before the other precepts of the law are given, right faith concerning God is put in first place; moreover, it is said: "Hear, O Israel: the Lord thy God is one" (Deut. 6:4).

[7]   Through this consideration we exclude the error of those who say that it makes no difference to the salvation of man whatever be the faith with which he serves God.[4]

2. See above, ch. 116.
3. Aristotle, Nicomachean Ethics, VI, 2 (1139a 28).
4. The Bishop of Paris, in 1277, condemned this proposition "that there are fables and errors in the Christian religion, as in others" (Fontes Vitae S. Thomae, ed. M. H. Laurent [Saint-Maximin: 1937], VI, p. 610, prop. 174). It is not known who held such a position in the thirteenth century. See Gilson, History of Christian Philosophy, p. 406.

Chapter 119.

THAT OUR MIND IS DIRECTED TO GOD BY CERTAIN SENSE OBJECTS

[1] Since it is connatural for man to receive knowledge through his senses, and since it is very difficult to transcend sensible objects, divine provision has been made for man so that a reminder of divine things might be made for him, even in the order of sensible things. The purpose of this is that the intention of man might be better recalled to divine matters, even in the case of the man whose mind is not strong enough to contemplate divine things in themselves.

[2] And it was for this reason that sensible sacrifices were instituted: man offers these to God, not because God needs them, but so that man may be reminded that he ought to refer both his own being and all his possessions to God as end, and thus to the Creator, Governor, and Lord of all.

[3] In fact, certain blessings using sensible things are provided for man, whereby man is washed, or anointed, or fed, or given drink, along with the expression of sensible words, so that man may be reminded through sensible things that intelligible gifts come to him from without, and from God, Whose name is expressed in sensible words.

[4] So, certain sensible works are performed by man, not to stimulate God by such things, but to awaken man himself to divine matters by these actions, such as prostrations, genuflections, vocal ejaculations, and hymns. These things are done not because God needs them, for He knows all things, and His will is immutable, and the disposition of His mind does not admit of movement from a body for His own sake; rather, we do these things for our sakes, so that our attention may be directed to God by these sensible deeds and that our love may be aroused. At the same time,

then, we confess by these actions that God is the author of soul and body, to Whom we offer both spiritual and bodily acts of homage.

[5]   For this reason, it is not astonishing if heretics who deny that God is the author of our body condemn such manifestations. This condemnation shows that they have not remembered that they are men when they judge that the representation of sensible objects to themselves is not necessary for inner knowledge and for love. For it is evident from experience that the soul is stimulated to an act of knowledge or of love by bodily acts. Hence, it is obvious that we may quite appropriately use even bodily things to elevate our mind to God.

[6]   Now, the *cult* of God is said to consist in these bodily manifestations to God. For we are said to *cultivate* those things to which we devote effort through our works. Indeed, we show our zeal in regard to God by our activity, not, of course, to benefit Him (as we are said to do, when we cultivate other things by our actions), but because we approach more closely to God by such acts. And since we directly tend toward God through interior acts, we therefore properly give cult to God by interior acts. Yet exterior acts also pertain to the cult of God, according as our mind is lifted up to God by such acts, as we have said.

[7]   Also, this cult of God is called *religion*, because in some way man *binds*[1] himself by such acts, so that he will not wander away from God, and also because man feels that he is *obligated* by some sort of natural prompting to pay, in his own way, reverence to God, from Whom comes the beginning of man's being and of all good.

[8]   As a consequence, too, religion takes the name *piety*. For piety is the means whereby we pay due honor to our parents. Hence, the fact that honor is rendered to God, the Parent of all beings, seems appropriately to be attributed to

1. In Latin, *religio* may have the same root as the verb "to bind" (*ligare*); see St. Augustine, *De vera religione*, 55 (PL, 34, col. 172).

piety. And for this reason, those who are opposed to these things concerned with the cult of God are called *impious*.

[9]   And because God is not only the cause and source of our being, but also because our entire existence is within His power, and because we owe Him everything that is present in us, and as a consequence He is truly our Lord, what we offer Him in homage is called *service*.

[10]   Of course, God is not a lord in the accidental sense, as one man is over another; He is so through nature. And so, service is owed to God in one way, and to man in another, for we are accidentally subject to a man whose lordship over things is limited and also derivative from God. Hence, the service which is owed to God is technically called *latria* among the Greeks.

Chapter 120.

THAT THE CULT PROPER TO LATRIA IS TO BE OFFERED TO GOD ALONE

[1]   There have been some who have thought that the cult of latria should be offered not only to the first principle of things, but even to all creatures which exist above man. Hence, some, though of the opinion that God is the one, first, and universal principle of things, have nevertheless thought that latria should be offered, first of all, after the highest God, to celestial intellectual substances whom they called *gods*, whether they were substances completely separated from bodies or whether they were the souls of the spheres or the stars.

[2]   Secondly, they thought that it should be offered also to certain intellectual substances united, as they believed, to aerial bodies; and these they called *daemons*. Yet, because they believed them to be above men, as an aerial body is above a terrestrial body, they claimed that even these substances are to be honored with divine cult by men. And in

relation to men they said that those substances are *gods*,
being intermediaries between men and the gods. Moreover, because the souls of good men, through their separa-
tion from the body, have passed over into a state higher
than that of the present life, they held the opinion in their
belief that divine cult should be offered to the souls of the
dead, whom they called *heroes*, or *manes*.[1]

[3]   In fact, some people, holding the view that God is the
World Soul,[2] have believed that the cult of divinity is to be
offered to the entire world and to each of its parts; not, of
course, for the sake of the bodily part, but for the sake of
the "Soul," which they said was God, just as honor is
rendered to a wise man, not because of his body, but because of his soul.

[4]   Indeed, some men said that even things below man's
level in nature are to be honored with divine cult because
some power of a higher nature is participated by them.
Hence, since they believed that certain idols made by men
receive a supernatural power, either from the influence of
celestial bodies or from the presence of certain spirits, they
said that divine cult should be offered to images of this
kind. And they even called these idols gods. For which
reason they are also said to be *idolaters*, since they offer the
cult of latria to *idols*, that is, to images.[3]

[5]   Now, it is unreasonable for people who maintain only
one, separate, first principle to offer divine cult to another
being. For we render cult to God, as we have said,[4] not because He needs it, but so that a true opinion concerning
God may be strengthened in us, even by means of sensible

1. See St. Augustine, *De civitate Dei*, VII, 6 (*PL*, 41, col. 199)
   for the source of this pagan "theology" which had been de-
   scribed earlier in a now lost work of M. T. Varro.
2. *Ibid*.
3. See St. Thomas, *Summa Theologiae*, II-II, 94, 1; and the full
   historical documentation in this place, in the Ottawa edition
   (tome III, p. 1910, footnotes).
4. See above, ch. 119.

things. But an opinion on the point that God is one, exalted above all things, cannot be established in us through sensible things unless we honor Him with something unique, which we call *divine cult*. So, it is evident that a true opinion concerning the one principle is weakened if divine cult is offered to several beings.

[6] Again, as we said above,[5] this kind of exterior worship is necessary to man so that man's mind may be aroused to a spiritual reverence for God. Now, for the mind of man to be moved toward something custom plays a great part, since we are easily moved toward objectives that have become customary. Of course, human custom supports this practice, in that the honor which is offered to the person holding the highest office in the state, for example, the king or emperor, should be offered to no other person. Therefore, man's mind ought to be stimulated so that he will think that there is but one highest principle of things by means of his offering something to this principle which is offered to none other. This we call the *cult of latria*.

[7] Besides, if the cult of latria were owed to any person because of his superiority and not because he is the highest being, then since one man may be superior to another, and there is the same possibility among angels, it would follow that one man ought to offer latria to another, and one angel to another angel. And since, among men, he who is superior in one way may be inferior in another way, it would follow that men should mutually offer latria to each other. This is not appropriate.

[8] Moreover, by human custom, special repayment should be made for special benefit. Now, there is a special benefit which man receives from the highest God, namely, man's own creation, for it has been shown in Book Two[6] that God alone is the Creator. Therefore, man ought to return something special to God in acknowledgment of this special benefit. This is the cult of latria.

5. *Ibid.*
6. *SCG*, II, ch. 21.

[9] Furthermore, latria implies *service*.[7] But service is owed to a lord. Now, a lord is properly and truly one who gives precepts of action to others and who takes his own rule of action from no one else. On the other hand, one who carries out what has been ordered by a superior is more a minister than a lord. But God, Who is the highest principle of reality, disposes all things to their proper actions through His providence, as we showed above.[8] Hence, in Sacred Scripture both angels and celestial bodies are said *to minister* to God, Whose order they carry out; and also to us, for it is to our advantage that their actions accrue (Ps. 112:21; Heb. 1:14). Therefore, the cult of latria which is owed to the highest Lord is not to be offered except to the highest principle of things.

[10] Again, among other items which pertain to latria, *sacrifice* may be seen to have a special place, for genuflections, prostrations, and other manifestations of this kind of honor may also be shown to men, though with a different intention than in regard to God. But it is agreed by any man that sacrifice should be offered to no person unless he is thought to be God or unless one pretends to think so. Now, external sacrifice is representative of true, interior sacrifice, by which the human mind offers itself to God. Indeed, our mind offers itself to God as the principle of its creation, the author of its actions, the end of its happiness. These attributes are, in fact, appropriate to the highest principle of things only. For we have showed above[9] that the creative cause of the rational soul is the highest God alone; moreover, He alone is able to incline the will of man to whatever He wishes, as was shown above;[10] so also it is evident from our preceding considerations[11] that man's ultimate felicity consists solely in the enjoyment of Him. Therefore, man ought to offer sacrifice and the cult of

7. See above, ch. 119.
8. See above, ch. 64.
9. *SCG*, II, ch. 87.
10. See above, ch. 88.
11. See above, ch. 37.

latria only to the highest God, and not to any other kind of spiritual substances.

[11] Now, though the theory which claims that God is nothing but the world soul is a departure from the truth, as we showed above,[12] while the other position is true which maintains that God is a separate being and that all other intellectual substances depend on Him for their existence, whether separated from, or joined to, a body—still, the first theory provides a more rational basis for offering the cult of latria to different things. For, in offering the cult of latria to a variety of things one appears to be offering it to the one highest God, since, according to their theory, the different parts of the world are related to Him as the different members of the human body are to the human soul. But reason is also opposed to this view. For they say that the cult of latria should not be offered to the world by reason of its body, but because of its soul, which they assert to be God. Thus, though the bodily part of the world is divisible into different parts, the world soul is, however, indivisible. So, the cult of divinity ought not be offered to a variety of things, but to one only.

[12] Besides, if the world be supposed to have a soul which animates the whole and all its parts, this cannot be understood as a nutritive or sensitive soul, because the operations of these parts of the soul are not suitable to all parts of the universe. And even granting that the world might have a sensitive or nutritive soul, the cult of latria would not be due it because of such souls, for this cult is not due to brute animals or to plants. The conclusion remains, then, that their assertion that God, to Whom latria is owed, is the world soul must be understood of the intellectual soul. In fact, this soul is not the perfection of individually distinct parts of the body, but in some way has reference to the whole. This is even evident in the case of our soul which is less noble, for the intellect has no corporeal organ, as is proved in Book III of *On the Soul.*[13]

12. *SCG*, I, ch. 27.

13. See Aristotle, *De anima*, III, 4 (429a 25).

Therefore, even on the basis of their theory, the cult of divinity should not be offered to the various parts of the world, but to the entire world because of its soul.

[13]   Moreover, if in their theory there be but one soul which animates the whole world and all its parts, and if the world is not termed God except on account of the soul, then there will be but one God. And thus the cult of divinity will be owed to one being only. On the other hand, if there be but one soul for the whole, and if the different parts, in turn, have different souls, they have to say that the souls of the parts are subordinated to the soul of the whole; for the same proportion holds between perfections as between perfectible things. Now, supposing that a number of intellectual substances exist in an ordered hierarchy, the cult of latria will be due only to the one which holds the highest rank among them, as we showed in opposing the previous theory.[14] Therefore, the cult of latria should not be offered to the parts of the world, but only to the whole.

[14]   Furthermore, it is evident that some parts of the world have no soul of their own. Therefore, this cult should not be offered to them. Yet these men had the practice of honoring all the elements of the world, namely, earth, water, fire, and other inanimate bodies of like kind.

[15]   Again, it is obvious that a superior does not owe the cult of latria to an inferior. Now, man is superior in the order of nature, at least in regard to all lower bodies, to the extent that he has a more perfect form. Therefore, the cult of latria should not be offered by man to lower bodies, even if some cult were owed them on the supposition that they possessed souls of their own.

[16]   The same inappropriate conclusion must follow if someone were to say that the individual parts of the world have their own souls but the whole does not possess one common soul. For it will still remain necessary for the

14. Above, ¶6.

highest part of the world to have a more noble soul, to which alone, according to the premises, the cult of latria will be owed.

[17]   But more unreasonable than these theories is the one which states that the cult of latria should be offered to images. For, if images of this sort have power or worth of any kind derived from celestial bodies, then the cult of latria is not due them on this basis, because such worship is not even due to those celestial bodies, unless, perchance, because of their souls, as some have claimed.[15] But these images are claimed to have received some power from celestial bodies through the physical power of these bodies.

[18]   Again, it is evident that they do not obtain from celestial bodies any perfection which is as noble as is the rational soul. So, they are inferior in degree of worth to any man. Therefore, no cult is owed them by man.

[19]   Besides, a cause is more powerful than its effect. Now, the makers of these images are men. So, man owes no cult to them.

[20]   But, if it be said that these images have some virtue or worth due to the fact that certain spiritual substances are connected with them, even this will not suffice, because the cult of latria is owed to no spiritual substance except the highest.

[21]   Moreover, the rational soul is combined with man's body in a more noble way than that whereby a spiritual substance might be attached to the aforesaid images. So, man will still remain on a higher level of dignity than the aforesaid images.

[22]   Furthermore, since these images at times admit of harmful effects, it is evident that, if they derive their result from some spiritual substances, then those spiritual substances are vicious. This can also be clearly proved from this fact: they are deceptive in their answers and they

15. Above, ¶2.

demand certain actions contrary to virtue from their devotees. And so, they are inferior to good men. Therefore,
the cult of latria is not owed to them.

[23]   Therefore, it is clear from what we have said that
the cult of latria is due to the one, highest God only. Thus
it is said in Exodus (22:20): "He that sacrificeth to the
gods shall be put to death, save only to the Lord"; and in
Deuteronomy (6:13): "Thou shalt fear the Lord thy God,
and shalt serve Him only." And in Romans (1:22–23) it is
said of the Gentiles: "For, professing themselves to be
wise, they became fools, and they changed the glory of
the incorruptible God into the likeness of the image of a
corruptible man and of birds, and of fourfooted beasts and
of creeping things"; and later (verse 25; Douay modified):
"Who changed the truth of God into a lie and worshiped
and served the creature rather than the Creator, Who is
God above all blessed for ever."

[24]   So, since it is unfitting for the cult of latria to be
offered to any other being than the first principle of things,
and since to incite to unworthy deeds can only be the work
of a badly disposed rational creature, it is evident that men
have been solicited by the urging of demons to develop the
aforesaid unworthy cults, and these demons have been presented in place of God as objects of men's worship because
they craved divine honor. Hence it is said in the Psalm
(95:5): "All the gods of the Gentiles are devils"; and in
I Corinthians (10:20): "the things which the heathens
sacrifice, they sacrifice to devils and not to God."

[25]   Therefore, since this is the chief intent of divine law:
that man be subject to God and that he should offer special
reverence to Him, not merely in his heart, but also orally
and by bodily works, so first of all, in Exodus 20, where the
divine law is promulgated, the cult of many gods is forbidden when it is said:[16] "Thou shalt not have strange gods
before me" and "thou shalt not make to thyself a graven

16. Several modifications of the Douay version have been re-
    quired in the following verses.

thing, nor any likeness" (20:3–4). Secondly, it is forbidden man to pronounce vocally the divine name without reverence, that is, in order to lend support to anything false; and this is what is said: "Thou shalt not take the name of God in vain" (20:7). Thirdly, rest is prescribed at certain times from outward works, so that the mind may be devoted to divine contemplation; and thus it is stated: "Remember that thou keep holy the sabbath day" (20:8).

Chapter 121.

THAT DIVINE LAW ORDERS MAN ACCORDING TO REASON IN REGARD TO CORPOREAL AND SENSIBLE THINGS

[1] Now, just as man's mind may be raised up to God by means of corporeal and sensible things, if one use them in a proper way to revere God, so, too, the improper use of them either completely distracts the mind from God, and so the end of the will is fixed in inferior things, or such abuse slows down the inclination of the mind toward God so that we become attached to things of this kind to an extent greater than is necessary. But the divine law was given for this chief purpose: so that man might cling to God.[1] Therefore, it does pertain to the divine law to order man in regard to his love and use of bodily and sensible things.

[2] Again, as man's mind is subordinated to God, so is the body subordinated to the soul, and the lower powers to reason. But it pertains to divine providence, of which divine law is but a rational plan proposed by God to man, to see that individual things keep their proper order. Therefore, man must be so ordered by divine law that his lower powers may be subject to reason, and his body to his soul, and so that external things may subserve the needs of man.

1. See above, ch. 115.

[3]   Besides, any law that is rightly established promotes virtue. Now, virtue consists in this: that both the inner feelings and the use of corporeal things be regulated by reason. So, this is something to be provided for by divine law.

[4]   Moreover, it is the function of every lawmaker to determine by law the things without which observation of the law is impossible. Now, since law is proposed to reason, man would not follow the law unless all the other things which belong to man were subject to reason. So, it is the function of divine law to command the submission to reason of all the other factors proper to man.

[5]   Thus it is said: "Let your service be reasonable" (Rom. 12:1); and again: "This is the will of God, your sanctification" (I Thess. 4:3).

[6]   Now, by this conclusion we refute the error of some who say that those acts only are sinful whereby one's neighbor is offended or scandalized.

Chapter 122.

THE REASON WHY SIMPLE FORNICATION IS
A SIN ACCORDING TO DIVINE LAW,
AND THAT MATRIMONY IS NATURAL

[1]   From the foregoing we can see the futility of the argument of certain people who say that simple fornication is not a sin.[1] For they say: Suppose there is a woman who is not married, or under the control of any man, either her father or another man. Now, if a man performs the sexual act with her, and she is willing, he does not injure her, because she favors the action and she has control over her own body. Nor does he injure any other person, because

1. That this view still remained a problem in 1277 is evidence by Bishop Tempier's condemned proposition 183 (*Fontes Vitae S. Thomae*, VI, 611).

she is understood to be under no other person's control. So, this does not seem to be a sin.

[2]   Now, to say that he injures God would not seem to be an adequate answer. For we do not offend God except by doing something contrary to our own good, as has been said.[2] But this does not appear contrary to man's good. Hence, on this basis, no injury seems to be done to God.

[3]   Likewise, it also would seem an inadequate answer to say that some injury is done to one's neighbor by this action, inasmuch as he may be scandalized. Indeed, it is possible for him to be scandalized by something which is not in itself a sin. In this event, the act would be accidentally sinful. But our problem is not whether simple fornication is accidentally a sin, but whether it is so essentially.

[4]   Hence, we must look for a solution in our earlier considerations. We have said that God exercises care over every person on the basis of what is good for him.[3] Now, it is good for each person to attain his end, whereas it is bad for him to swerve away from his proper end. Now, this should be considered applicable to the parts, just as it is to the whole being; for instance, each and every part of man, and every one of his acts, should attain the proper end. Now, though the male semen is superfluous in regard to the preservation of the individual, it is nevertheless necessary in regard to the propagation of the species. Other superfluous things, such as excrement, urine, sweat, and such things, are not at all necessary; hence, their emission contributes to man's good. Now, this is not what is sought in the case of semen, but, rather, to emit it for the purpose of generation, to which purpose the sexual act is directed. But man's generative process would be frustrated unless it were followed by proper nutrition, because the offspring would not survive if proper nutrition were withheld. Therefore, the emission of semen ought to be so ordered that it

2. See above, ch. 121.
3. See above, ch. 112ff.

will result in both the production of the proper offspring and in the upbringing of this offspring.

[5]   It is evident from this that every emission of semen, in such a way that generation cannot follow, is contrary to the good for man. And if this be done deliberately, it must be a sin. Now, I am speaking of a way from which, *in itself*, generation could not result: such would be any emission of semen apart from the natural union of male and female. For which reason, sins of this type are called *contrary to nature*. But, if by accident generation cannot result from the emission of semen, then this is not a reason for it being against nature, or a sin; as for instance, if the woman happens to be sterile.

[6]   Likewise, it must also be contrary to the good for man if the semen be emitted under conditions such that generation could result but the proper upbringing would be prevented. We should take into consideration the fact that, among some animals where the female is able to take care of the upbringing of offspring, male and female do not remain together for any time after the act of generation. This is obviously the case with dogs. But in the case of animals of which the female is not able to provide for the upbringing of offspring, the male and female do stay together after the act of generation as long as is necessary for the upbringing and instruction of the offspring. Examples are found among certain species of birds whose young are not able to seek out food for themselves immediately after hatching. In fact, since a bird does not nourish its young with milk, made available by nature as it were, as occurs in the case of quadrupeds, but the bird must look elsewhere for food for its young, and since besides this it must protect them by sitting on them, the female is not able to do this by herself. So, as a result of divine providence, there is naturally implanted in the male of these animals a tendency to remain with the female in order to bring up the young. Now, it is abundantly evident that the female in the human species is not at all able to take care of the upbringing of offspring by herself, since the

needs of human life demand many things which cannot be provided by one person alone. Therefore, it is appropriate to human nature that a man remain together with a woman after the generative act, and not leave her immediately to have such relations with another woman, as is the practice with fornicators.

[7] Nor, indeed, is the fact that a woman may be able by means of her own wealth to care for the child by herself an obstacle to this argument. For natural rectitude in human acts is not dependent on things accidentally possible in the case of one individual, but, rather, on those conditions which accompany the entire species.

[8] Again, we must consider that in the human species offspring require not only nourishment for the body, as in the case of other animals, but also education for the soul. For other animals naturally possess their own kinds of prudence whereby they are enabled to take care of themselves. But a man lives by reason, which he must develop by lengthy, temporal experience so that he may achieve prudence. Hence, children must be instructed by parents who are already experienced people. Nor are they able to receive such instruction as soon as they are born, but after a long time, and especially after they have reached the age of discretion. Moreover, a long time is needed for this instruction. Then, too, because of the impulsion of the passions, through which prudent judgment is vitiated,[4] they require not merely instruction but correction. Now, a woman alone is not adequate to this task; rather, this demands the work of a husband, in whom reason is more developed for giving instruction and strength is more available for giving punishment. Therefore, in the human species, it is not enough, as in the case of birds, to devote a small amount of time to bringing up offspring, for a long period of life is required. Hence, since among all animals it is necessary for male and female to remain together as long as the work of the father is needed by the offspring, it

4. Aristotle, *Nicomachean Ethics*, VI, 5 (1140b 19).

is natural to the human being for the man to establish a lasting association with a designated woman, over no short period of time. Now, we call this society *matrimony*. Therefore, matrimony is natural for man, and promiscuous performance of the sexual act, outside matrimony, is contrary to man's good. For this reason, it must be a sin.

[9]   Nor, in fact, should it be deemed a slight sin for a man to arrange for the emission of semen apart from the proper purpose of generating and bringing up children, on the argument that it is either a slight sin, or none at all, for a person to use a part of the body for a different use than that to which it is directed by nature (say, for instance, one chose to walk on his hands, or to use his feet for something usually done with the hands) because man's good is not much opposed by such inordinate use. However, the inordinate emission of semen is incompatible with the natural good; namely, the preservation of the species. Hence, after the sin of homicide whereby a human nature already in existence is destroyed, this type of sin appears to take next place, for by it the generation of human nature is precluded.

[10]   Moreover, these views which have just been given have a solid basis in divine authority. That the emission of semen under conditions in which offspring cannot follow is illicit is quite clear. There is the text of Leviticus (18:22–23): "thou shalt not lie with mankind as with womankind . . . and thou shalt not copulate with any beast." And in I Corinthians (6:10): "Nor the effeminate, nor liers with mankind . . . shall possess the kingdom of God."

[11]   Also, that fornication and every performance of the act of reproduction with a person other than one's wife are illicit is evident. For it is said: "There shall be no whore among the daughters of Israel, nor whoremonger among the sons of Israel" (Deut. 23:17); and in Tobias (4:13): "Take heed to keep thyself from all fornication,

and beside thy wife never endure to know a crime"; and in I Corinthians (6:18): "Fly fornication."

[12] By this conclusion we refute the error of those who say that there is no more sin in the emission of semen than in the emission of any other superfluous matter, and also of those who state that fornication is not a sin.

Chapter 123.

THAT MATRIMONY SHOULD BE INDIVISIBLE

[1] If one will make a proper consideration, the preceding reasoning will be seen to lead to the conclusion not only that the society of man and woman of the human species, which we call matrimony, should be long lasting, but even that it should endure throughout an entire life.

[2] Indeed, possessions are ordered to the preservation of natural life, and since natural life, which cannot be preserved perpetually in the father, is by a sort of succession preserved in the son in its specific likeness, it is naturally fitting for the son to succeed also to the things which belong to the father. So, it is natural that the father's solicitude for his son should endure until the end of the father's life. Therefore, if even in the case of birds the solicitude of the father gives rise to the cohabitation of male and female, the natural order demands that father and mother in the human species remain together until the end of life.

[3] It also seems to be against equity if the aforesaid society be dissolved. For the female needs the male, not merely for the sake of generation, as in the case of other animals, but also for the sake of government, since the male is both more perfect in reasoning and stronger in his powers. In fact, a woman is taken into man's society for the needs of generation; then, with the disappearance of a woman's fecundity and beauty, she is prevented from association with another man. So, if any man took a woman

in the time of her youth, when beauty and fecundity were hers, and then sent her away after she had reached an advanced age, he would damage that woman contrary to natural equity.

[4] Again, it seems obviously inappropriate for a woman to be able to put away her husband, because a wife is naturally subject to her husband as governor, and it is not within the power of a person subject to another to depart from his rule. So, it would be against the natural order if a wife were able to abandon her husband. Therefore, if a husband were permitted to abandon his wife, the society of husband and wife would not be an association of equals, but, instead, a sort of slavery on the part of the wife.

[5] Besides, there is in men a certain natural solicitude to know their offspring. This is necessary for this reason: the child requires the father's direction for a long time. So, whenever there are obstacles to the ascertaining of offspring they are opposed to the natural instinct of the human species. But, if a husband could put away his wife, or a wife her husband, and have sexual relations with another person, certitude as to offspring would be precluded, for the wife would be united first with one man and later with another. So, it is contrary to the natural instinct of the human species for a wife to be separated from her husband. And thus, the union of male and female in the human species must be not only lasting, but also unbroken.

[6] Furthermore, the greater that friendship is, the more solid and long-lasting will it be. Now, there seems to be the greatest friendship between husband and wife, for they are united not only in the act of fleshly union, which produces a certain gentle association even among beasts, but also in the partnership of the whole range of domestic activity. Consequently, as an indication of this, man must even "leave his father and mother" for the sake of his wife, as is said in Genesis (2:24). Therefore, it is fitting for matrimony to be completely indissoluble.

[7] It should be considered, further, that generation is the only natural act that is ordered to the common good, for

eating and the emission of waste matters pertain to the individual good, but generation to the preservation of the species. As a result, since law is established for the common good, those matters which pertain to generation must, above all others, be ordered by laws, both divine and human. Now, laws that are established should stem from the prompting of nature, if they are human; just as in the demonstrative sciences, also, every human discovery takes its origin from naturally known principles. But, if they are divine laws, they not only develop the prompting of nature but also supplement the deficiency of natural instinct, as things that are divinely revealed surpass the capacity of human reason. So, since there is a natural prompting within the human species, to the end that the union of man and wife be undivided, and that it be between one man and one woman, it was necessary for this to be ordered by human law. But divine law supplies a supernatural reason, drawn from the symbolism of the inseparable union between Christ and the Church, which is a union of one spouse with another (Eph. 5:24–32). And thus, disorders connected with the act of generation are not only opposed to natural instinct, but are also transgressions of divine and human laws. Hence, a greater sin results from a disorder in this area than in regard to the use of food or other things of that kind.

[8] Moreover, since it is necessary for all other things to be ordered to what is best in man, the union of man and wife is not only ordered in this way because it is important to the generating of offspring, as it is in the case of other animals, but also because it is in agreement with good behavior, which right reason directs either in reference to the individual man in himself, or in regard to man as a member of a family, or of civil society. In fact, the undivided union of husband and wife is pertinent to good behavior. For thus, when they know that they are indivisibly united, the love of one spouse for the other will be more faithful. Also, both will be more solicitous in their care for domestic possessions when they keep in mind

that they will remain continually in possession of these same things. As a result of this, the sources of disagreements which would have to come up between a man and his wife's relatives, if he could put away his wife, are removed, and a more solid affection is established among the relatives. Removed, also, are the occasions for adultery which are presented when a man is permitted to send away his wife, or the converse. In fact, by this practice an easier way of arranging marriage with those outside the family circle is provided.

[9]   Hence it is said in Matthew (5:31) and in I Corinthians (7:10): "But I say to you . . . that the wife depart not from her husband."

[10]   By this conclusion, moreover, we oppose the custom of those who put away their wives, though this was permitted the Jews in the old Law, "by reason of the hardness of their hearts" (Matt. 19:8); that is, because they were ready to kill their wives. So, the lesser evil was permitted them in order to prevent a greater evil.

Chapter 124.

THAT MATRIMONY SHOULD BE BETWEEN
ONE MAN AND ONE WOMAN

[1]   It seems, too, that we should consider how it is inborn in the minds of all animals accustomed to sexual reproduction to allow no promiscuity; hence, fights occur among animals over the matter of sexual reproduction. And, in fact, among all animals there is one common reason, for every animal desires to enjoy freely the pleasure of the sexual act, as he also does the pleasure of food; but this liberty is restricted by the fact that several males may have access to one female, or the converse. The same situation obtains in the freedom of enjoying food, for one animal is obstructed if the food which he desires to eat is taken over

by another animal. And so, animals fight over food and sexual relations in the same way. But among men there is a special reason, for, as we said,[1] man naturally desires to know his offspring, and this knowledge would be completely destroyed if there were several males for one female. Therefore, that one female is for one male is a consequence of natural instinct.

[2] But a difference should be noted on this point. As far as the view that one woman should not have sexual relations with several men is concerned, both the aforementioned reasons apply. But, in regard to the conclusion that one man should not have relations with several females, the second argument does not work, since certainty as to offspring is not precluded if one male has relations with several women. But the first reason works against this practice, for, just as the freedom of associating with a woman at will is taken away from the husband, when the woman has another husband, so, too, the same freedom is taken away from a woman when her husband has several wives. Therefore, since certainty as to offspring is the principal good which is sought in matrimony, no law or human custom has permitted one woman to be a wife for several husbands. This was even deemed unfitting among the ancient Romans, of whom Maximus Valerius reports that they believed that the conjugal bond should not be broken even on account of sterility.[2]

[3] Again, in every species of animal in which the father has some concern for offspring, one male has only one female; this is the case with all birds that feed their young together, for one male would not be able to offer enough assistance to bring up the offspring of several females. But in the case of animals among whom there is no concern on the part of the males for their offspring, the male has promiscuous relations with several females and the female with plural males. This is so among dogs, chickens, and the

1. See above, ch. 123.
2. Maximus Valerius, *Factorum et dictorum memorabilium*, II, 1, 4 (Paris: 1841, p. 623).

like. But since, of all animals, the male in the human species has the greatest concern for offspring, it is obviously natural for man that one male should have but one wife, and conversely.

[4]   Besides, friendship consists in an equality.[3] So, if it is not lawful for the wife to have several husbands, since this is contrary to certainty as to offspring, it would not be lawful, on the other hand, for a man to have several wives, for the friendship of wife for husband would not be free, but somewhat servile. And this argument is corroborated by experience, for among husbands having plural wives the wives have a status like that of servants.

[5]   Furthermore, strong friendship is not possible in regard to many people, as is evident from the Philosopher in Ethics VIII.[4] Therefore, if a wife has but one husband, but the husband has several wives, the friendship will not be equal on both sides. So, the friendship will not be free, but servile in some way.

[6]   Moreover, as we said,[5] matrimony among humans should be ordered so as to be in keeping with good moral customs. Now, it is contrary to good behavior for one man to have several wives, for the result of this is discord in domestic society, as is evident from experience. So, it is not fitting for one man to have several wives.

[7]   Hence it is said: "They shall be two in one flesh" (Gen. 2:24).

[8]   By this, the custom of those having several wives is set aside, and also the opinion of Plato who maintained that wives should be common.[6] And in the Christian period he was followed by Nicolaus, one of the seven deacons.[7]

3. See Aristotle, *Nicomachean Ethics*, VIII, 5 (1157b 36).
4. Aristotle, *Nicomachean Ethics*, VIII, 6 (1158a 10).
5. See above, ch. 123.
6. Plato, *Republic*, V, 449Dff; *Timaeus*, 18C.
7. See St. Augustine, *De haeresibus*, 5 (PL, 42, col. 26).

Chapter 125.

THAT MATRIMONY SHOULD NOT TAKE PLACE BETWEEN CLOSE RELATIVES

[1]   Moreover, because of reasonable considerations of this kind it has been ordered by the laws that certain persons, related by their origin, are excluded from matrimony.

[2]   In fact, since there is in matrimony a union of diverse persons, those persons who should already regard themselves as one because of having the same origin are properly excluded from matrimony, so that in recognizing themselves as one in this way they may love each other with greater fervor.

[3]   Again, because the acts performed by husband and wife are associated with a certain natural shame, it is necessary that those persons to whom respect is due because of the bond of blood should be prohibited from performing such actions with each other. Indeed, this reason seems to have been suggested in the Old Testament law, in the text which states: "Thou shalt not uncover the nakedness of thy sister" (Lev. 18:9), and also in other texts.

[4]   Besides, for man to be much given to sexual pleasures contributes to the dissolution of good moral behavior; because, since this pleasure greatly occupies the mind, reason is withdrawn from things which should be done rightly. Now, if a man were permitted sexual relations with those persons with whom he must live, such as sisters and other relatives, excessive indulgence in this pleasure would result, for the occasion for sexual relations with such persons could not be removed. Therefore, it was suitable to good moral behavior for such union to be prohibited by laws.

[5]   Furthermore, the enjoyment of sexual relations "greatly corrupts the judgment of prudence."[1] So, the mul-

1. Aristotle, *Nicomachean Ethics*, VI, 5 (1140b 19).

tiplication of such pleasure is opposed to good behavior. Now, such enjoyment is increased through the love of the persons who are thus united. Therefore, intermarriage between relatives would be contrary to good behavior, for, in their case, the love which springs from community of origin and upbringing would be added to the love of concupiscence, and, with such an increase of love, the soul would necessarily become more dominated by these pleasures.

[6]   Moreover, in human society it is most necessary that there be friendship among many people. But friendship is increased among men when unrelated persons are bound together by matrimony. Therefore, it was proper for it to be prescribed by laws that matrimony should be contracted with persons outside one's family and not with relatives.

[7]   Besides, it is unfitting for one to be conjugally united with persons to whom one should naturally be subject. But it is natural to be subject to one's parents. Therefore, it would not be fitting to contract matrimony with one's parents, since in matrimony there is a conjugal union.

[8]   Hence it is said: "No man shall approach to her that is near of kin to him" (Lev. 18:6).

[9]   By these arguments the custom of those who practice carnal relations with their relatives is refuted.

[10]   Moreover, we should note that just as natural inclination tends toward things which happen in most cases, so also positive law depends on what happens in most cases. It is not contrary to the foregoing arguments if in a particular case the outcome might be otherwise, for the good of many should not be sacrificed for the sake of one person's good, because "the good of many is always more divine than the good of one person."[2] However, lest the disadvantage which could occur in the individual case be altogether without remedy, there remains with lawmakers and others of similar function the authority to grant a dispensation from what is generally required by law, in view of

2. Aristotle, *Nicomachean Ethics*, I, 2 (1094b 19).

what is necessary in any particular case. For, if the law be a human one, it can be dispensed by men who have such power. But, if the law be divinely given, dispensation can be granted by divine authority; as, in the Old Law, permission seems to have been granted by dispensation to have several wives and concubines and to put away one's wife.

Chapter 126.

THAT NOT ALL SEXUAL INTERCOURSE IS SINFUL

[1]   Now, just as it is contrary to reason for a man to perform the act of carnal union contrary to what befits the generation and upbringing of offspring, so also is it in keeping with reason for a man to exercise the act of carnal union in a manner which is suited to the generation and upbringing of offspring. But only those things that are opposed to reason are prohibited by divine law, as is evident from what we said above.[1] So, it is not right to say that every act of carnal union is a sin.

[2]   Again, since bodily organs are the instruments of the soul, the end of each organ is its use, as is the case with any other instrument. Now, the use of certain bodily organs is carnal union. So, carnal union is the end of certain bodily organs. But that which is the end of certain natural things cannot be evil in itself, because things that exist naturally are ordered to their end by divine providence, as is plain from what was said above.[2] Therefore, it is impossible for carnal union to be evil in itself.

[3]   Besides, natural inclinations are present in things from God, Who moves all things. So, it is impossible for the natural inclination of a species to be toward what is evil in

1. See above, ch. 121.
2. See above, ch. 64.

itself. But there is in all perfect animals a natural inclination toward carnal union. Therefore, it is impossible for carnal union to be evil in itself.

[4]   Moreover, that without which a thing cannot be what is good and best is not evil in itself. But the perpetuation of the species can only be preserved in animals by generation, which is the result of carnal union. So, it is impossible for carnal union to be evil in itself.

[5]   Hence it is said in I Corinthians (7:28): "if a virgin marry, she hath not sinned."

[6]   Now, this disposes of the error of those who say that every act of carnal union is illicit, as a consequence of which view they entirely condemn matrimony and marriage arrangements. In fact, some of these people say this because they believe that bodily things arise, not from a good, but from an evil, source.[3]

Chapter 127.

THAT THE USE OF FOOD IS NOT
A SIN IN ITSELF

[1]   Just as the exercise of sexual capacities is without sin, provided it be carried on with reason, so also in the case of the use of food. Now, any action is performed in accord with reason when it is ordered in keeping with what befits its proper end. But the proper end of taking food is the preservation of the body by nutrition. So, whatever food can contribute to this end may be taken without sin. Therefore, the taking of food is not in itself a sin.

3. On this view of the Albigensians, or *Cathari*, see C. J. H. Hayes and M. W. Baldwin, *History of Europe* (New York: 1949), I, 304–306; for the role of St. Thomas' Order, the Dominicans, in opposing this heresy, see C. Douais, *Essai sur l'organisation des études dans l'ordre des Frères Prêcheurs* (Toulouse: 1884), pp. 4–8.

[2] Again, no use of a thing is evil in itself unless the thing itself is evil in itself. Now, no food is by nature evil, for everything is good in its own nature, as we showed above.[1] But a certain article of food may be bad for a certain person because it is incompatible with his bodily state of health. So, no taking of food is a sin in itself, by virtue of the type of thing that it is; but it can be a sin if in opposition to reason a person uses it in a manner contrary to his health.

[3] Besides, to use things for the purpose for which they exist is not evil in itself. But plants exist for the sake of animals; indeed, some animals exist for the sake of others, and all exist for the sake of man, as is evident from earlier considerations.[2] Therefore, to use either plants or the flesh of animals for eating or for whatever other utility they may have for man is not a sin in itself.

[4] Moreover, a sinful defect may be transferred from the soul to the body, but not conversely, for we call something sinful according as there is a deordination of the will. Now, food pertains immediately to the body, not to the soul. So, the taking of food cannot be a sin in itself unless, of course, it be incompatible with rectitude. It could be so, in one way, by virtue of incompatibility with the proper end of food: thus, for the sake of the pleasure associated with eating food a man might eat food which works against the health of his body, either because of the kind of food or the quantity. This could be so in another way, because it is opposed to the situation of the person who uses the food or of those with whom he lives; for instance, a man might eat finer foods than his circumstances could well provide and in a manner different from the customs of the people with whom he lives. It is possible in a third way, by virtue of food being prohibited by law for some special reason: thus, in the Old Law, certain kinds of food were prohibited for a symbolic reason; and in Egypt the eating

1. See above, ch. 7.
2. See above, ch. 22.

of the flesh of the ox was prohibited in olden times so that agriculture would not be hindered; or even because certain rules prohibit the use of certain foods, with a view to the restraint of concupiscence.

[5]   Hence, the Lord says: "Not that which goeth into the mouth defileth a man" (Matt. 15:11). And in I Corinthians (10:25) it is said: "Whatever is sold in the shambles, eat; asking no question for conscience' sake." And in I Timothy (4:4) it is said: "Every creature of God is good, and nothing to be rejected that is received with thanksgiving."

[6]   By this conclusion we refute the error of some people who say that the use of certain foods is illicit in itself. Of these the Apostle speaks in the same place (I Tim. 4:1-3): "in the last times some shall depart from the faith . . . forbidding to marry, to abstain from meats which God hath created to be received with thanksgiving."

[7]   Now, since the use of food and sexual capacities is not illicit in itself, but can only be illicit when it departs from the order of reason, and since external possessions are necessary for the taking of food, for the upbringing of offspring and the support of a family, and for other needs of the body, it follows also that the possession of wealth is not in itself illicit, provided the order of reason be respected. That is to say, a man must justly possess what he has; he must not set the end of his will in these things, and he must use them in a fitting way for his own and others' benefit. Hence, the Apostle does not condemn the rich, but he gives them a definite regulation for the use of their wealth, when he says: "Charge the rich of this world not to be highminded, nor to trust in the uncertainty of riches, but . . . to be rich in good works, to give easily, to communicate to others" (I Tim. 6:17-18); and in Ecclesiasticus (31:8): "Blessed is the rich man that is found without blemish, and that hath not gone after gold, nor put his trust in money nor in treasure."

[8] By this we also set aside the error of those who, as Augustine says in his book *On Heresies*, "most arrogantly call themselves Apostolics, because they refuse to accept into their communion those who practice marriage, and who possess goods of their own (practices which the Catholic Church has), and also many monks and clerics. But these men are thereby heretics, for, in separating themselves from the Church, they think that there is no hope for those who use these things which they do without."[3]

Chapter 128.

HOW MAN IS ORDERED BY THE LAW OF GOD IN REGARD TO HIS NEIGHBOR

[1] From the things that we have said[1] it is clear that man is directed by the divine law to observe the order of reason in regard to all things that can come to his use. Among all those things which come within the use of man, the most important are other men. "For man is by nature a social animal,"[2] because he needs many things which cannot be provided by one man alone. Therefore, it is necessary for man to be instructed by divine law, so that he may live in relation to other men, according to the order of reason.

[2] Again, the end of divine law is for man to cling to God.[3] But one man may be aided to this end by another man, both in regard to knowledge and to love. For men are of mutual assistance to each other in the knowing of truth, and one man may stimulate another toward the good, and also restrain him from evil. Hence it is said: "Iron sharpeneth iron, so a man sharpeneth the countenance of his

3. St. Augustine, *De haeresibus*, 40 (*PL*, 42, col. 32).
1. See above, ch. 121ff.
2. Aristotle, *Politics*, I, 2 (1253a 2).
3. See above, ch. 115.

friend" (Prov. 27:17). And it is said in Ecclesiastes
(4:9–12): "It is better therefore that two should be together than one, for they have the advantage of their society;
if one fall, he shall be supported by the other. Woe to him
that is alone; for, when he falleth, he hath none to lift
him up. And if two lie together, they shall warm one another. How shall one alone be warmed? And if a man
prevail against one, two shall withstand him." Therefore,
it was necessary for the society of men, in their mutual
interrelations, to be ordered by divine law.

[3]   Besides, divine law is a certain plan of divine providence for the purpose of governing men.[4] Now, it is the
function of divine providence to maintain the individuals
subject to it under proper order, in such a way that each
may take its proper place and level. Therefore, divine law
so orders men in regard to each other that each man may
keep his order. This is for men to be at peace with each
other, for "peace among men is nothing but ordered concord," as Augustine says.[5]

[4]   Moreover, whenever certain things are subordinated
to another, they must be ordered in a manner concordant
to each other; otherwise, they might hinder each other in
the attaining of their common end. This is clear in the
case of an army which is concordantly ordered to victory,
the end of the commander. Now, each man is ordered to
God by divine law, so there must be among men, according to divine law, an ordered concord, peace that is, so
that they may not hinder each other.

[5]   Hence it is said in the Psalm (147:14): "Who hath
placed peace in thy borders." And the Lord said: "These
things I have spoken to you, that in Me you may have
peace" (John 16:33).

[6]   Now, an ordered concord is preserved among men
when each man is given his due, for this is justice. And so,

---

4. See above, ch. 114ff.
5. St. Augustine, *De civitate Dei*, XIX, 13 (PL, 41, col. 640).

it is said in Isaias (32:17): "the work of justice shall be peace." Therefore, by divine law precepts had to be given, so that each man would give his neighbor his due and would abstain from doing injuries to him.

[7] Moreover, among men a person is most in debt to his parents. And so, among the precepts of the law ordering us in regard to our neighbor, Exodus (20:12–17) puts first: "Honor thy father and thy mother." In this text it is understood to be commanded that each man must render what he owes, both to his parents and to other persons, in accord with another text: "Render to all men their dues" (Rom. 13:7). Next to be put down are the precepts commanding abstinence from causing various sorts of harm to one's neighbor. For instance, that we must not offend him by any deeds against his person; thus it was said: "Thou shalt not kill"; nor against a person associated with him, for it was written: "Thou shalt not commit adultery"; nor against his external goods, for it was written: "Thou shalt not steal." We are also prohibited from offending our neighbor by words that are contrary to justice, for it was written: "Thou shalt not bear false witness against thy neighbor." And since God is the judge, even of our hearts, we are prohibited from offending our neighbor in our heart, "by desiring his wife" or any of his goods.

[8] Now, that he may observe this kind of justice which is prescribed by divine law man is impelled in two ways: in one, from within; in the other way, from without. From within, of course, man is voluntary in regard to observing what divine law prescribes. In fact, this is accomplished by man's love of God and his neighbor, for he who loves a person gives him his due spontaneously and joyfully, and he even adds something in excess by way of liberality. So, the complete fulfillment of the law depends on love, according to the text of the Apostle: "Love is the fulfilling of the law" (Rom. 13:10). And the Lord says that, "on these two commandments," that is, on the love of God and of neighbor, "dependeth the whole law" (Matt. 22:40). But since some people are not so disposed internally

that they will do spontaneously what the law orders, they must be forced from without to fulfill the justice of the law. Of course, since this is done only from fear of punishments, they do not fulfill the law in freedom, but in servility. Hence it is said in Isaias (26:9): "When Thou shalt do Thy judgments on the earth," that is, by punishing the wicked, "all the inhabitants of the world shall learn justice."

[9]   The first, then, "are a law unto themselves" (Rom. 2:14), for they have charity which impels them in place of law and makes them act with liberality. So, it was not necessary to promulgate an external law for their sake, but for the sake of those who are not inclined of themselves toward the good. Hence it is said in I Timothy (1:9): "The law is not made for the just man, but for the unjust." This should not be understood as if the just were not obliged to obey the law, as some have badly understood it, but that these people are inclined of themselves to do what is just, even without a law.

Chapter 129.

THAT SOME HUMAN ACTS ARE RIGHT ACCORDING TO NATURE AND NOT MERELY BECAUSE THEY ARE PRESCRIBED BY LAW

[1]   From the foregoing it is apparent that things prescribed by divine law are right, not only because they are put forth by law, but also because they are in accord with nature.

[2]   Indeed, as a result of the precepts of divine law, man's mind is subordinated to God, and all other things that are in man's power are ordered under reason.[1] Now, the natural order requires that lower things be subject to higher things. Therefore, the things prescribed by divine law are naturally right in themselves.

1. See above, ch. 121.

[3] Again, men receive from divine providence a natural capacity for rational judgment, as a principle for their proper operations. Now, natural principles are ordered to natural results. So, there are certain operations that are naturally suitable for man, and they are right in themselves, not merely because they are prescribed by law.

[4] Besides, there must be definite kinds of operations which are appropriate to a definite nature, whenever things have such a definite nature. In fact, the operation appropriate to a given being is a consequent of that nature. Now, it is obvious that there is a determinate kind of nature for man. Therefore, there must be some operations that are in themselves appropriate for man.

[5] Moreover, whenever a certain thing is natural to any being, that without which this certain thing cannot be possessed must also be natural, "for nature is not defective in regard to necessary things."[2] But it is natural for man to be a social animal, and this is shown by the fact that one man alone does not suffice for all the things necessary to human life. So, the things without which human society cannot be maintained are naturally appropriate to man. Examples of such things are: to preserve for each man what is his own and to refrain from injuries. Therefore, there are some things among human acts that are naturally right.

[6] Furthermore, we showed above[3] that man has this natural endowment, he may use lower things for the needs of his life. Now, there is a definite measure according to which the use of the aforesaid things is proper to human life, and if this measure is set aside the result is harmful to man, as is evident in the immoderate eating of food. Therefore, there are some human acts that are naturally fitting and others that are naturally unfitting.

[7] Again, according to the natural order, the body of man is for the sake of his soul and the lower powers of the

2. Aristotle, *De anima*, III, 9 (432b 21).
3. See above, ch. 121 and 127.

soul are for the sake of reason, just as in other things matter is for the sake of form and instruments are for the sake
of the principal agent. But, because of one thing being
ordered to another, it ought to furnish help to that other,
and not offer it any hindrance. So, it is naturally right for
the body and the lower powers of the soul to be so managed by man that thereby his activity of reason, and his
good, are least hindered and are, instead, helped. But, if it
happens otherwise, the result will naturally be sinful.
Therefore, drinking bouts and feastings, and inordinate
sexual activities through which rational activity is hindered,
and domination by the passions which do not permit free
judgment of reason—these are naturally evil things.

[8] Besides, those acts by which he inclines toward his
natural end are naturally appropriate to an agent, but those
that have the contrary effect are naturally inappropriate to
the agent. Now, we showed above[4] that man is naturally
ordered to God as his end. Therefore, the things by which
man is brought to the knowledge and love of God are
naturally right, but whatever things have the contrary effect
are naturally evil for man.

[9] Therefore, it is clear that good and evil in human activities are based not only on the prescription of law, but
also on the natural order.

[10] Hence it is said in the Psalm (18:10): "the judgments of the Lord are true, justified in themselves."

[11] By this conclusion we set aside the position of those
who say that things are just and right only because they are
prescribed by law.

4. See above, ch. 17 and 25.

Chapter 130.

ON THE COUNSELS THAT ARE GIVEN IN DIVINE LAW

[1] Since the best thing for man is to become attached in his mind to God and divine things, and since it is impossible for man intensively to busy himself with a variety of things in order that man's mind may be applied to God with greater liberty, counsels are given in the divine law whereby men are withdrawn from the busy concerns of the present life as far as is possible for one who is living an earthly life. Now, this detachment is not so necessary to man for justice that its absence makes justice impossible; indeed, virtue and justice are not removed if man uses bodily and earthly things in accord with the order of reason. And so, divine law admonitions of this kind are called *counsels*, not *precepts*, inasmuch as man is urged to renounce lesser goods for the sake of better goods.

[2] Moreover, in the general mode of human life, human concern is devoted to three items: first, to one's own person, what he should do, or where he should spend his time; second, to the persons of those connected with him, chiefly his wife and children; and third, to the acquisition of external things, which a man needs for the maintenance of life. So, to cut off solicitude for external things the counsel of *poverty* is given in the divine law, that is to say, so that one may cast off the things of this world with which his mind could be involved with some concern. Hence, the Lord says: "If thou wilt be perfect, go sell what thou hast and give to the poor . . . and come, follow me" (Matt. 19:21). And to cut off concern for wife and children there is given man the counsel of *virginity* or *continence*. Hence, it is said in I Corinthians (7:25): "Now, concerning virgins, I have no commandment of the Lord, but I give counsel." And giving the reason for this counsel, he adds: "He

that is without a wife is solicitous for the things that belong
to the Lord: how he may please God. But he that is with a
wife is solicitous for the things of the world: how he may
please his wife, and he is divided" (I Cor. 7:32–33).
Finally, to cut off man's solicitude even for himself there
is given the counsel of obedience, through which man
hands over the control of his own acts to a superior. Concerning which it is said: "Obey your prelates and be subject
to them. For they watch as being ready[1] to render an account of your souls" (Heb. 13:17).

[3]   But, since the highest perfection of human life consists in the mind of man being detached from care, for the
sake of God, and since the three counsels mentioned above
seem most definitely to prepare one for this detachment,
they appear to belong quite appropriately to the state of
perfection; not as if they were perfections themselves, but
that they are dispositions to perfection, which consists in
being detached from care, for the sake of God. And the
words of our Lord, when He advises poverty, definitely
show this, for He says: "If thou wilt be perfect, go sell what
thou hast and give to the poor . . . and follow me" (Matt.
19:21), thus putting the perfection of life in the following
of Him.

[4]   They may also be called the effects and signs of perfection. When the mind becomes attached to a thing with
intense love and desire, the result is that it sets aside other
things. So, from the fact that man's mind is fervently inclined by love and desire to divine matters, in which it is
obvious that perfection is located, it follows that he casts
aside everything that might hold him back from this inclination to God: not only concern for things, for wife, and the
love of offspring, but even for himself. And the words of
Scripture suggest this, for it is said in the Canticle of
Canticles (8:7): "if a man should give all the substance of
his house for love, he will account it as nothing"; and in
Matthew (13:45): "the kingdom of heaven is like to a
merchant seeking good pearls, who, when he had found one

1. Douay omits "ready."

pearl of great price, went his way and sold all that he had and bought it"; and also in Philippians (3:7–8; Douay modified): "the things that were gain to me . . . I counted them but as dung, that I might gain Christ."

[5] So, since the aforesaid three counsels are dispositions to perfection, and are the effects and signs of perfection, it is fitting that those who pledge themselves to these three by a vow to God should be said to be *in the state of perfection*.[2]

[6] Now, the perfection to which these three counsels give a disposition consists in detachment of the mind for God. Hence, those who profess the aforesaid vows are called *religious*, in the sense that they offer themselves and their goods to God, as a special kind of sacrifice: as far as goods are concerned, by poverty; in regard to their body, by continence; and in regard to their will, by obedience. For religion consists in a divine cult, as was said above.[3]

Chapter 131.

ON THE ERROR OF THE ATTACKERS
OF VOLUNTARY POVERTY

[1] There have been some people who, in opposition to the teaching of the Gospel, have disapproved the practice of voluntary poverty. The first of these to be found is Vigilantius,[1] whom, however, some others[2] have followed later, "calling themselves teachers of the law, understanding

2. See St. Thomas, *De perfectione vitae spiritualis* (ed. P. Mandonnet, in *Opuscula Omnia* [Paris: 1927], IV, pp. 196–264).

3. See above, ch. 119.

1. See St. Jerome, *Contra Vigilantium*, 14 (*PL*, 23, col. 366); also, St. Thomas, *Summa Theologiae*, II-II, 186, 4.

2. William of St. Amour and his associates criticized the religious life of poverty, in Paris, a few years before the writing of *SCG*; St. Thomas wrote against them in *Contra impugnantes Dei cultum et religionem* (ed. Mandonnet, *Opuscula Omnia*, IV, pp. 1–195).

neither the things they say, nor whereof they affirm"
(I Tim. 1:7). They were led to this view by these and
similar arguments.[3]

[2]   Natural appetite requires every animal to provide for
itself in regard to the necessities of its life; thus, animals
that are not able to find the necessities of life during every
period of the year, by a certain natural instinct gather the
things needed for life during the season when they can be
found, and they keep them; this practice is evident in the
case of bees and ants. But men need many things for the
preservation of life which cannot be found in every season.
So, there is a natural tendency in man to gather and keep
things necessary to him. Therefore, it is contrary to natural
law to throw away, under the guise of poverty, all that one
has gathered together.

[3]   Again, all have a natural predilection for the things
whereby their being may be preserved, because all things
desire to be. But man's life is preserved by means of the
substance of external goods. So, just as each man is obliged
by natural law to preserve his life, so is he obliged to preserve external substance. Therefore, as it is contrary to the
law of nature for a man to injure himself, so, too, is it for a
man to deprive himself by voluntary poverty of the necessities of life.

[4]   Besides, "man is by nature a social animal," as we
said above.[4] But society could not be maintained among
men unless one man helped another. So, it is natural to
men for one to help another in need. But those who discard external substance, whereby most help can be given
others, render themselves by this practice unable to give
help. Therefore, it is against natural instinct, and against
the good of mercy and charity, for a man to discard all
worldly substance by voluntary poverty.

[5]   Moreover, if it be evil to possess the substance of this
world, but if it be good to deliver one's neighbors from evil

3. See below, ch. 134, for St. Thomas' answers.
4. See above, ch. 128.

and bad to lead them into evil, the conclusion is that to give the substance of this world to a needy person is an evil and to take from an owner is a good. Now, this is not right. So, it is a good thing to possess the substance of this world. Therefore, to throw it away entirely is an evil thing.

[6]   Furthermore, occasions of evil are to be avoided. But poverty is an occasion of evil, since some are induced, as a result of it, to acts of theft, of false praise and perjury, and the like. Therefore, poverty should not be embraced voluntarily; rather, should care be taken to avoid its advent.

[7]   Again, since virtue lies in a middle way, corruption comes from both extremes. Now, there is a virtue of liberality, which gives what should be given and retains what should be retained. But the vice of defect is illiberality, which retains both the things that should and should not be retained. So, too, it is a vice of excess, for all things to be given away. This is what the people do who assume poverty voluntarily. Therefore, this is vicious, and similar to prodigality.

[8]   Moreover, these arguments seem to be confirmed by the text of Scripture. For it is said: "Give me neither beggary nor riches; give me only the necessaries of life, lest perhaps being filled, I should be tempted to deny, and say: Who is the Lord? Or being compelled by poverty, I should steal, and forswear the name of my God" (Prov. 30:8–9).

Chapter 132.

ON THE WAYS OF LIFE OF THOSE WHO PRACTICE VOLUNTARY POVERTY

[1]   Now, it seems that this problem may be better treated if we examine in greater detail the ways in which those who practice voluntary poverty must live.[1]

1. For St. Thomas' eventual estimate of the five ways discussed here, see below, ch. 135.

[2]   The *first* way of so living is for each person to sell his possessions, and for all to live in common on the proceeds. This appears to have been the practice under the Apostles in Jerusalem, for it is said: "As many as were owners of lands or houses sold them and brought the price of the things they sold, and laid it down before the feet of the Apostles. And distribution was made to every one as he had need" (Acts 4:34–35). But it does not seem that effective provision is made for human life, according to this way.

[3]   First, because it is not easy to get a number of persons who have large possessions to adopt this life. So, if distribution is made among many of the proceeds derived from a few rich people, the amount will not be sufficient for any length of time.

[4]   Next, because it is possible and easy for such a fund to disappear, either through fraud on the part of the managers or by theft or robbery. So, those who follow this kind of poverty will be left without support for life.

[5]   Again, many things happen whereby men are forced to change their location. It will not be easy, then, to provide from the common fund gathered from such sale of possessions for those who will perhaps be scattered in various places.

[6]   Then, there is a *second* way of so living: this is to hold common possessions, from which provision is made for individual persons, according to their needs, as is the practice in many monasteries. But even this way of living does not seem appropriate.

[7]   In fact, earthly possessions are the source of worry, both in regard to taking care of their revenues and in regard to their protection against frauds and attacks. Moreover, the larger they are, the more people are required to take care of them, and, so, the larger must these possessions be to give adequate support to all these people. And thus, in this way, the very purpose of voluntary poverty vanishes, at least in

regard to the many men who must concern themselves with the management of the possessions.

[8] Again, common possession is usually a cause of disagreement. People who hold nothing in common, such as the Spaniards and Persians, do not seem to get into legal disputes, but, rather, those who do hold something in common. This is why there are disagreements even among brothers. Now, discord is the greatest impediment to giving over one's mind to divine matters, as we said above.[2] So, it seems that this way of living obstructs the end of voluntary poverty.

[9] There is still a *third way* of living: that is for those who practice voluntary poverty to live from the labor of their hands. Indeed, this was the way of life followed by the Apostle Paul, and he recommended his practice to others by his example and by his teaching. For it is stated in II Thessalonians (3:8–10): "Neither did we eat any man's bread for nothing, but in labor and toil we worked night and day, lest we should be chargeable to any of you. Not as if we had not power, but that we might give ourselves a pattern unto you, to imitate us. For also, when we were with you, this we declared to you, that, if any man will not work, neither let him eat." But even this way of living does not seem to be appropriate.

[10] As a matter of fact, manual labor is necessary for the support of life, because by it anything may be acquired. Now, it seems foolish for a man to give away what is needed and then to work to get it again. If, then, it is necessary after the adoption of voluntary poverty again to acquire by manual labor that by which a man may support himself, it was useless to give up all that he had for the support of life.

[11] Again, voluntary poverty is counseled, so that a person may be disposed by it to follow Christ in a better way, because he is freed by it from worldly concerns. But it

2. See above, ch. 128; the reference may be to a deleted chapter, following ch. 129; see the *Prefatio* to the Leonine edition, tome XIV, pp. 47*b, XIIIa, XVIIb.

seems to require greater concern for a person to get his food by his own labor than for him to use what he possesses for the support of his life, and especially if he has possessions of modest size, or that are capable of being moved, from which something would be available to provide for the needs of life. Therefore, to live by the labor of one's hands does not seem to be suitable to the intention of those embracing voluntary poverty.

[12]   Added to this is the fact that even our Lord, while taking away from his disciples solicitude for earthly things, in the parable of the birds and the lilies of the field seems to forbid them manual labor. For He says: "Behold the birds of the air, for they neither sow, nor do they reap nor gather into barns"; and again: "Consider the lilies of the field, how they grow: they labor not, neither do they spin" [Matt. 6:26–28].

[13]   Moreover, this way of life seems inadequate. In fact, there are many who desire perfection of life, for whom neither the ability nor the skill is available to enable them to spend their lives in manual labor, because they are neither brought up, nor informed, in such pursuits. Indeed, in this case, country people and workmen would be in a better position to embrace perfection of life than those who have devoted themselves to the pursuit of wisdom, but who have been reared in wealth and comfort, which they have left behind for the sake of Christ. It is also possible for some who embrace voluntary poverty to become disabled or to be otherwise prevented from the possibility of working. So, in such a case, they would become destitute of the necessities of life.

[14]   Again, the labor of no small amount of time is requisite for gaining the necessities of life; this is obvious in the case of many who devote all their time to it, yet hardly manage to make an adequate living. Now, if it were necessary for followers of voluntary poverty to make their living by manual labor, the result would be that they might take up the greater part of their lives in this kind of work; con-

sequently, they would be kept away from other, more necessary activities, such as the pursuit of wisdom, and teaching, and other such spiritual exercises. In this way, voluntary poverty would be an impediment to perfection of life rather than a disposition helpful to it.

[15] Moreover, if someone says that manual labor is necessary in order to avoid idleness, this is not an adequate objection to the argument. For it would be better to avoid idleness by occupations under the moral virtues, in which riches serve an instrumental role, for instance, in giving alms and things like that, rather than by manual labor. Besides, it would be futile to counsel poverty simply because men who have become poor would refrain from idleness and devote their lives to manual labors, unless it were done in such a way that they could devote themselves to more noble activities than those which are customary in the ordinary lives of men.

[16] But, if someone says that manual labor is necessary for the mastering of fleshly concupiscences, this is not a pertinent objection. Our question is: whether it is necessary for followers of voluntary poverty to make their living by manual labor. Besides, it is possible to control the concupiscences of the flesh in many other ways, namely, by fasting, vigils, and other such practices. Moreover, they could use manual labor for this purpose even if they were rich and did not need to work to gain a living.

[17] Then, there is still a *fourth* way of living: that is, the followers of voluntary poverty may live on the goods which are offered them by others, who, while keeping their own wealth, wish to make a contribution to this perfection of voluntary poverty. And it seems that our Lord and His disciples practiced this way of life, for we read in Luke (8:2-3) that certain women followed Christ and "ministered to Him out of their substance." However, even this way of life does not seem proper.

[18] For it does not seem reasonable for a person to part with his own goods and then live off another man.

[19]   Besides, it seems improper for a person to take from another and make no repayment to him, for, in giving and receiving, the equality of justice should be observed. But it can be maintained that some of those recipients who live on the bounty of others may render some sort of service to these others. This is why ministers of the altar, and preachers who supply the people with teaching and other divine services, are observed accepting, not inappropriately, the means of livelihood from them. "For the workman is worthy of his meat," as the Lord says in Matthew (10:10). For which reason, the Apostle says in I Corinthians (9:13–14) that "the Lord ordained that they who preach the gospel should live by the gospel . . . just as they who work in the holy place eat the things that are of the holy place." So, it seems improper for those who serve the people in no special function to take the necessities of life from the people.

[20]   Again, this way of living seems to be a source of loss to others. For there are people who, of necessity, must be supported by the benefactions of others and who cannot provide for themselves because of poverty and sickness. The alms received by them must be decreased if those who embrace poverty voluntarily have to be supported on the gifts of others, because there are not enough men, nor are men much inclined, to support a great number of poor people. Consequently, the Apostle commands in I Timothy (5:16; Douay modified) that, if anyone have a widow related to him, "let him minister to her, that the Church may be sufficient for them that are widows indeed." So, it is improper for men who choose poverty to take over this way of living.

[21]   Besides, freedom of mind is absolutely necessary for perfection in virtue, for, when it is taken away, men easily become "partakers of other men's sins" (see I Tim. 5:22), either by evident consent, or by flattering praise, or at least by pretended approval. But much that is prejudicial to this freedom of mind arises from the aforesaid way of life; indeed, it is not possible for a man not to shrink from offend-

ing a person on whose bounty he lives. Therefore, the way of life under discussion is a hindrance to perfection of virtue, which is the purpose of voluntary poverty. Thus, it does not seem to suit those who are voluntarily paupers.

[22] Moreover, we do not control what depends on the will of another person. But what a giver gives of his own goods depends on his will. So, insufficient provision is made for the control of their means of livelihood by voluntary paupers living in this way.

[23] Furthermore, paupers who are supported by the gifts of others have to reveal their needs to others and beg for necessities. Now, this kind of begging makes mendicants objects of contempt, and even nuisances. In fact, men think themselves superior to those who have to be supported by them, and many give with reluctance. But those who embrace perfection of life should be held in reverence and love, so that men may more readily imitate them and emulate their state of life. Now, if the opposite happens, even virtue itself may be held in contempt. Therefore, to live by begging is a harmful way of life for those who embrace poverty voluntarily for the sake of perfect virtue.

[24] Besides, for perfect men, not only evils must be avoided, but even things that have an appearance of evil, for the Apostle says in Romans 12:17 (I Thess. 5:22): "From all appearance of evil refrain yourselves." And the Philosopher says[3] that the virtuous man should not only avoid disgraceful actions, but also those which appear disgraceful. Now, mendicancy has the appearance of an evil, since many people beg because of greed. Therefore, this way of life should not be adopted by perfect men.

[25] Moreover, the counsel of voluntary poverty was given in order that man's mind might be withdrawn from solicitude for earthly things and more freely devoted to God. But this way of living by begging requires a great deal of solicitude; in fact, there seems to be greater solicitude involved in getting things from others than in using what is one's own.

3. Aristotle, *Nicomachean Ethics*, IV, 9 (1128b 20).

So, this way of living does not seem appropriate for those taking on voluntary poverty.

[26]   Now, if anyone wants to praise mendicancy because of its humility, he would seem to be speaking quite unreasonably. For humility is praised because earthly exaltation is held in contempt, and it consists in riches, honors, renown, and things like that; but it is not praised for contemning the loftiness of virtue, in regard to which we should be magnanimous. So, it would contribute to the bad repute of humility if anyone in the name of humility did anything derogatory to the higher character of virtue. But mendicancy is derogatory to it: both because "it is better to give than to receive" (Acts 20:35) and because it has the appearance of something disgraceful, as we said. Therefore, mendicancy should not be praised because of its humility.

[27]   There have been some, finally, who asserted that followers of perfection in life should have no concern at all, either to beg, or to work, or to keep anything for themselves, but that they should look to God alone for the support of life—because of what is said in Matthew (6:25; Douay modified): "Be not solicitous for your life, what you shall eat or drink, nor for your body, what you shall put on"; and later: "Be not solicitous for tomorrow" (Matt. 6:24). Now, this seems completely unreasonable.

[28]   Indeed, it is foolish to wish for an end, and then to neglect the things that are related to the end. But human solicitude is related to the end of eating, for by it one obtains food for oneself. So, those who cannot live without eating ought to have some concern about obtaining food.

[29]   Besides, solicitude for earthly things need not be avoided, unless it hinders the contemplation of eternal matters. But a man endowed with mortal flesh cannot live unless he does many things whereby contemplation is interrupted, things like sleeping, eating, and other such actions. Therefore, solicitude for the necessities of life is not to be set aside on this basis, that it is an impediment to contemplation.

[30]   Moreover, there is a marvelously absurd consequence. For, on the same reasoning, one could say that he does not wish to walk, or to open his mouth to eat, or to avoid a falling stone or a plunging sword, but would rather wait for God to do something. This is to tempt God. Therefore, solicitude for the means of living is not to be rejected entirely.

Chapter 133.

IN WHAT WAY POVERTY IS GOOD

[1]   So, then, in order to show the truth in regard to the foregoing arguments, and what view we should take regarding poverty, we shall make a consideration of riches. As a matter of fact, external riches are necessary for the good of virtue; since by them we support our body and give assistance to other people. Now, things that are means to an end must derive their goodness from the end. So, external riches must be a good for man; not, of course, the principal one, but as a secondary good. For the end is the principal good, while other things are good because they are ordered to the end. This is why it has seemed to some people that the virtues are the greatest goods for man, while external riches are his least important goods. Now, things that are means to an end must be measured in accord with the requirements of the end. Therefore, riches are good, to the extent that they advance the practice of virtue, but if this measure is departed from, so that the practice of virtue is hindered by them, then they are not to be numbered among goods, but among evils. Hence, it happens to be a good thing for some people to possess riches, for they use them for the sake of virtue, but for others it is a bad thing to have them, for these people are taken away from virtue by them, either through too much solicitude or affection for them, or also because of mental pride resulting from them.

[2]   However, since there are virtues of the active and the contemplative life, both types have a different need for external riches. For the contemplative virtues need them only for the support of nature, but the active virtues need them for this, and also for the helping of others with whom one must live. Hence, the contemplative life is more perfect, even on this point, for it needs fewer things. Now, it seems proper to this kind of life for a man to devote himself entirely to divine things, which perfection the teaching of Christ urges on man. Hence, for followers of this type of perfection a very small amount of external riches suffices, that is, just the amount needed to support nature. And so, the Apostle says, in I Timothy (6:8): "Having food and wherewith to be covered, with these we are content."

[3]   So, poverty is praiseworthy according as it frees man from the vices in which some are involved through riches. Moreover, in so far as it removes the solicitude which arises from riches, it is useful to some, namely, those disposed to busy themselves with better things. However, it is harmful to others, who, being freed from this solicitude, fall into worse occupations. Hence, Gregory says: "Often, those who have lived a life of human activities have been well occupied, but have been killed by the sword of their own retirement."[1] However, in so far as poverty takes away the good which results from riches, namely, the assisting of others and the support of oneself, it is purely an evil; except in the case where the temporal help that is offered to neighbors can be compensated for by a greater good, that is, by the fact that a man who lacks riches can more freely devote himself to divine and spiritual matters. But the good of supporting oneself is so necessary that it can be compensated for by no other good, since no man should take away from himself the support of life, under the pretext of obtaining another good.

[4]   And so, such poverty is praiseworthy when a man is freed by it from earthly concerns and devotes himself more freely to divine and spiritual things, provided, of course,

1. St. Gregory, Moralia, VI, 37 (PL, 75, col. 761).

that the ability remains along with it in man to support himself in a lawful manner, for which support not many things are needed. Thus, the less one's way of living in poverty requires of solicitude, the more praiseworthy it is. For poverty in itself is not good, but only in so far as it liberates from those things whereby a man is hindered from intending spiritual things. Hence, the measure of its goodness depends on the manner in which man is freed by means of it from the aforementioned obstacles. And this is generally true of all external things: they are good to the extent that they contribute to virtue, but not in themselves.

Chapter 134.

ANSWERS TO THE ARGUMENTS BROUGHT FORWARD ABOVE AGAINST POVERTY

[1] Now that these things have been seen, it is not difficult to answer the foregoing arguments by which poverty is attacked.[1]

[2] Although there is naturally present in man a desire to gather the things necessary for life, as the first argument suggested,[2] it is not, however, such that every man must be occupied with this work. Indeed, not even among the bees do all have the same function; rather, some gather honey, others build their homes out of wax, while the rulers are not occupied with these works. And the same should hold in the case of man. In fact, since many things are needed for man's life, for which one man could not suffice of himself, it is necessary for different jobs to be done by different people.[3] For some should be farmers, some caretakers of animals, some builders, and so on for the other tasks. And since the life of man requires not only corporeal but, even

1. See above, ch. 131.
2. *Ibid.*, ¶2.
3. For an earlier statement of the division of labor, see Plato, *Republic*, II, 370B.

more, spiritual goods, it is also necessary for some men to devote their time to spiritual things, for the betterment of others; and these must be freed from concern over temporal matters. Now, this division of various tasks among different persons is done by divine providence, inasmuch as some people are more inclined to one kind of work than to another.

[3] In this way, then, it is clear that those who abandon temporal things do not take away from themselves their life support, as the *second* argument implies.[4] For there remains with them a good expectation of supporting their lives, either from their own labors, or from the benefactions of others, whether they take them as common possessions or for daily need. Thus, indeed, "what we can do through our friends, we do by ourselves, in a sense," as the Philosopher says,[5] and so, what is possessed by friends is possessed by us, in a way.

[4] Moreover, there should be mutual friendship among men, in accord with which they assist each other either in spiritual or in earthly functions. Of course, it is a greater thing to help another in spiritual matters than in temporal affairs, as much greater as spiritual things are more important than temporal ones, and more necessary for the attainment of the end which is beatitude. Hence, he who gives up, through voluntary poverty, the possibility of succoring others in temporal things, so that he may acquire spiritual goods whereby he may more beneficially help others, he does not work against the good of human society, as the *third* argument concludes.[6]

[5] It is clear from things said earlier that riches are a definite good for man, when they are ordered to the good of reason, though not in themselves. Hence, nothing prevents poverty from being a greater good, provided one is

4. See above, ch. 131, ¶3.
5. Aristotle, *Nicomachean Ethics*, III, 3 (1112b 28).
6. See above, ch. 131, ¶4.

ordered to a more perfect good by it. And thus, the *fourth* argument is answered.[7]

[6]   And since neither riches, nor poverty, nor any external thing is in itself man's good, but they are only so as they are ordered to the good of reason, nothing prevents a vice from arising out of any of them, when they do not come within man's use in accord with the rule of reason. Yet they are not to be judged evil in themselves; rather, the use of them may be evil. And so, neither is poverty to be cast aside because of certain vices which may be at times occasioned by it, as the *fifth* argument tried to show.[8]

[7]   Hence, we must consider that the mean of virtue is not taken according to the amount of exterior goods that come into use, but according to the rule of reason. So, it sometimes happens that what is excessive in relation to the quantity of an external thing may be moderate in relation to the rule of reason. For no one inclines to greater things than does the magnanimous man; nor is there anyone who surpasses in greatness of expenditures the magnificent man. So, they adhere to a mean that does not consist in the amount of expense, or anything like that, but in so far as they neither exceed the rule of reason, nor fall short of it. Indeed, this rule measures not only the size of a thing that is used, but also the circumstances of the person, and his intention, the fitness of place and time, and other such things that are necessary in acts of virtue. So, no one runs counter to virtue through voluntary poverty, even if he abandons everything. Nor does he do this wastefully, since he does it with a proper end, and with due attention to other circumstances. For it is a greater thing to risk one's life, which, of course, a person may do under the virtue of fortitude if he observes the proper circumstances, than to abandon all his goods for a due end. And so, the *sixth* argument is answered.[9]

7. *Ibid.*, ¶5.
8. *Ibid.*, ¶6.
9. *Ibid.*, ¶7.

[8]   What is suggested on the basis of the words of Solomon[10] is not to the contrary. For it is evident that he speaks of forced poverty, which is often the occasion for thievery.

Chapter 135.

ANSWER TO THE OBJECTIONS AGAINST THE DIFFERENT WAYS OF LIFE OF THOSE WHO EMBRACE VOLUNTARY POVERTY

[1]   After these answers, we must make a consideration of the ways in which devotees of voluntary poverty must live.

[2]   Now, the first way,[1] that is, for all to live in common on the proceeds of possessions that are sold, is one which will work, but not for a long time. So, the Apostles instituted this way of living for the faithful in Jerusalem, because they foresaw through the Holy Spirit that they would not remain together for long in Jerusalem, both because of the persecutions to come from the Jews and because of the imminent destruction of the city and its people. As a result, it was not necessary to provide for the faithful, except for a short time. Consequently, when they went out to other peoples, among whom the Church was to be established and to continue to endure, there is no account of their establishing this mode of living.

[3]   But the fraud which can be committed by the distributors is no argument against this way of life. For, this is common to all modes of living in which people dwell together—less so, in this way, since it seems more difficult for followers of perfection in life to commit fraud. Also, a remedy is provided against this, in the prudent selection of trustworthy distributors. Thus, under the Apostles, Stephen and others were chosen who were deemed worthy of this office (Acts 6:3ff.).

10. *Ibid.*, ¶8.
1. See above, ch. 132, ¶2-5.

[4] Then, the *second way*[2] is also suitable for those who embrace voluntary poverty: that is, for them to live on common possessions.

[5] Nor is any of the perfection to which devotees of voluntary poverty tend lost by this way. For it is possible for it to be arranged that possessions be obtained in a proper manner through the effort of one of them, or of a small number of men, and so the others who remain without solicitude for temporal things may freely give their time to spiritual matters, which is the fruit of voluntary poverty. Nor, in fact, do those who take over this solicitude for the others lose anything of their perfection of life, because what they appear to lose by a lack of free time they gain in the service of charity, in which perfection of life also consists.

[6] Nor, indeed, in this way of life, is concord taken away as a result of common possessions. People should embrace voluntary poverty who are of the type that hold temporal things in contempt, and such people cannot disagree about temporal goods that are common, especially since they ought to look for nothing from these temporal things except the necessities of life, and, besides, the distributors ought to be trustworthy. Nor can this way of life be disapproved because certain people abuse it, for bad men use even good things badly, just as good men use bad things in a good way.

[7] Moreover, the *third way*[3] of living is appropriate to those who embrace voluntary poverty; namely, they may live by the labor of their hands.

[8] Indeed, it is not foolish to give away temporal things so that they may again be acquired by manual labor, as the first argument to the contrary suggested,[4] because the possession of riches required solicitude in getting them, or

2. *Ibid.*, ¶6–8.
3. *Ibid.*, ¶9–16.
4. *Ibid.*, ¶10.

even in keeping them, and they attracted the love of man to them; and this does not happen when a person applies himself to the gaining of his daily bread by manual labor.

[9]   Besides, it is clear that but a little time is enough for the acquisition of food sufficient for the support of nature by means of manual labor, and not much solicitude is needed. However, to amass riches or to acquire a large amount of supplies, as worldly workmen propose, requires the spending of much time and the application of great care. In this, the answer to the *second* argument is evident.[5]

[10]   However, we should bear in mind that the Lord in the Gospel did not prohibit labor, but only mental solicitude for the necessities of life. For He did not say: "Do not work," but, rather: "Be not solicitous." This He proves from a weaker case. For, if birds and lilies are sustained by divine providence, things which are of lower estate and unable to labor at those tasks whereby men gain their living, it is much more likely that He will provide for men who are of more worthy estate and to whom He has given the capacity to seek their livelihood through their own labors. Thus, it is not necessary to be afflicted by anxious concern for the needs of this life. Hence, it is evident that there is nothing derogatory to this way of life in the words of the Lord which were cited.

[11]   Nor, in fact, can this way of living be rejected because it is inadequate. The fact that in a few cases a man may be unable to gain what suffices for the needs of life by manual labor alone is due either to sickness or some like disability. However, an arrangement is not to be rejected because of a defect which occurs rarely, for such things happen in nature and in the order of voluntary acts. Nor is there any way of living whereby things may be so arranged that failure cannot occur at times, for even riches can be taken away by theft or robbery; so, also, the man who lives from the work of his hands can grow feeble. Yet

5. *Ibid.*, ¶11.

there is a remedy in connection with the way of life that we are talking about; namely, that help be given him whose labor is not enough to provide his living, either by other men in the same society who can do more work than is necessary for them or else by those who have riches. This is in accord with the law of charity and natural friendship whereby one man comes to the assistance of another who is in need. Hence, while the Apostle said, in II Thessalonians (3:10): "if any man will not work, neither let him eat"—for the sake of those who are not able to gain a living by their own labor—he adds a warning to others, saying: "But you, brethren, be not weary in well doing" (II Thess. 3:13).

[12] Moreover, since a few things suffice for the needs of life, those who are satisfied with little need not spend a great deal of time in gaining what is necessary by manual labor. So, they are not much hindered from the spiritual works on account of which they embraced voluntary poverty, especially since, while working with their hands, they may think about God and praise Him and do other practices like this which people living alone should do. However, so that they may not altogether be precluded from spiritual works, they can also be helped by the benefactions of the rest of the faithful.

[13] Now, although voluntary poverty is not adopted for the purpose of getting rid of idleness or controlling the flesh by manual work, since this even possessors of riches could do, there is no doubt that manual labor is useful for that purpose, even without the need of gaining a living. However, idleness can be avoided by other more useful occupations, and concupiscence of the flesh conquered by stronger remedies. Hence, the need to work does not apply, for these reasons, to people who have, or can have, other means on which they may properly live. For, only the necessity of livelihood forces one to work with his hands, and thus the Apostle says, in II Thessalonians (3:10): "if any man will not work, neither let him eat."

[14] The *fourth* way[6] of living, from those things that are offered by others, is also suitable for those who embrace voluntary poverty.

[15] For, it is not inappropriate that he who has given away his own goods for the sake of an objective which contributes to the benefit of others should be supported by the gifts of these others. Indeed, unless this were so, human society could not endure, because, if every man took care of his own possessions only, there would be no one to serve the common welfare. So, it is quite fitting to human society that those who have set aside concern for their own goods, and who serve the common welfare, should be supported by those whose welfare they serve. Indeed, it is for this same reason that soldiers live on stipends paid by others and that the rulers of a republic are provided for from the common funds. As a matter of fact, those who adopt voluntary poverty in order to follow Christ renounce all things so that they may serve the common welfare, enlightening the people by their wisdom, learning, and examples, or strengthening them by prayer and intercession.

[16] As a result, it is clear that there is nothing disgraceful in their living on the gifts of others, because they make a greater return: on their part, receiving temporal support; but in regard to others, contributing to progress in spiritual matters. Hence, the Apostle says, in II Corinthians (8:14): "Let your abundance," that is, in temporal things, "supply their want," of the same things, "that their abundance," that is, in spiritual goods, "also may supply your want." For he who helps another shares in his work, both in its good and in its evil.

[17] Now, by their examples they incite others to virtue, for it develops that those who profit by their examples become less attached to riches when they observe other people completely abandoning their wealth for the sake of perfection in life. But the less a man loves riches, and the more intent on virtue he is, the more readily, also, does he dis-

6. *Ibid.*, ¶17-26.

tribute his wealth for the needs of others. As a result, those who embrace voluntary poverty and live on the gifts of others, rather than causing loss to the poor by taking the benefactions which would support the lives of others, become more beneficial to other poor people, because they by words and examples stimulate other men to works of mercy.

[18] Moreover, it is clear that men of perfect virtue, such as they must be who adopt voluntary poverty, since they hold riches in contempt, do not lose their freedom of mind because of the petty amount that they accept from others for the maintenance of life. As a matter of fact, a man does not lose his independence of mind unless it be because of things which are dominant in his affections. Hence, a man does not lose his independence because of things he despises, even if they are given to him.

[19] Now, although the maintenance of those who live on the gifts of others depends on the will of the givers, this is not, for that reason, an inadequate way of supporting the life of Christ's poor. For it does not depend on the will of one man but on the will of many. Hence, it is not probable that, among the vast number of the faithful, there would not be many people who would readily supply the needs of those whom they hold in reverence because of the perfection of their virtue.

[20] Nor is it unfitting for them to declare their needs and ask for what is necessary, whether for others or for themselves. Indeed, we read that even the Apostles did this: not only did they receive what was necessary from those to whom they preached, which was rather a matter of rightful authority than of mendicancy, because of the rule of the Lord that they who serve, "the gospel should live by the gospel" (I Cor. 9:13–14), but they also did it for the poor who were in Jerusalem (Acts 9:27ff.; II Cor. 8 and 9) and who, having given up their possessions, were living in poverty, yet were not preaching to the Gentiles; rather, their spiritual manner of living entitled them to such support. Hence, the Apostle urges, not as a matter

of obligation but of good will on the part of the givers (II Cor. 9:7), the aiding of such people by means of alms; and this is nothing but begging. Now, this begging does not make men objects of contempt, provided it is done with moderation, for need and not to excess, and without undue insistence, with consideration for the circumstances of the persons from whom the request is made, and for the place and time—all of which must be observed by those devoted to perfection in life.

[21]   As a result, it is clear that such begging has no appearance of the disgraceful. It would have, if it were done with insistence and lack of discretion for the sake of pleasure or superfluity.

[22]   Of course, it is evident that mendicancy is associated with a certain humiliation. For, as to suffer an action is less noble than to do it, so to receive is less noble than to give, and to be ruled and obedient is less noble than to govern and command, although by virtue of some added circumstance this evaluation may be reversed.

[23]   However, it is the mark of humility to accept humiliations without hesitation; not in all cases, of course, but when it is necessary. For, since humility is a virtue, it does not work without discretion. So, it is not proper to humility, but to stupidity, for a man to accept every kind of humiliation, but what must be done for the sake of virtue a person does not reject because of humiliation. For example, if charity demands that some humiliating duty be performed for a neighbor, one will not refuse it through humility. Therefore, if it is necessary for the adoption of the perfection of the life of poverty that a man beg, then to suffer this humiliation is proper to humility. Sometimes, too, it is virtuous to accept humiliations even though our job does not require it, in order by our example to encourage others who have such a burden, so that they may bear it readily. For, a general may at times serve like an ordinary soldier, in order to spur on others. Sometimes, moreover, we use humiliations virtuously for their medicinal

value. For instance, if a man's mind is prone to undue pride, he may make beneficial use, in due moderation, of humiliations, either self-imposed or caused by others, in order to restrain this tendency to pride, provided that through bearing these things he puts himself on a level, as it were, with even the lowliest men who perform low-grade tasks.

[24] Now, the error of those who regard all solicitude for the gaining of a living for oneself as forbidden by God is altogether unreasonable.[7] Indeed, every act requires solicitude. So, if a man ought to have no concern for corporeal things, then it follows that he ought not to be engaged in corporeal action, but this is neither possible nor reasonable. In fact, God has ordained activity for each thing in accord with the proper perfection of its nature. Now, man was made with a spiritual and bodily nature. So, he must by divine disposition both perform bodily actions and keep his mind on spiritual things. However, this way of human perfection is not such that one may perform no bodily actions, because, since bodily actions are directed to things needed for the preservation of life, if a man fail to perform them he neglects his life which every man is obliged to preserve. Now, to look to God for help in those matters in which a man can help himself by his own action, and to omit one's own action, is the attitude of a fool and a tempter of God. Indeed, this is an aspect of divine goodness, to provide things not by doing them directly, but by moving others to perform their own actions, as we showed above.[8] So, one should not look to God in the hope that, without performing any action by which one might help oneself, God will come to one's aid, for this is opposed to the divine order and to divine goodness.

[25] But since, in spite of our having the power to act, we do not have the power to guarantee the success of our actions in attaining their proper end, because of impedi-

7. See above, ch. 132, ¶27–30.
8. See above, ch. 77.

ments which may occur, this success that may come to each man from his action lies within the disposition of divine providence. Therefore, the Lord commands us not to be solicitous concerning what pertains to God, namely, the outcome of our actions. But He has not forbidden us to be concerned about what pertains to us, namely, our own work. So, he who is solicitous about things that he can do does not act against the Lord's precept. Rather, he does who is solicitous concerning the things which can result, even if he carries out his own actions, so that he omits the actions that are required to avoid these eventualities, against which we must rather place our hope in God's providence, by which even the birds and the flowers are supported. To have solicitude of this kind seems to pertain to the error of the Gentiles who deny divine providence. This is why the Lord concludes that we must not be "solicitous for to-morrow." He did not forbid us, by this injunction, from taking care in time of the things necessary for the future, but, rather, from being concerned about future events in despair of divine help. Or, perhaps, He forbade preoccupation today with the solicitude which one should have to-morrow, for each day has its own concerns; hence, He adds: "Sufficient for the day is the evil thereof" (Matt. 6:34).

[26]   And thus, it is clear that those who adopt voluntary poverty can live in various appropriate ways. Among these ways, that is more praiseworthy which makes man's mind free, to a greater degree, from solicitude about temporal matters and from activity in connection with them.

Chapter 136.

ON THE ERROR OF THOSE WHO ATTACK
PERPETUAL CONTINENCE

[1]   Now, just as in the case of the opposition to the per-fection of poverty, so also have some perverse-minded men

spoken against the good of continence. Some of them try to destroy the good of continence by these and like arguments.[1]

[2] In fact, the union of husband and wife is directed to the good of the species. For the good of the species is more godlike than the good of the individual.[2] Therefore, he who completely abstains from the act whereby the species is preserved commits a greater sin than he would if he abstained from an act by which the individual is preserved, such as eating and drinking and the like.

[3] Again, by the divine order, organs are given man that are suited for procreation, and so are the concupiscible power that stimulates him and also other similar endowments related to it. Hence, he who completely abstains from the act of generation seems to act against the divine ordinance.

[4] Besides, if it is a good thing for one man to be continent, it is better for many, and best for all to do so. But the conclusion of this would be the extinction of the human race. So, it is not good for any man to be completely continent.

[5] Moreover, chastity, like the other virtues, lies in a mean. Therefore, just as a man acts against virtue and is intemperate if he devotes himself entirely to matters of concupiscence, so also does he act against virtue and is he without feeling who totally abstains from matters of concupiscence.

[6] Furthermore, it is impossible for some feelings of sexual concupiscence to fail to arise in a man, for they are natural. Now, to resist these feelings of concupiscence fully and, as it were, to wage a continuous fight against them

1. Here, again, it may be noted that one of the propositions condemned by Bishop Tempier at Paris in 1277 (*Fontes Vitae S. Thomae*, VI, 610, No. 168) was: "That continence is not essentially a virtue."
2. See Aristotle, *Nicomachean Ethics* I, 2 (1094b 8–10).

192 ON THE TRUTH OF THE CATHOLIC FAITH

produces more disturbance than if a man indulges moderately in concupiscent activities. Therefore, since mental disturbance is most incompatible with perfection of virtue, it appears to be opposed to virtue for a man to observe perpetual continence.

[7]   Such, then, seem to be the objections against perpetual continence. It is also possible to add to them the command of the Lord which, we read, was given to our first parents in Genesis (1:28; 9:1): "Increase and multiply, and fill the earth." This was not revoked, but seems rather to have been confirmed by the Lord in the Gospel, where it is said: "What therefore God hath joined together, let no man put asunder" (Matt. 19:6), when He speaks of the matrimonial union. But those who observe perpetual continence clearly act against this precept. So, it seems to be illicit to observe perpetual continence.

[8]   However, it is not difficult to answer these objections in terms of the things that were established above.[3]

[9]   For we should keep in mind that one type of rational explanation is to be used for things which belong to the needs of the individual man, while a different one applies to the things that pertain to the needs of the group. In regard to things pertinent to the needs of the individual man, it is necessary to make provision for each person. Now, of this type are food and drink, and other goods having to do with the maintenance of the individual. Hence, each man must make use of food and drink. But, in the case of things that are necessary for the group, it is not necessary for the assignment to be given to each person in the group; indeed, this is not even possible. For it is clear that many things are needed by a group of men, such as food, drink, clothing, housing and the like, which cannot all be procured by one man. And so, different tasks must be given to different persons, just as different organs of the body are directed to different functions. So, since procreation is not a matter of the need of the individual but of the need of the whole

3. See above, ch. 135.

species, it is not necessary for all men to devote themselves to acts of generation; instead, certain men, refraining from these acts, undertake other functions, such as the military life or contemplation.

[10] From this the answer to the *second* argument[4] is clear. Indeed, the things that are necessary for the entire species are given man by divine providence, but it is not necessary for each man to use every one of them. For man has been given skill in building and strength for fighting; however, this does not mean that all men must be builders or soldiers. Likewise, though the generative power and things related to its act have been divinely provided, it is not necessary for each man to direct his intention to the generative act.

[11] As a result, the answer to the *third* objection[5] is also evident. Though it is better for some individuals to abstain from the things that are necessary for the group, it is not good for all to abstain. The same situation is apparent in the order of the universe, for, although spiritual substance is better than the corporeal, that universe in which there are spiritual substances only would not be better but more imperfect. And even though an eye is better than a foot in the body of an animal, the animal would not be perfect unless it had both eye and foot. So, too, the community of mankind would not be in a perfect state unless there were some people who direct their intention to generative acts and others who refrain from these acts and devote themselves to contemplation.

[12] Moreover, what is objected *fourthly*,[6] that virtue must lie in the mean, is answered by what was said above[7] in regard to poverty. For the mean of virtue is not always taken according to the quantity of the thing that is ordered by reason, but, rather, according to the rule of reason which

4. Above, ¶3.
5. Above, ¶4.
6. Above, ¶5.
7. See above, ch. 134.

takes in the proper end and measures the appropriate circumstances. And so, to abstain from all sexual pleasures, without a reason, is called the vice of insensibility. But, if it be done in accord with reason, it is a virtue which surpasses man's ordinary way of life, for it makes men share somewhat in the divine likeness; hence, virginity is said to be related to the angels (Matt. 22:30).

[13] In regard to the *fifth* argument,[8] it should be said that the solicitude and occupation which encumber those who are married, concerning their wives, children and the procuring of the necessities of life, are continuous. But the disturbance which a man suffers in the fight against concupiscent tendencies is for a limited time. For this decreases as a result of a man refusing to consent to it; in fact, the more a person indulges in pleasures, the more does the desire for pleasure grow in him.[9] Thus, concupiscent feelings are weakened by acts of abstinence and other corporeal practices suitable to those who have the vow of continence. Moreover, the enjoyment of corporeal delights distracts the mind from its peak activity and hinders it in the contemplation of spiritual things much more than the disturbance that results from resisting the concupiscent desires for these pleasures, because the mind becomes very strongly attached to carnal things through the enjoyment of such pleasures, especially those of sex. For enjoyment makes the appetite become fixed on the thing that is enjoyed. And so, for those people who devote their attention to the contemplation of divine things and of every kind of truth, it is especially harmful to have been addicted to sexual pleasures and particularly beneficial to abstain from them. Now, this is not to suggest that, although it is generally better for the individual man to observe continence than to engage in matrimony, the latter may not be better in a particular case. Hence, the Lord, having mentioned continence, says: "All men take not this word, but they to whom it is given" (Matt. 19:11).

8. Above, ¶6.
9. See Aristotle, *Nicomachean Ethics*, III, 12 (1119b 10).

[14] To what is asserted in the *last* objection,[10] on the ground of the precept given to our first parents, the reply is evident from what has been said. Indeed, that precept is concerned with the natural inclination in man to preserve the species by the act of generation; however, this need not be carried out by all men, but by some, as we said.

[15] Now, just as it is not expedient for every man to abstain from matrimony, so also it is not a good thing to do so at all times, if the increase of the race requires matrimony: whether because of a lack of men, as in the beginning when the human race began to multiply; or because of the small number of the faithful, in which situation they should multiply by carnal generation, as was the case in the Old Testament. Thus, the counsel of practicing perpetual continence was reserved to the New Testament, when the faithful are multiplied by a spiritual generation.

Chapter 137.

ANOTHER ERROR CONCERNING PERPETUAL CONTINENCE[1]

[1] Moreover, there have been some others who, though not disapproving perpetual continence, have, however, put the state of matrimony on the same level with it. This is the heresy of the Jovinians.[2] But the falsity of this error is quite apparent from the foregoing, since by continence man is made more skillful in raising his mind to spiritual and divine matters, and so he is placed, in a way, above the level of a man and in a certain likeness to the angels.

[2] Nor is it any objection that some men of most perfect virtue have practiced matrimony, such as Abraham, Isaac,

10. Above, ¶7.

1. Title supplied by translator.

2. See St. Jerome, *Adversus Jovinianum*, I (*PL*, 23, col. 224); St. Augustine, *De haeresibus*, 82 (*PL*, 42, col. 46); see also, St. Thomas, *Summa Theologiae*, II-II, 186, 4c.

and Jacob, for, the stronger the power of the mind is, the less likely is it to be cast down from its heights by any things whatsoever. So, though they were married, they did not love the contemplation of truth and divine things any less. Rather, as the state of their times demanded, they embraced matrimony for the sake of increasing the numbers of the faithful.

[3] Nor, in fact, is the perfection of one person a sufficient argument for the perfection of a state of life, since one man can use a minor good with a more perfect intention than another man could use a greater good. Therefore, the fact that Abraham or Moses was more perfect than many men who observe continence does not mean that the state of matrimony is more perfect than the state of continence, or even equal to it.

Chapter 138.

AGAINST THOSE WHO ATTACK VOWS

[1] It has seemed foolish to some people to bind oneself by a vow to obey anyone, or to any kind of practice. In fact, the more freely any good action is done, the more virtuous it seems to be. On the other hand, the more and the greater the necessity whereby a man is constrained to a certain practice, the less freely does it seem to be performed. So, it appears derogatory to the praiseworthy character of virtuous acts for them to be done under the necessity of obedience or a vow.

[2] Now, these men seem to ignore the meaning of necessity. In fact, there are two kinds of necessity. One is that of coaction. This kind decreases the value of virtuous acts, because it is contrary to the voluntary, for what is done under coaction is what is against the will. But there is another necessity that results from interior inclination. This does not diminish the value of a virtuous act, but increases

it, for it makes the will incline more intensely toward an act of virtue. Indeed, it is evident that the more perfect a habit of virtue is, the more forcefully does it make the will tend to the good of virtue, and less likely to fall short of it. So that, if it reaches the end of perfection, it confers a certain necessity of acting well, as in the case of the blessed who are not able to sin, as will appear later.[1] Yet, because of this, neither is any freedom of will lost, nor goodness of the act.

[3]   However, there is still another necessity resulting from the end, as when we say that someone must have a ship in order to cross the sea. Again it is evident that this necessity does not decrease freedom of will or the goodness of the acts. Rather, the fact that a man does something that is necessary for an end is praiseworthy in itself; and the better the end, the more praiseworthy it is.

[4]   Now, it is clear that the necessity of practicing what one has vowed to do, or of obeying a person to whom one has subjected himself, is not the necessity of coaction or even that resulting from interior inclination, but it is from a relation to the end. For it is necessary for a person who takes a vow to do this or that thing if he is to fulfill the vow or practice obedience. So, since these ends are praiseworthy, inasmuch as by them man subjects himself to God, the aforesaid necessity in no way diminishes the value of virtue.

[5]   We should further consider that the carrying out of things which a person has vowed, or the fulfilling of the orders of a man to whom the person has subjected himself for God's sake, are actions worthy of greater praise and reward. It is possible, of course, for one act to pertain to two vices, provided the act of one vice be directed to the end of another vice. For instance, when a man steals so that he may fornicate, the act is specifically one of avarice, but by its intention it belongs to lust.[2] In the same way, it also

1. *SCG*, IV, ch. 92.
2. See Aristotle, *Nicomachean Ethics*, V, 2 (1130a 24).

happens in the case of virtues that the act of one virtue is ordered to another virtue. Thus, when one gives away his possessions so that he may enjoy the friendship of charity with another man, this act specifically belongs to liberality, but from its end it pertains to charity. Now, acts of this kind acquire greater value from the greater virtue, that is, from charity rather than from liberality. Hence, though it loses its character as an exclusive act of liberality by virtue of its ordination to charity, it will be more praiseworthy and worthy of greater reward than if it were done liberally, with no relation to charity.

[6]   So, let us suppose a man performing some work of a definite virtue, say a man who is fasting or restraining himself continently from sexual pleasure—now, if he does this without a vow it will be an act of chastity or of abstinence, but if he does it as a result of a vow it is referred further to another virtue whose scope includes the vowing of something to God; that is, to the virtue of religion which is better than chastity or abstinence, inasmuch as it makes us rightly disposed in relation to God.[3] So, the act of abstinence or continence will be more praiseworthy in the case of the man who performs it under a vow, even though he does not take so much delight in abstinence or continence due to the fact that he is taking his delight in a higher virtue, that is, religion.

[7]   Again, what is most important in virtue is a proper end, for the rational character of a good act stems chiefly from the end. So, if the end is more eminent, then, even if one is somewhat less than perfect in the act, it will be for him a more virtuous act. For example, take the case of a man who proposes to make a long journey for a virtuous purpose, while another man undertakes a short one; he who proposes to do more for the sake of virtue will be more praiseworthy, even though he makes slower progress on the trip. But suppose a man does something for God's sake, offering this act to God: if he does this under a vow he

3. See St. Thomas, *Summa Theologiae*, II-II, q. 81, a. 1, c.

offers God not only the act, but also his power. Thus, it is evident that his intention is to offer something greater to God. So, his act will be more virtuous by reason of his intention for a greater good, even if, in the execution of it, another man might appear more fervent.

[8] Besides, the act of will which precedes an act continues in its power through the whole performance of the act, and renders it worthy of praise, even when the agent is not thinking during the execution of the work of the commitment of will from which the act began. In fact, it is not necessary for a man who undertakes a journey for God's sake actually to think about God during every part of the trip. Now, it is clear that the man who vows that he will do a certain thing wills it more intensely than one who simply decides to do it, for the first man not only wills to do it, but he wills to strengthen himself so that he will not fail to act. So, by this act of voluntary intention there is produced a praiseworthy execution of the vow accompanied by a certain fervor, even when the will-act is not actually continued during the operation, or is continued in a slack way.

[9] And so, what is done as a result of a vow becomes more praiseworthy than what is done without a vow, provided other conditions are equal.

Chapter 139.

THAT NEITHER MERITORIOUS ACTS
NOR SINS ARE EQUAL

[1] Next, it is plain that neither all good works, nor all sins, are equal. Indeed, counsel is given only in regard to the better good.[1] Now, counsels are given in the divine law concerning poverty, continence, and other like things, as we said above.[2] So, these are better than the practice of

1. See above, ch. 130, ¶1.
2. *Ibid.*, ¶2.

matrimony and the possession of temporal things, but it is possible to act virtuously according to these latter, provided the order of reason be observed, as we showed above.[3] Therefore, not all acts of the virtues are equal.

[2]   Again, acts get their species from their objects. So, the better the object is, the more virtuous the act will be in its species. Now, the end is better than the means to the end; and of the means, the closer one is to the end, the better it is. Hence, among human acts, that one is best which is directed immediately to the ultimate end, namely, God. After that, an act is better in its species the closer its object is to God.

[3]   Besides, the good in human acts is dependent on their being regulated by reason. But it happens that some acts come nearer to reason than others. The more definitely these acts pertain to reason itself, the more they share in the good of reason, in comparison with the acts of the lower powers which reason commands. Therefore, there are some human acts that are better than others.

[4]   Moreover, the precepts of the law are best fulfilled as a result of love, as we said above.[4] But it happens that one man does what is prescribed for him to do with greater love than another man. So, one virtuous act will be better than another.

[5]   Furthermore, while man's acts are rendered good as a result of virtue, it is possible for the same virtue to be more intensified in one man than in another. So, one human act must be better than another.

[6]   Again, if human acts are made good by the virtues, then that act must be better which belongs to the better virtue. But it is possible for one virtue to be better than another; for instance, magnificence than liberality, and magnanimity than moderation. So, one human act will be better than another.

3. See above, ch. 133, 136 and 137.
4. See above, ch. 116 and 128.

[7] Hence, it is said, I Cor. (7:38): "He that giveth his virgins in marriage doth well: and he that giveth them not, doth better."

[8] Moreover, it is apparent for the same reason that not all sins are equal, since one gets farther away from the end through one sin than through another, and the order of reason may be more perverted, and more harm may be done one's neighbor.

[9] Hence, it is said, in Ezechiel (16:47): "thou hast done almost more wicked things than they in all thy ways."

[10] Now, by this consideration we refute the error of those who say that all meritorious acts and all sins are equal.

[11] As a matter of fact, the view that all virtuous acts are equal seems to have a certain reasonableness, since every act is virtuous as a result of the goodness of its end. Hence, if there is some end of goodness for all good acts, then all must be equally good.

[12] However, although there is but one ultimate end for the good, the acts that derive their goodness from it receive different degrees of goodness. For, there is in the goods that are ordered to the ultimate end a difference of degree, in so far as some are better and nearer to the ultimate end than others. Hence, there will be degrees of goodness both in the will and in its acts, depending on the diversity of goods in which the will and its act terminate, even though the ultimate end be the same.

[13] Similarly, also, the notion that all sins are equal seems to have some reasonableness, since sin occurs in human acts solely because a person overlooks the rule of reason. But a man who departs a little from reason overlooks its rule, just as one who misses it by a wide margin. So, it would seem that a sin is equal whether the wrong done was small or great.

[14] Now, support for this argument seems to come from the practice in human courts of law. In fact, if a boundary

line is set up which a certain man is not to cross, it makes
no difference to the judge whether he trespassed for a large
distance or a small one; just as it is unimportant, when a
fighter goes over the ropes, whether he goes very far. So, in
the case of a man overstepping the rule of reason, it makes
no difference whether he bypasses it a little or a great deal.

[15]   However, if one takes a more careful look at it, in all
matters in which the perfect and the good consists in some
sort of commensuration, the greater the departure from the
proper measurement, the worse will it be. Thus, health consists in a properly measured amount of humors, and beauty
in a due proportion of bodily members, while truth lies in
a measured relation of the understanding, or of speech, to
the thing. Now, clearly, the more inequality there is in the
humors, the greater the sickness; and the greater the disorder in the members of the body, the greater is the ugli-
ness; and the farther one departs from the truth, the greater
is the falsity. For instance, the man who thinks that three
is five is not as wrong as the one who thinks three is a
hundred. Now, the good pertaining to virtue consists in a
certain commensuration, for there is a mean that is set up
between opposed vices according to a proper judgment of
the limiting circumstances. Therefore, the more it departs
from this harmonious balance, the greater the evil is.

[16]   Moreover, it is not the same thing to transgress virtue and to trespass over boundaries set up by a judge. Virtue is, in fact, good in itself, and so to depart from virtue is
an evil in itself. Hence, to go farther away from virtue is a
greater evil. But to pass over a boundary line set up by a
judge is not essentially evil, but accidentally so—to the extent, that is, that it is prohibited. But in the case of events
that are accidental, it is not necessary that "if one event
taken without qualification follows another event without
qualification, then an increase in the first event is followed
by an increase in the second."⁵ This only follows in things
which exist of themselves. For instance, it does not follow

5. Aristotle, Topics, V, 8 (137b 34).

that, if a white man is musical, then a whiter man will be more musical, but it does follow that, if a white thing is a distinctive object of sight, a whiter thing is a more distinctive object for sight.[6]

[17] Yet there is this point to be noted regarding the differences among sins: that one kind is mortal and another venial. Now, the mortal is that which deprives the soul of spiritual life. The meaning of this life may be taken from two points in the comparison with natural life. In fact, a body is naturally alive because it is united to a soul which is the source of life for it. Moreover, a body that is made alive by a soul moves by itself, but a dead body either remains without movement or is only moved from outside. So, too, the will of man, when united by a right intention to its ultimate end, which is its object and, in a sense, its form, is also enlivened. And when it adheres to God and neighbor through love, it moves from an interior principle to do the right things. But when the intention and love of the ultimate end are removed, the soul becomes, as it were, dead, since it does not move of itself to do right actions, but either entirely ceases to do them or is led to do them solely by something external, namely, the fear of punishments. So, whatever sins are opposed to the intending and loving of the ultimate end are mortal. But, if a man is properly disposed in regard to them, yet falls somewhat short of the right order of reason, his sin will not be mortal but venial.

6. The meaning of *disgregativum visus* is not clear. I am taking Rickaby's suggestion that the phrase is equivalent to the Aristotelian διακριτικὸν ὄψεως (*God and His Creatures*, p. 310) and rejecting Gerlaud's "dissolvant de la vue" (*Contra Gentiles, Livre Troisième*, p. 675); which reading is, however, more in accord with the meaning of *disgregatio* in thirteenth-century physics (A. C. Crombie, *Grosseteste and Experimental Science* [Oxford: 1953], p. 87, note 1). See the same example in St. Thomas, *Summa Theologiae*, I-II, 30, 4 c.

Chapter 140.

THAT A MAN'S ACTS ARE PUNISHED
OR REWARDED BY GOD

[1]   It is apparent from the foregoing that man's acts are punished or rewarded by God.

[2]   For the function of punishing and rewarding belongs to him whose office it is to impose the law; indeed, lawmakers enforce observance of the law by means of rewards and punishments. But it belongs to divine providence to lay down the law for men, as is clear from the previous statements.[1] Therefore, it belongs to God to punish and reward men.

[3]   Again, wherever there is a proper order to an end, this order must lead to the end, while a departure from this order prevents the attainment of the end. For things which depend on the end derive their necessity from the end; that is to say, this means is necessary if the end is to be attained —and under these conditions, if there be no impediment, the end is achieved. Now, God has imposed on men's acts a certain order in relation to the final good, as is evident from preceding statements.[2] So, it must be, if this order is rightly laid down, that those who proceed according to this order will attain the final good, and this is to be rewarded; but those who depart from this order by means of sin must be cut off from the final good, and this is to be punished.

[4]   Besides, as things in nature are subject to the order of divine providence, so are human acts, as is clear from what was said earlier.[3] In both cases, however, it is possible for the proper order to be observed or overlooked. Yet there

1. See above, ch. 114.
2. See above, ch. 115.
3. See above, ch. 90.

is this difference: the observance or trangression of the due order is put within the control of the human will, but it is not within the power of things in nature to fall short of or to follow the proper order. Now, effects must correspond in an appropriate way with their causes. Hence, just as when natural things adhere to a due order in their natural principles and actions, the preservation of their nature and the good in them necessarily follows, while corruption and evil result when there is a departure from the proper and natural order—so also, in human affairs, when a man voluntarily observes the order of divinely imposed law, good must result, not as if by necessity, but by the management of the governor, and this is to be rewarded. On the contrary, evil follows when the order of the law has been neglected, and this is to be punished.

[5] Moreover, to leave nothing unordered among things pertains to the perfect goodness of God; as a result, we observe that every evil in things of nature is included under the order of something good. So, the corruption of air is the generation of fire and the killing of a sheep is the feeding of a wolf. Hence, since human acts are subject to divine providence, just as things in nature are, the evil which occurs in human acts must be contained under the order of some good. Now, this is most suitably accomplished by the fact that sins are punished. For in that way those acts which exceed the due measure are embraced under the order of justice which reduces to equality. But man exceeds the due degree of his measure when he prefers his own will to the divine will by satisfying it contrary to God's ordering. Now, this inequity is removed when, against his will, man is forced to suffer something in accord with divine ordering. Therefore, it is necessary that human sins be given punishment of divine origin and, for the same reason, that good deeds receive their reward.

[6] Furthermore, divine providence not only arranges the order of things, it also moves all things to the execution of the order thus arranged, as we showed above.[4] Now, the

4. See above, ch. 67.

will is moved by its object, which is a good or bad thing.
Therefore, it is the function of divine providence to offer
men good things as a reward, so that their will may be
moved to make right progress, and to set forth evil things as
punishment, so that their will may avoid disorder.

[7]   Besides, divine providence has so ordered things that
one will be useful to another.[5] But it is most appropriate
for man to derive profit for his final good, both from another man's good and another man's evil, in the sense that
he may be stimulated to good action by seeing that others
who do good are rewarded, and that he may be turned
back from evil action by observing that those who do evil
are punished. So, it is proper to divine providence that evil
men be punished and good men rewarded.

[8]   Hence, it is said, in Exodus (20:5–6): "I am thy God
. . . visiting the iniquity of the fathers upon the children
. . . and showing mercy . . . to them who love me and keep
my commandments." And again, in the Psalm (61:13):
"For Thou wilt render to every man according to his
works." And in Romans (2:6–8; Douay modified): "Who
will render to every man according to his works; to them
indeed who, according to patience in good work, glory and
honor . . . but to them . . . who obey not the truth but
give credit to iniquity, wrath and indignation."

[9]   Now, by this we set aside the error of some people
who assert that God does not punish. In fact, Marcion and
Valentine said that there is one good God, and another God
of justice Who punishes.[6]

5. See above, ch. 77ff.
6. See St. Augustine, De haeresibus, 21–22 (PL, 42, col. 29).

Chapter 141.

ON THE DIVERSITY AND ORDER
OF PUNISHMENTS

[1]   As we have just seen, since a reward is what is set before the will as an end whereby one is stimulated to good action, punishment, on the contrary, in the guise of some evil that is to be avoided, is set before the will to restrain it from evil. So, just as it is essential to a reward that it be a good that is agreeable to the will, so is it essential to punishment that it be an evil and contrary to will. Now, evil is a privation of the good.[1] Hence, the diversity and order of punishments must depend on the diversity and order of goods.

[2]   Now, felicity is the highest good for man, for it is his ultimate end, and the nearer anything is to this end, the higher the place that it occupies among man's goods. But the nearest thing to it is virtue,[2] and any other thing, if there be such, which helps man in good action whereby he attains happiness. Next comes the proper disposition of his reason and of the powers subject to it. After this comes soundness of body, which is needed for ready action. In final place are external things which we use as aids to virtue.

[3]   So, the greatest punishment will be for man to be cut off from happiness. After this ranks deprivation of virtue and of any perfection of the natural powers of the soul that is related to good action. Next comes the disorder of the natural powers of the soul; then, bodily injury; and finally, the taking away of exterior goods.

[4]   However, because it is essential not only that punishment by a privation of the good, but also that it be contrary to the will, for not every man's will regards good things

1. See above, ch. 6.
2. Aristotle, *Nicomachean Ethics*, I, 9 (1099b 9–32).

as they really are, it happens at times that what deprives one of the greater good is less repugnant to the will and thus seems to be less punishing. Hence it is that a good many men who think better of and know more about sensible and corporeal things than they do about intellectual and spiritual goods have a greater fear of bodily punishments than of spiritual ones. In the opinion of these people the order of punishments seems the reverse of the above-mentioned ranking. With them, injuries of the body are deemed the greatest punishment, together with the loss of external things; whereas they regard disorder of soul, loss of virtue, and the deprivation of the divine enjoyment, in which man's ultimate felicity consists, as of slight or no importance.

[5]   Now, the result of this is that they do not think that men's sins are punished by God, for they see many sinners enjoying bodily vigor, highly favored by external good fortune, of which goods virtuous men are sometimes deprived.

[6]   To people who consider the matter rightly this should not seem astonishing. For, since external goods are subordinated to internal goods, and body to soul, external and bodily goods are good for man to the extent that they contribute to the good of reason, but to the extent that they hinder the rational good they turn into evils for man. Now, God, the disposer of things, knows the measure of human virtue. Hence, He at times provides corporeal and external goods for the virtuous man as an aid to his virtue, and in this He confers a benefit on him. At other times, however, He takes away these things from man, because He considers such things to be for him a hindrance to virtue and divine enjoyment. Indeed, from the fact that external goods may turn into evils for man, as we said, their loss may consequently become, by the same reasoning, a good thing for man.

So, if every punishment is an evil, and if it is not a bad thing for a man to be deprived of external and corporeal goods in accord with what is helpful to progress in virtue, then it will not be a punishment for a virtuous man if he be deprived of external goods as an aid to virtue. On the contrary, however, it will be for the punishment of evil men if external goods are granted them, for by them they are incited to evil. Hence it is said in Wisdom (14:11) that "the creatures of God are turned to an abomination, and a temptation to the souls of men, and a snare to the feet of the unwise."

However, since it is essential to punishment that it be not only an evil but that it be against the will, the loss of corporeal and external things, even when it helps man toward virtue and not toward evil, is called a punishment, in an improper sense, because it is contrary to will.

[7] Still, as a result of the disorder in man, it happens that a man may not judge things as they are, but may set corporeal things above spiritual ones. Now, such a disorder is either a fault or it stems from some preceding fault. Consequently, it is evident that there is no punishment for man, even in the sense of being contrary to will, without a prior fault.

[8] This is also clear from another fact: these things that are good in themselves would not turn into evils for man, because of their abuse, unless some disorder were present within man.

[9] Besides, the fact that the things which the will favors because they are naturally good must be taken away from man for the advancement of virtue arises from a disorder in man which is either a fault or the result of a fault. Indeed, it is obvious that some disorder in the affections of man is caused by a previous sin, and so afterwards he is more easily inclined to sin. So, man is not without fault, also, in the fact that he must be helped to the good of virtue by what is for him something of a punishment, inasmuch as it is absolutely against his will, even though it be desired sometimes, in a relative way, because reason looks to the end. But, we shall talk later[3] about this disorder in human nature which results from original sin. However, it is now evident to

3. *SCG*, IV, ch. 50.

what extent God punishes men for their sins, and that He does not punish unless there be some fault.

Chapter 142.

THAT NOT ALL REWARDS AND PUNISHMENTS ARE EQUAL

[1]   Since divine justice requires, for the preservation of equality in things, that punishments be assigned for faults and rewards for good acts, then, if there are degrees in virtuous acts and in sins, as we showed,[1] there must also be degrees among rewards and punishments. Otherwise, equality would not be preserved, that is, if a greater punishment were not given to one who sins more, or a greater reward to one who acts better. Indeed, the same reasoning seems to require different retribution on the basis of the diversity of good and evil, and on the basis of the difference between the good and the better, or between the bad and the worse.

[2]   Again, the equality proper to distributive justice is such that unequal things are assigned to unequal persons. Therefore, there would not be a just compensation by punishments and rewards if all rewards and all punishments were equal.[2]

[3]   Besides, rewards and punishments are set up by a lawmaker so that men may be drawn away from evil things and toward good things, as is evident from what was said above.[3] But it is not only necessary for men to be attracted to goods

1. See above, ch. 139.
2. For an expansion of this highly condensed statement on distributive justice, see *Summa Theologiae,* I, 21, 1, c. (in Pegis, *Basic Writings of St. Thomas,* I, 223-224). Consult also, Martinez, M. L., "Distributive Justice according to St. Thomas," *Modern Schoolman,* 24 (1947), 208-223, or V. J. Bourke, *Ethics,* pp. 334-337.
3. See above, ch. 140.

and drawn away from evils, but also good men must be encouraged to better things and evil men discouraged from worse things. This could not be done if rewards and punishments were equal. Therefore, punishments and rewards must be unequal.

[4] Moreover, just as a thing is disposed toward a form by natural dispositions, so is a man disposed toward punishments and rewards by good and bad works. But the order which divine providence has established in things has this feature: things that are better disposed obtain a more perfect form. Therefore, depending on the diversity of good or bad works, there must be a diversity of punishments and rewards.

[5] Furthermore, it is possible for variations of degree to apply to good and bad works in two ways: in one way, numerically, in the sense that one man has more good or bad works than another; in a second way, qualitatively, in the sense that one man accomplishes a better or worse work than another. Now, to the increase which depends on the number of works there must be a corresponding increase in rewards and punishments; otherwise, there would not be a compensation under divine justice for all the things that a person does, if some evils remained unpunished and some goods unrewarded. So, by equivalent reasoning, for the increase which depends on the different quality of the works there must be a corresponding inequality of rewards and punishments.

[6] Hence, it is said in Deuteronomy (25:2): "According to the measure of the sin shall the measure also of the stripes be." And in Isaias (27:8; Douay modified): "In measure against measure, when it shall be cast off, I shall judge it."

[7] By this we dispose of the error of those who say that in the future all rewards and punishments will be equal.

Chapter 143.

ON THE PUNISHMENT DUE TO MORTAL AND VENIAL SIN IN RELATION TO THE ULTIMATE END

[1]   Now, it is obvious from the foregoing that it is possible to sin in two ways.[1] One way is such that the mental intention is entirely broken away from the order to God, Who is called the ultimate end of all good people; and this is mortal sin. The second way is such that, while the ordering of the human mind to the ultimate end remains, some impediment is brought in whereby one is held back from freely tending toward the end; and this is called venial sin. So, if there must be a difference of punishments depending on a difference of sins,[2] it follows that he who commits a mortal sin must be punished in such a way that he may be cut off from the end of man, but he who sins venially must not be punished so that he is cut off but so that he is retarded or made to suffer difficulty in acquiring the end. For, thus is the equality of justice preserved: in whatever way man voluntarily turns away from his end by sinning, in the same way in the order of punishment, involuntarily, he is impeded in regard to the attainment of his end.

[2]   Again, as will is in men, so is natural inclination in the things of nature. Now, if the inclination toward its end be taken away from a natural thing, it becomes altogether unable to reach its end. For example, when a heavy body loses its weight through corruption and becomes light, it will not reach its proper place. But, if there be an impediment to its motion, while its inclination to the end remains, then, when the obstacle is removed, it will reach its end. Now, in the man who commits a mortal sin, the intention

1. See above, ch. 139.
2. See above, ch. 142.

of his will is completely turned away from his ultimate end; while in the man who commits a venial sin, his intention continues to be fixed on the end, but he is somewhat hindered in that he improperly fixes his intention on the means to the end. Therefore, for the one who sins mortally, this is the proper punishment: to be completely cut off from the attainment of the end. But for the one who sins venially, he must suffer some difficulty before he reaches the end.

[3] Besides, when a person obtains some good that he did not intend, this is due to fortune and chance.[3] So, if he whose intention is turned away from the ultimate end is to attain the ultimate end, this will be due to fortune and chance. But this is not right. In fact, the ultimate end is a good of the understanding. Now, fortune is repugnant to understanding, since fortuitous events occur apart from the ordering of understanding. Moreover, it is not appropriate for the understanding to attain its end in an unintelligent manner. Therefore, he will not attain his ultimate end who, by sinning mortally, has his intention turned away from the ultimate end.

[4] Moreover, matter does not get its form from the agent unless it be disposed to the form. Now, the end or the good is a perfection of the will, just as form is for matter. Hence, the will is not going to obtain its ultimate end unless it be appropriately disposed. But the will is disposed toward its end by the intention and desire for the end. Therefore, he whose intention is averted from the end will not obtain that end.

[5] Furthermore, in the case of things ordered to an end, the relationship is such that, if the end occurs or will occur, then the means to the end must also be available, but if the means to the end are not available, then the end will not occur. For, if the end can occur even without the presence of the means to the end, it is futile to seek the end by such means. But it is admitted by all men that man, through

3. See above, ch. 74 and 92.

works of virtue, among which the chief one is the intention of the proper end, may attain his ultimate end which is felicity. So, if a person acts against virtue, with his intention turned away from the ultimate end, it is fitting that he be deprived of his ultimate end.

[6]   Hence, it is said, Matthew (7:23; Douay modified): "Depart from me, all you who work iniquity."

Chapter 144.

THAT BY MORTAL SIN A MAN IS ETERNALLY DEPRIVED OF HIS ULTIMATE END

[1]   This punishment by which a person is deprived of the ultimate end should be interminable.

[2]   For there is no privation of a thing unless one is born to possess that thing; in fact, a newborn puppy is not said to be deprived of sight. But man is not born with a natural aptitude to attain his end in this life, as we have proved.[1] So, the privation of this kind of end must be a punishment after this life. But after this life there remains in man no capacity to acquire the ultimate end. The soul needs a body for the obtaining of its end, in so far as it acquires perfection through the body, both in knowledge and in virtue. But the soul, after it has been separated from its body, will not again return to this state in which it receives perfection through the body, as the reincarnationists claimed. We have argued against them above.[2] Therefore, he who is punished by this punishment, so that he is deprived of the ultimate end, must remain deprived of it throughout eternity.

[3]   Again, if there is a privation of something which is naturally required, it is impossible for this to be restored

1. See above, ch. 47ff.
2. SCG, II, ch. 44.

unless there be a breaking down of the subject to the underlying matter, so that another subject may again be generated
anew, as is the case when an animal loses the power of sight
or any other sense power. Now, it is impossible for what
has been already generated to be again generated, unless it
is first corrupted. In that case, from the same matter it is
possible for another whole being to be generated, not the
same numerically but in species. But spiritual things, such
as a soul or an angel, cannot be broken down by corruption
into an underlying matter so that another member of the
same species may in turn be generated. So, if such a being
is deprived of what it must have in its nature, then such a
privation has to continue perpetually. But there is in the
nature of a soul and of an angel an ordering toward the
ultimate end Who is God. So, if it departs from this order
by virtue of some punishment, this punishment will endure
perpetually.

[4] Besides, natural equity seems to demand that each
person be deprived of the good against which he acts, for
by this action he renders himself unworthy of such a good.
So it is that, according to civil justice, he who offends
against the state is deprived completely of association with
the state, either by death or by perpetual exile. Nor is any
attention paid to the extent of time involved in his wrongdoing, but only to what he sinned against. There is the same
relation between the entirety of our present life and an
earthly state that there is between the whole of eternity
and the society of the blessed who, as we showed above,[3]
share in the ultimate end eternally. So, he who sins against
the ultimate end and against charity, whereby the society
of the blessed exists and also that of those on the way
toward happiness, should be punished eternally, even
though he sinned for but a short space of time.

[5] Moreover, "before the divine seat of judgment the
will is counted for the deed,"[4] since, "just as man seeth

3. See above, ch. 62ff.
4. St. Augustine, *Enarrationes in Psalmos*, LVII, 3 (PL, 36, col.
675–676).

those things that are done outwardly, so doth God behold the heart of men" (I Kings 16:7; Douay modified). Now, he who has turned aside from his ultimate end for the sake of a temporal good, when he might have possessed his end throughout eternity, has put the temporal enjoyment of this temporal good above the eternal enjoyment of the ultimate end. Hence, it is evident that he much preferred to enjoy this temporal good throughout eternity. Therefore, according to divine judgment, he should be punished in the same way as if he had sinned eternally. But there is no doubt that an eternal punishment is due an eternal sin. So, eternal punishment is due to him who turns away from his ultimate end.

[6]   Furthermore, by the same principle of justice, punishments are assigned to wrongdoings and rewards to good acts.[5] "Now, the reward for virtue is happiness."[6] And this is, of course, eternal, as we showed above.[7] Therefore, the punishment whereby one is cut off from happiness should be eternal.

[7]   Hence, it is said, in Matthew (25:46): "And these shall go into everlasting punishment, but the just, into life everlasting."

[8]   Now, by this conclusion we set aside the error of those who say that the punishments of the wicked are to be ended at some time. In fact, this view seems to have originated from the theory of certain philosophers who said that all punishments are for purposes of purification and so are to terminate at some time.[8]

[9]   This view seemed persuasive on the basis of human custom. Indeed, the punishments under human law are applied for the remedy of vices, and so they are like medicines. On the basis of reason, also, if a punishment were assigned

5. See above, ch. 140.
6. Aristotle, *Nicomachean Ethics*, I, 9 (1099b 15).
7. See above, ch. 140.
8. See Aristotle, *Nicomachean Ethics*, II, 3 (1104b 17).

by a punishing agent, not for the sake of something else, but for its own sake alone, it would follow that the agent takes pleasure in punishments for their own sake, which is not in keeping with divine goodness. So, punishments must be inflicted for the sake of something else. And there seems to be no other more suitable end than the correction of vices. So, it seems that all punishments may fittingly be said to be purgatorial and, consequently, requiring termination at some time, since what can be purged out is accidental to a rational creature and may be removed without consuming the substance.

[10] Now, we have to concede that punishments are not inflicted by God for their own sake, as if God delighted in them, but they are for something else; namely, for the imposing of order on creatures, in which order the good of the universe consists. Now, this order of things demands that all things be divinely arranged in a proportionate way. This is why it is said in the Book of Wisdom (11:21) that God made all things, "in weight, number and measure." Now, just as rewards are in proportional correspondence with the acts of the virtues, so are punishments with sins. And to some sins are proportioned eternal punishments, as we showed. So, God inflicts eternal punishments for certain sins so that due order may be observed in things, which order manifests His wisdom.

[11] However, if one concede that all punishments are applied for the correction of behavior and not for anything else, one is still not forced by this admission to assert that all punishments are purgatorial and terminable. For even according to human laws some people are punished with death, not, of course, for their own improvement, but for that of others. Hence, it is said in Proverbs (19:25): "the wicked man being scourged, the fool shall be wiser." Then, too, some people, in accord with human laws, are perpetually exiled from their country, so that, with them removed, the state may be purer. Hence, it is said in Proverbs (22:10): "Cast out the scoffer, and contention shall go with him, and quarrels and reproaches shall cease." So, even

if punishments are used only for the correction of behavior, nothing prevents some people, according to divine judgment, from having to be separated perpetually from the society of good men and to be punished eternally, so that men may refrain from sinning, as a result of their fear of perpetual punishment, and thus the society of good men may be made purer by their removal. As it is said in the Apocalypse (21:27): "There shall not enter it," that is, into the heavenly Jerusalem, by which the society of good men is designated, "anything defiled or that worketh abomination or maketh a lie."

Chapter 145.

THAT SINS ARE PUNISHED ALSO BY THE EXPERIENCE OF SOMETHING PAINFUL

[1]   Those who sin against God are not only to be punished by their exclusion from perpetual happiness, but also by the experience of something painful. Punishment should proportionally correspond to the fault, as we said above.[1] In the fault, however, the mind is not only turned away from the ultimate end, but is also improperly turned toward other things as ends. So, the sinner is not only to be punished by being excluded from his end, but also by feeling injury from other things.

[2]   Again, punishments are inflicted for faults so that men may be restrained from sins by the fear of these punishments, as we said above.[2] But no one fears to lose what he does not desire to obtain. So, those who have their will turned away from the ultimate end do not fear to be cut off from it. Thus, they cannot be restrained from sinning simply by exclusion from the ultimate end. Therefore, another punishment must also be used for sinners, which they may fear while they are sinners.

1. See above, ch. 42.
2. See above, ch. 144.

[3]   Besides, if a man makes inordinate use of a means to the end, he may not only be deprived of the end, but may also incur some other injury. This is exemplified in the inordinate eating of food, which not only fails to maintain strength, but also leads to sickness. Now, the man who puts his end among created things does not use them as he should, namely, by relating them to his ultimate end. So, he should not only be punished by losing happiness, but also by experiencing some injury from them.

[4]   Moreover, as good things are owed to those who act rightly, so bad things are due to those who act perversely. But those who act rightly, at the end intended by them, receive perfection and joy. So, on the contrary, this punishment is due to sinners, that from those things in which they set their end they receive affliction and injury.

[5]   Hence, divine Scripture not only threatens sinners with exclusion from glory, but also with affliction from other things. For it is said, in Matthew (25:41): "Depart from me you cursed into everlasting fire, which was prepared for the devil and his angels." And in the Psalm (10:7), "He shall rain snares upon sinners, fire and brimstone and storms of winds shall be the portion of their cup."

[6]   By this we refute the error of Algazel, who claimed that this punishment only is applied to sinners, that they are afflicted with the loss of their ultimate end.[3]

Chapter 146.

THAT IT IS LAWFUL FOR JUDGES
TO INFLICT PUNISHMENTS

[1]   Since some people pay little attention to the punishments inflicted by God, because they are devoted to the

3. See Algazel, *Metaphysics*, II, 5, 4–5 (ed. J. T. Muckle [Toronto: 1933], pp. 186–190).

objects of sense and care only for the things that are seen, it has been ordered accordingly by divine providence that there be men in various countries whose duty it is to compel these people, by means of sensible and present punishments, to respect justice. It is obvious that these men do not sin when they punish the wicked, for no one sins by working for justice. Now, it is just for the wicked to be punished, since by punishment the fault is restored to order, as is clear from our statements above.[1] Therefore, judges do no wrong in punishing the wicked.

[2]   Again, in various countries, the men who are put in positions over other men are like executors of divine providence; indeed, God through the order of His providence directs lower beings by means of higher ones, as is evident from what we said before.[2] But no one sins by the fact that he follows the order of divine providence. Now, this order of divine providence requires the good to be rewarded and the evil to be punished, as is shown by our earlier remarks.[3] Therefore, men who are in authority over others do no wrong when they reward the good and punish the evil.

[3]   Besides, the good has no need of evil, but, rather, the converse. So, what is needed to preserve the good cannot be evil in itself. Now, for the preservation of concord among men it is necessary that punishments be inflicted on the wicked. Therefore, to punish the wicked is not in itself evil.

[4]   Moreover, the common good is better than the particular good of one person.[4] So, the particular good should be removed in order to preserve the common good. But the life of certain pestiferous men is an impediment to the common good which is the concord of human society. Therefore, certain men must be removed by death from the society of men.

1. See above, ch. 140.
2. See above, ch. 77ff.
3. See above, ch. 140.
4. See above, ch. 69, ¶16, with the accompanying note.

[5]   Furthermore, just as a physician looks to health as the end in his work, and health consists in the orderly concord of humors, so, too, the ruler of a state intends peace in his work, and peace consists in "the ordered concord of citizens."[5] Now, the physician quite properly and beneficially cuts off a diseased organ if the corruption of the body is threatened because of it. Therefore, the ruler of a state executes pestiferous men justly and sinlessly in order that the peace of the state may not be disrupted.

[6]   Hence, the Apostle says, in I Corinthians (5:6): "Know you not that a little leaven corrupteth the whole lump?" And a little later he adds: "Put away the evil one from among yourselves" (I Cor. 5:13). And in Romans (13:4) it is said of earthly power that "he beareth not the sword in vain: for he is God's minister, an avenger to execute wrath upon him that doth evil." And in I Peter (2:13–14) it is said: "Be ye subject therefore to every human creature for God's sake: whether it be to the king as excelling, or to governors as sent by him for the punishment of evildoers and for the praise of the good."

[7]   Now, by this we set aside the error of some who say that corporeal punishments are illicit to use. These people adduce as a basis for their error the text of Exodus (20:13): "Thou shalt not kill," which is mentioned again in Matthew (5:21). They also bring up what is said in Matthew (13:30), that the Lord replied to the stewards who wanted to gather up the cockle from amidst the wheat: "Suffer both to grow until the harvest." By the cockle we understand the children of the wicked one, whereas by the harvest we understand the end of the world, as is explained in the same place (Matt. 13:38–40). So, the wicked are not to be removed from among the good by killing them.

[8]   They also allege that so long as a man is existing in this world he can be changed for the better. So, he should not be removed from the world by execution, but kept for punishment.

5. See above, ch. 128.

[9]   Now, these arguments are frivolous. Indeed, in the law which says "Thou shalt not kill" there is the later statement: "Wrongdoers[6] thou shalt not suffer to live" (Exod. 22:18). From this we are given to understand that the unjust execution of men is prohibited. This is also apparent from the Lord's words in Matthew 5. For, after He said: "You have heard that it was said to them of old: Thou shalt not kill" (Matt. 5:21), He added: "But I say to you that whosoever is angry with his brother," etc. From this He makes us understand that the killing which results from anger is prohibited, but not that which stems from a zeal for justice. Moreover, how the Lord's statement, "Suffer both to grow until the harvest," should be understood is apparent through what follows: "lest perhaps, gathering up the cockle, you root up the wheat also together with it" (Matt. 13:29). So, the execution of the wicked is forbidden wherever it cannot be done without danger to the good. Of course, this often happens when the wicked are not clearly distinguished from the good by their sins, or when the danger of the evil involving many good men in their ruin is feared.

[10]   Finally, the fact that the evil, as long as they live, can be corrected from their errors does not prohibit the fact that they may be justly executed, for the danger which threatens from their way of life is greater and more certain than the good which may be expected from their improvement. They also have at the critical point of death the opportunity to be converted to God through repentance. And if they are so stubborn that even at the point of death their heart does not draw back from evil, it is possible to make a highly probable judgment that they would never come away from evil to the right use of their powers.

6. Douay has "wizards" for "wrongdoers" (*maleficos*); Rickaby, *op. cit.*, p. 318, suggests "poisoners," under the influence of the Greek text, which has φαρμακούς.

Chapter 147.

THAT MAN NEEDS DIVINE HELP
TO ATTAIN HAPPINESS

[1]   Since it is plain from earlier chapters[1] that divine providence controls rational creatures in a different way from other things, because they differ from other things in the way that their own nature was established, it remains to be shown that, by virtue of the dignity of their end, a higher mode of governance is used by divine providence in their case.[2]

[2]   Now, it is obvious that, according to what befits their nature, they achieve a higher participation in the end. In fact, since they have an intellectual nature, they are able by its operation to attain to intelligible truth, and this is not possible for other things that are devoid of understanding. And, of course, because they can reach intelligible truth by their natural operation, it is clear that divine provision is made for them in a different way than for other things. Inasmuch as man is given understanding and reason, by which he can both discern and investigate the truth; as he is also given sensory powers, both internal and external, whereby he is helped to seek the truth; as he is also given the use of speech, by the functioning of which he is enabled to convey to another person the truth that he conceives in his mind—thus constituted, men may help themselves in the process of knowing the truth, just as they may in regard to the other needs of life for man is "a naturally social animal."[3]

[3]   But, beyond this, man's ultimate end is fixed in a certain knowledge of truth which surpasses his natural ca-

---

1. See above, ch. 112ff.
2. See above, ch. 111.
3. Aristotle, *Politics*, I, 2 (1253a 2).

pacity: that is, he may see the very First Truth in Itself, as we showed above.[4] Now, this is not granted to lower creatures, that is, the possibility of their reaching an end which exceeds their natural capacity. So, the different mode of governance in regard to men and in regard to other, lower creatures must be noted as a result of this end. For, the things that are related to an end must be proportionate to that end. So, if man is ordered to an end which exceeds his natural capacity, some help must be divinely provided for him, in a supernatural way, by which he may tend toward his end.

[4]   Again, a thing of an inferior nature cannot be brought to what is proper to a higher nature except by the power of that higher nature. For example, the moon, which does not shine by its own light, becomes luminous by the power and action of the sun, and water, which is not hot of itself, becomes hot by the power and action of fire. Now, to see the very First Truth in Itself so transcends the capacity of human nature that it is proper to God alone, as we showed above.[5] Therefore, man needs divine help so that he may reach this end.

[5]   Besides, each thing attains its ultimate end by its own operation. Now, operation gets its power from the operating principle; thus, by the action of the semen there is generated a being in a definite species, whose power preexists in the semen. Therefore, man is not able by his own operation to reach his ultimate end, which transcends the capacity of his natural powers, unless his operation acquires from divine power the efficacy to reach the aforesaid end.

[6]   Moreover, no instrument can achieve its ultimate perfection by the power of its own form, but only by the power of the principal agent, although by its own power it can provide a certain disposition to the ultimate perfection. Indeed, the cutting of the lumber results from the saw according to the essential character of its own form, but the

4. See above, ch. 50ff.
5. See above, ch. 52.

form of the bench comes from the skilled mind which uses the tool. Likewise, the breaking down and consumption of food in the animal body is due to the heat of fire, but the generation of flesh, and controlled growth and similar actions, stem from the vegetative soul which uses the heat of fire as an instrument. Now, all intellects and wills are subordinated as instruments under a principal agent to God, Who is the first intellect and will. So, their operations must have no efficacy in regard to the ultimate perfection which is the attainment of final happiness, except through the divine power. Therefore, a rational nature needs divine help to obtain the ultimate end.

[7] Furthermore, there are many impediments presented to man in the attaining of his end. For he is hindered by the weakness of his reason, which is easily drawn into error by which he is cut off from the right way of reaching his end. He is also hindered by the passions of his sensory nature, and by the feelings whereby he is attracted to sensible and lower things; and the more he attaches himself to these, the farther he is removed from his ultimate end, for these things are below man, whereas man's end is above him. He is further hindered by frequent bodily illness from the carrying out of his virtuous activities whereby he may tend toward happiness. Therefore, man needs divine help, but he may fall completely short of the ultimate end as a result of these obstacles.

[8] Hence, it is said, in John (6:44): "No man can come to Me, except the Father, Who hath sent Me, draw him," and again: "As the branch cannot bear fruit of itself, unless it abide in the vine, so neither can you, unless you abide in Me" (John 15:4).

[9] By this we set aside the error of the Pelagians, who said that man could merit the glory of God by his free choice alone.[6]

6. See St. Augustine, *De haeresibus*, 88 (PL, 42, col. 47); see also Pelagius, *Epist.* I, ad Demetriadem (inter oper. Pseudo-Jerome PL, 30, col. 32). For a later treatment of Pelagianism by St.

Chapter 148.

THAT BY THE HELP OF DIVINE GRACE MAN IS NOT FORCED TOWARD VIRTUE

[1]   Now, it might seem to someone that by divine help some external compulsion to good action is exercised on man, because it has been said: "No man can come to Me, except the Father, Who hath sent Me, draw him" (John 6:44); and because of the statement in Romans (8:14): "Whosoever are led by the Spirit of God, they are the sons of God"; and in II Corinthians (5:14): "the charity of Christ presseth us." Indeed, to be drawn, to be led, and to be pressed seem to imply coaction.

[2]   But that this is not true is clearly shown. For divine providence provides for all things according to their measure, as we have shown above.[1] But it is proper to man, and to every rational nature, to act voluntarily and to control his own acts, as it is clear from what we have said before.[2] But coaction is contrary to this. Therefore, God by His help does not force men to right action.

[3]   Again, that divine help is provided man so that he may act well is to be understood in this way: it performs our works in us, as the primary cause performs the operations of secondary causes, and as a principal agent performs the action of an instrument. Hence, it is said in Isaias (26:12–13): "Thou hast wrought all our works for us, O Lord." Now, the first cause causes the operation of the secondary cause according to the measure of the latter. So, God also causes our works in us in accord with our measure, which

---

Thomas, see *Summa Theologiae*, I-II, q. 109, art. 4–5 (in Pegis, *Basic Writings*, II, 985–987).

1. See above, ch. 71.
2. See *SCG*, II, ch. 47ff.

means that we act voluntarily and not as forced. Therefore, no one is forced to right action by the divine help.

[4] Besides, man is ordered to his end by his will, for the object of the will is the good and the end. Now, divine help is chiefly afforded us so that we may obtain our end. So, this help does not exclude from us the act of our will, but, rather, in a special way, produces this act in us. Hence, the Apostle says, in Philippians (2:13; Douay modified): "it is God Who worketh in you, both to will and to accomplish, according to good will." But coaction excludes the act of the will in us, since we do under force that whose contrary we will. Therefore, God does not force us by His help to act rightly.

[5] Moreover, man reaches his ultimate end by acts of the virtues, for felicity is assigned as a reward for virtue. Now, forced acts are not acts of the virtues, since the main thing in virtue is choice, which cannot be present without voluntariness to which violence is opposed. Therefore, man is not divinely compelled to act rightly.

[6] Furthermore, the means to the end should be in proportion to the end. But the ultimate end which is felicity is appropriate only to voluntary agents, who are masters of their acts. Hence, we call neither inanimate things nor brute animals, happy, just as they are neither fortunate nor unfortunate, except metaphorically. Therefore, the help that is divinely given men to attain felicity is not coactive.

[7] Hence, it is said in Deuteronomy (30:15–18; Douay modified): "Consider that the Lord has set before thee this day life and good, and on the other hand death and evil; that thou mayest love the Lord thy God, and walk in His ways . . . But if thy heart be turned away so that thou wilt not hear . . . I foretell thee this day that thou shalt perish." And in Ecclesiasticus (15–18): "Before man is life and death, good and evil; that which he shall choose shall be given him."

Chapter 149.

THAT MAN CANNOT MERIT DIVINE HELP IN ADVANCE

[1]   From what has been said it is quite manifest that man cannot merit divine help in advance. For everything is related as matter to what is above it. Now, matter does not move itself to its own perfection; rather, it must be moved by something else. So, man does not move himself so as to obtain divine help which is above him; rather, he is moved by God to obtain it.[1] Now, the movement of the mover precedes the movement of the movable thing in reason and causally. Therefore, divine help is not given to us by virtue of the fact that we initially move ourselves toward it by good works; instead, we make such progress by good works because we are preceded by divine help.

[2]   Again, an instrumental agent is not disposed to be brought to perfection by the principal agent, unless it acts by the power of the principal agent. Thus, the heat of fire no more prepares matter for the form of flesh than for any other form, except in so far as the heat acts through the power of the soul. But our soul acts under God, as an instrumental agent under a principal agent.[2] So, the soul cannot prepare itself to receive the influence of divine help except in so far as it acts from divine power. Therefore, it is preceded by divine help toward good action, rather than preceding the divine help and meriting it, as it were, or preparing itself for it.

[3]   Besides, no particular agent can universally precede the action of the first universal agent, because the action of a particular agent takes its origin from the universal agent; just as in things here below, all motion is preceded by

1. See above, ch. 147.
2. See above, ch. 147.

celestial motion. But the human soul is subordinated to God as a particular agent under a universal one. So, it is impossible for there to be any right movement in it which divine action does not precede. Hence, the Lord says, in John (15:5): "without Me you can do nothing."

[4] Moreover, compensation is in proportion to merit, because in the repaying of compensation the equality of justice is practiced. Now, the influence of divine help which surpasses the capacity of nature is not proportionate to the acts that man performs by his natural ability. Therefore, man cannot merit the aforesaid help by acts of that kind.

[5] Furthermore, knowledge precedes the movement of the will. But the knowledge of the supernatural end comes to man from God, since man could not attain it by natural reason because it exceeds his natural capacity. So, divine help must precede the movements of our will toward the ultimate end.

[6] Hence, it is said in Titus (3:5): "Not by the works of justice which we have done, but according to His mercy, He saved us." And in Romans (9:16) the action of willing is "not of him that willeth," nor is the action of running "of him that runneth," but both are "of God that showeth mercy." For, to perform a good act of willing and of doing, man must be preceded by divine help. For instance, it is customary to attribute an effect not to the proximate agent of operation, but to the first mover; thus, the victory is ascribed to the general even though it is accomplished by the work of the soldiers. Not that free choice of the will is excluded by these words, as some have wrongly understood them, as if man were not the master of his own internal and external acts; the text shows that man is subject to God. And it is said in Lamentations (5:21): "Convert us, O Lord, to Thee, and we shall be converted." From which it is clear that our conversion to God is preceded by God's help which converts us.

[7] However, we read in Zacharias (1:3; Douay modified) a statement made in the name of God: "Turn ye to me

. . . and we shall turn to you." Not, of course, that the working of God fails to precede our conversion, as we said, but that He subsequently assists our conversion, whereby we turn to Him, by strengthening it so that it may reach its result and by confirming it so that it may obtain its proper end.

[8]   Now, by this we set aside the error of the Pelagians,[3] who said that this kind of help is given us because of our merits, and that the beginning of our justification is from ourselves, though the completion of it is from God.

Chapter 150.

THAT THE AFORESAID DIVINE HELP IS CALLED GRACE, AND WHAT SANCTIFYING GRACE IS

[1]   Since what is given a person, without any preceding merit on his part, is said to be given to him *gratis*, and because the divine help that is offered to man precedes all human merit, as we showed,[1] it follows that this help is accorded *gratis* to man, and as a result it quite fittingly took the name *grace*. Hence, the Apostle says, in Romans (11:6): "And if by grace, it is not now by works: otherwise grace is no more grace."

[2]   But there is another reason why the aforesaid help of God has taken the name *grace*. In fact, a person is said to be in the "good graces" of another because he is well liked by the other. Consequently, he who is loved by another is said to enjoy his grace. Now, it is of the essence of love that the lover wishes good and does what is good for the object of his love. Of course, God wishes and does good things in regard to every creature, for the very being of the creature and all his perfection result from God's willing and

3. See above, ch. 147.
1. See above, ch. 149.

doing, as we showed above.[2] Hence, it is said in Wisdom
(11:25): "For Thou lovest all things that are, and hatest
none of the things which Thou hast made." But a special
mark of divine love is observable in the case of those to
whom He offers help so that they may attain a good which
surpasses the order of their nature, namely, the perfect enjoyment, not of some created good, but of Himself. So, this
help is appropriately called *grace*, not only because it is
given gratis, as we showed, but also because by this help
man is, through a special prerogative, brought into the good
graces of God. Hence, the Apostle says, in Ephesians
(1:5–6): "Who hath predestinated us unto the adoption
of children . . . according to the purpose of His will, unto
the praise of the glory of His grace, in which He hath
graced us in His beloved Son."

[3]   Now, this grace, within the man who is graced by it,
must be something, a sort of form and perfection for that
man. For, a thing that is directed toward an end must have
a continual relation to it, because the mover continually
moves the moved object, until the object comes to its end
as a result of the motion. Therefore, since man is directed
to the ultimate end by the help of divine grace, as we
showed,[3] man must continually enjoy this help until he
reaches his end. Now, this would not be if man participated
in the aforesaid help as a motion or passion and not as an
enduring form which is, as it were, at rest in him. In fact,
a motion and a passion would not be present in man except when he was actually converted to the end, and this
act is not continually performed by man, as is especially
evident in the case of sleeping man. Therefore, sanctifying
grace[4] is a form and perfection remaining in man even
when he is not acting.

2. *SCG*, II, ch. 15.

3. See above, ch. 147.

4. St. Thomas' expression *gratia gratum faciens* means, literally,
   "grace producing a graced state" (cf. Eph. 1:6). R. W.
   Schmidt, translating a parallel text (*De veritate*, 27, 1, in
   St. Thomas, *Truth* [Chicago: 1954], III, 307–310) uses the expression "ingratiatory grace." It is commonly called sanctifying,

[4]   Again, God's love is causative of the good which is in us, just as a man's love is called forth and caused by some good thing which is in the object of his love. But man is aroused to love someone in a special way because of some special good which pre-exists in the person loved. Therefore, wherever there is found a special love of God for man, there must consequently be found some special good conferred on man by God. Hence, since in accord with the preceding explanation sanctifying grace marks a special love of God for man, it must be that a special goodness and perfection is marked, as being present in man, by this term.

[5]   Besides, everything is ordered to an end suitable to it by the rational character of its form, for there are different ends for different species. But the end to which man is directed by the help of divine grace is above human nature. Therefore, some supernatural form and perfection must be superadded to man whereby he may be ordered suitably to the aforesaid end.

[6]   Moreover, man must reach his ultimate end by his own operations. Now, everything operates in accord with its own form. So in order that man may be brought to his ultimate end by his own operations, a form must be superadded to him from which his operations may get a certain efficacy in meriting his ultimate end.

[7]   Furthermore, divine providence makes provision for all things in accord with the measure of their nature, as is evident from preceding statements.[5] Now, this is the measure proper for man: for the perfection of their operations there must be present in them, above their natural potencies, certain perfections and habits whereby they may operate well and do the good, connaturally, easily and enjoyably, as it were. Therefore, the help of grace which man

---

or habitual grace today: see Garrigou-Lagrange, *Reality: A Synthesis of Thomistic Thought*, trans. P. Cummins (St. Louis: 1950), pp. 293–302.

5. See above, ch. 71.

obtains from God in order to reach the ultimate end designates a form and perfection present in man.

[8]   Hence, in Scripture, the grace of God is signified by some sort of light, for the Apostle says in Ephesians (5:8): "you were heretofore darkness, but now, light in the Lord." Properly enough, then, the perfection whereby man is initially moved to his ultimate end, which consists in the vision of God, is called *light*, for this is the principle of the act of seeing.

[9]   By this we set aside the opinion of certain men who say that the grace of God places nothing within man, just as something is not put into a person as a result of the statement that he has the good graces of a king, but only in the king who likes him. It is clear, then, that they were deceived by their failure to note the difference between divine and human love. For divine love is causative of the good which He loves in anything, but human love is not always so.

Chapter 151.

THAT SANCTIFYING GRACE CAUSES THE LOVE OF GOD IN US

[1]   From the foregoing it becomes evident that man achieves this result through the help of divine sanctifying grace: the fact that he loves God.

[2]   For sanctifying grace is an effect in man of divine love. But the proper effect in man of divine love seems to be the fact that he loves God. Indeed, this is the principal thing in the lover's intention: to be loved in turn by the object of his love. To this, then, the lover's main effort inclines, to attract his beloved to the love of himself; unless this occurs, his love must come to naught. So, this fact that he loves God is the result in man of sanctifying grace.

[3]   Again, there must be some union of things for which there is one end, as a result of their being ordered to this end. Thus, in a state men are unified by a certain concord, so that they may be able to attain the public good, and soldiers in combat must be united and act with one accord, so that victory, the common end, may be achieved. Now, the ultimate end, to which man is brought with the help of divine grace, is the vision of God in His essence, which is proper to God Himself. Thus, this final good is shared with man by God. So, man cannot be brought to this end unless he be united with God by the conformation of his will. And this is the proper effect of love, for "it is proper to friends to approve and disapprove the same things, and to be delighted in and to be pained by the same things."[1] Hence, by sanctifying grace man is established as a lover of God, since man is directed by it to the end that has been shared with him by God.

[4]   Besides, since the end and the good are the proper object of the appetite or affection, man's affections must be chiefly perfected by sanctifying grace, which directs man to his ultimate end. But the chief perfection of the affections is love. The mark of this is that every movement of feeling is derived from love, for no one desires, hopes, or rejoices except because of a good which is loved. Likewise, neither does anyone experience repugnance, fear, sorrow, or anger except because of what is opposed to the good that is loved. Therefore, the principal effect of sanctifying grace is for man to love God.

[5]   Moreover, the form whereby a thing is ordered to an end makes the thing somewhat like the end. For instance, a body acquires through the form of weight a likeness and conformity to the place toward which it is moved naturally. But we showed[2] that sanctifying grace is a certain form in man whereby he is ordered to his ultimate end, Who is God. So, man achieves the likeness to God through grace.

1. Aristotle, *Nicomachean Ethics*, IX, 3 (1165b 27).
2. See above, ch. 150.

Now, likeness is the cause of love, for everything loves its like (See Ecclus. 13:19). Therefore, by grace man is made a lover of God.

[6]   Furthermore, it is required for perfection of operation that a person act steadily and promptly. Now, love produces this result especially; because of it, even difficult things are lightly regarded. So, since man's operations must become perfect as a result of sanctifying grace, as appears from what we have said,[3] it is necessary for the love of God to be established in us through this grace.

[7]   Hence, the Apostle says, in Romans (5:5): "the charity of God is poured forth in our hearts by the Holy Ghost Who is given us." Moreover, the Lord has promised His vision to those who love Him, saying in John (14:21): "he that loveth Me shall be loved of My Father; and I will love him and will manifest Myself to him."

[8]   Thus, it is clear that grace, which directs us to the final divine vision, causes the love of God in us.

Chapter 152.

THAT DIVINE GRACE CAUSES FAITH IN US

[1]   Now, as a result of divine grace causing charity[1] in us, it is also necessary for faith to be caused in us by grace.

[2]   Indeed, the movement whereby we are directed by grace to our ultimate end is voluntary, not violent, as we showed above.[2] Now, there cannot be a voluntary movement toward something unless it is known. So, the knowledge of the ultimate end must be accorded us by grace, so that we may be voluntarily directed to it. But this knowl-

3. See above, ch. 150.
1. The "divine love" of the preceding chapter is called charity here.
2. See above, ch. 148.

edge cannot be by means of open vision in this life, as we showed above.[3] Therefore, this knowledge must be through faith.

[3]   Again, in every knowing being the mode of knowledge depends on the mode of its proper nature; hence, the mode of knowing is different for an angel, a man, and a brute animal, inasmuch as their natures are different, as is clear from things said earlier.[4] But to man, in order that he may attain his ultimate end, there is added a perfection higher than his own nature, namely, grace, as we have shown.[5] Therefore, it is necessary that, above man's natural knowledge, there also be added to him a knowledge which surpasses natural reason. And this is the knowledge of faith, which is of the things that are not seen by natural reason.

[4]   Besides, whenever something is moved by an agent to what is proper to the agent, the thing moved must be, at the start, imperfectly subject to the impulsions of the agent, impulsions that remain somewhat foreign and improper to it, until at the end of the movement they do become proper to it. For example, wood is first heated by fire, and that heat does not belong to the wood but is apart from its nature; at the end, however, when the wood is now ignited, the heat becomes proper and connatural to it. Likewise, when a person is being taught by a teacher, he must at the start accept the teacher's conceptions, not as one who understands them by himself, but by way of belief, as things which are beyond his capacity; but at the end, when he has become learned, he can understand them. Now, as is clear from what we have said,[6] we are directed by the help of divine grace to our ultimate end. But the ultimate end is an open vision of the First Truth in Itself, as we showed above.[7] Therefore, before it comes to this end, man's intellect must

3. See above, ch. 48 and 52.
4. SCG, II, 68, 82, and 96ff.
5. See above, ch. 150.
6. See above, ch. 147.
7. See above, ch. 50ff.

be subject to God by way of belief, under the influence of divine grace which accomplishes this.

[5]   Moreover, at the beginning of this work[8] we indicated the advantages which made it necessary for divine truth to be offered to men by way of belief. It is also possible to conclude from these reasons that it was necessary for faith to be a product in us of divine grace.

[6]   Hence, the Apostle says to the Ephesians (2:8): "by grace you are saved through faith; and that not of yourselves, for it is the gift of God."

[7]   By this conclusion we set aside the error of the Pelagians, who said that the beginning of faith in us was not from God but from ourselves.[9]

Chapter 153.

THAT DIVINE GRACE CAUSES HOPE IN US

[1]   On the same premises it can be shown that the hope of future happiness must be caused in us by grace.

[2]   In fact, the love that a man has for others arises in man from the love that he has for himself, for a man stands in relation to a friend as he does to himself. But a person loves himself inasmuch as he wishes the good for himself, just as he loves another person by wishing him good. So, by the fact that a man is interested in his own good he is led to develop an interest in another person's good. Hence, because a person hopes for good from some other person, a way develops for man to love that other person in himself, from whom he hopes to attain the good. Indeed, a person is loved in himself when the lover wishes the good for him, even if the lover may receive nothing from him. Now, since by sanctifying grace there is pro-

8. *SCG*, I, 3ff.
9. See above, ch. 147.

duced in man an act of loving God for Himself,[1] the result was that man obtained hope from God by means of grace. However, though it is not for one's own benefit, friendship, whereby one loves another for himself, has of course many resulting benefits, in the sense that one friend helps another as he helps himself. Hence, when one person loves another, and knows that he is loved by that other, he must get hope from him. Now, by grace man is so established as a lover of God, through the love of charity, that he is also instructed by faith that he is first loved by God: according to the passage found in I John (4:10): "In this is charity: not as though we had loved God, but because He hath first loved us." It follows, then, from the gift of grace that man gets hope from God. It is also clear from this that just as hope is a preparation of man for the true love of God, so also man is conversely strengthened in hope by charity.

[3]   Again, in every lover there is caused a desire to be united with his beloved, in so far as that is possible; as a result, it is most enjoyable to live with friends. So, if by grace man is made a lover of God, there must be produced in him a desire for union with God, according as that is possible. But faith, which is caused by grace, makes it clear that the union of man with God in the perfect enjoyment in which happiness consists is possible. Therefore, the desire for this fruition results in man from the love of God. But the desire for anything bothers the soul of the desirer, unless there be present some hope of attainment. So, it was appropriate that in man, in whom God's love and faith are caused by grace, there should also be caused a hope of acquiring future happiness.

[4]   Besides, if some difficulty should emerge among things ordered to a desired end, hope of attaining the end provides solace. For instance, a person suffers but slightly from the bitterness of medicine because of his hope for good health. But in our process of working toward happiness, which is the end of all our desires, many difficulties

1. See above, ch. 151.

present burdens to be borne, because virtue, by which one advances toward happiness, "is concerned with difficulties."[2] Therefore, in order that man may tend toward happiness smoothly and readily, it was necessary to provide him with the hope of obtaining happiness.

[5] Moreover, no one is moved toward an end that he judges impossible to attain. So, in order that a person may push forward toward the end, he must have a feeling toward the end as toward something possible of attainment, and this is the feeling of hope. Therefore, since man is directed toward his ultimate end of happiness by grace, it was necessary for the hope of attaining happiness to be impressed on man's power of feeling by means of grace.

[6] Hence, it is said in I Peter (1:3–4; Douay modified): "He hath regenerated us unto a lively hope . . . unto an inheritance incorruptible, reserved for heaven." And again in Romans (8:24) it is said: "we are saved by hope."

Chapter 154.

ON THE GIFTS OF GRATUITOUS GRACE, INCLUDING A CONSIDERATION OF THE DIVINATIONS OF DEMONS

[1] Since man can only know the things that he does not see himself by taking them from another who does see them, and since faith is among the things we do not see, the knowledge of the objects of faith must be handed on by one who sees them himself. Now, this one is God, Who perfectly comprehends Himself, and naturally sees His essence.[1] Indeed, we get faith from God. So, the things that we hold by faith must come to us from God. But, since the things that come from God are enacted in a definite order,

2. Aristotle, *Nicomachean Ethics*, II, 3 (1105a 9).
1. *SCG*, I, ch. 47.

as we showed above,[2] a certain order had to be observed in the manifestation of the objects of faith. That is to say, some persons had to receive them directly from God, then others from them, and so on in an orderly way down to the lowest persons.

[2]   Now, wherever there is an order among things, it is necessary that, the nearer one thing is to the first principle, the stronger it must be. This is apparent in the order of divine manifestation. For invisible things whose vision is beatifying, and to which faith applies, are first revealed by God to the blessed angels through open vision, as is clear from our previous statements.[3]

[3]   In turn, by the intermediary ministry of the angels they are manifested to certain men; not, of course, through open vision, but through a kind of certitude resulting from divine revelation.

[4]   This revelation, then, is accomplished by means of a certain interior and intelligible light, elevating the mind to the perception of things that the understanding cannot reach by its natural light. For, just as the understanding by its natural light is made certain concerning things that it knows by that light (for instance, concerning first principles), so also does it acquire certitude concerning things which it apprehends by supernatural light. Now, this latter certitude is needed so that the things that are grasped by divine revelation may be offered to others, for we cannot present things to others with assurance if we have not certain knowledge of them.[4] Now, accompanying this light that we have mentioned, which illumines the mind from within, there are at times in divine revelation other external or internal aids to knowledge; for instance, a spoken message, or something heard by the external senses which is produced by divine power, or something perceived internally

2. See above, ch. 77.
3. See above, ch. 79ff.
4. See F. A. Cunningham, "Certitudo in St. Thomas Aquinas," *Modern Schoolman*, 30 (1953), 297–324.

through imagination due to God's action, or also some things produced by God that are seen by bodily vision, or that are internally pictured in the imagination. From these presentations, by the light internally impressed on the mind, man receives a knowledge of divine things. Consequently, without the interior light, these aids do not suffice for a knowledge of divine things, but the interior light does suffice without them.

[5] However, this revelation of the invisible things of God belongs to *wisdom*, which is properly the knowledge of divine things. Thus, it is said in Wisdom (7:27-28; Douay modified) that the wisdom of God "conveyeth herself through nations into holy souls . . . for God loveth none but him that dwelleth with wisdom." And again in Ecclesiasticus (15:5; Douay modified) it is said: "the Lord hath filled him with the spirit of wisdom and understanding."

[6] But, since "the invisible things of God . . . are clearly seen, being understood by the things that are made,"[5] not only divine things are revealed to men by divine grace, but also some created things, and this seems to pertain to *knowledge*. Hence, it is said in Wisdom (7:17): "For He hath given me the true knowledge of the things that are: to know the disposition of the whole world, and the virtues of the elements." And in II Paralipomenon (1:12; Douay modified) the Lord said to Solomon: "Knowledge and wisdom are granted to thee."

[7] But the things that man knows he cannot properly convey to the knowledge of another man, except by speech. So, since those who receive a revelation from God, according to the divinely established order, should instruct others, it was necessary for them also to be given the *grace of speech*, in keeping with what the benefit of those who were to be instructed demanded. Hence, it is said in Isaias

5. See Rom. 1:20, which is modified to the formula given here, as early as the time of St. Augustine (*Confessions*, X, 6, 10, and in many other places).

(50:4): "The Lord hath given me a learned tongue, that I should know how to uphold by word him that is weary." And the Lord says to the disciples, in Luke (21:15): "I will give you a mouth and wisdom, which all your adversaries shall not be able to resist and gainsay." And also for this reason, when it was necessary for the truth of the faith to be preached by a few men to different peoples, some were divinely instructed to "speak with divers tongues," as is said in Acts (2:4): "They were all filled with the Holy Ghost: and they began to speak with divers tongues, according as the Holy Ghost gave them to speak."

[8]   But because oral teaching that is offered requires confirmation so that it may be accepted, unless it be evident in itself, and because things that are of faith are not evident to human reason, it was necessary for some means to be provided whereby the words of the preachers of the faith might be confirmed. Now, they could not be confirmed by any rational principles in the way of demonstration, since the objects of faith surpass reason. So, it was necessary for the oral teaching of the preachers to be confirmed by certain signs, whereby it might be plainly shown that this oral teaching came from God; so, the preachers did such things as *healing the sick*, and the *performance of other difficult deeds*, which only God could do. Hence, the Lord, sending forth His disciples to preach, said in Matthew (10:8): "Heal the sick, raise the dead, cleanse the lepers, cast out devils." And it is said at the end of Mark (16:20): "But they going forth preached everywhere: the Lord working withal, and confirming the word with signs that followed."

[9]   But there was still another way of confirmation, in so far as the preachers of truth were found to speak true things about hidden events which could be made evident later, so that credit was given them as speakers of truths about matters which men were not able to experience. Hence, the *gift of prophecy* was necessary, whereby they might know and reveal to others, through God's revelation, future events and things generally concealed from men. Thus, in this way, when they were discovered to tell about true events, belief

would be accorded them in regard to matters of faith. Hence, the Apostle says, in I Corinthians (14:24–25): "If all prophesy, and there come in one that believeth not or an unlearned person, he is convinced of all, he is judged of all; the secrets of his heart are made manifest; and so, falling down on his face, he will adore God, affirming that God is among you indeed."

[10] However, an adequate testimony to the faith is not supplied by this gift of prophecy unless it were concerned with things that can be known by God alone, just as miracles are of such nature that God alone can work them. Now, these things are especially, in the affairs of this world, the secrets of our hearts, which God alone can know, as we showed above,[6] and contingent future events which also come only under divine cognition, for He sees them in themselves because they are present to Him by reason of His eternity, as we showed above.[7]

[11] Of course, some contingent future events can also be foreknown by men; not, indeed, according as they are future, but inasmuch as they pre-exist in their causes. When these latter are known, either in themselves or through some of their evident effects, which are called signs, a foreknowledge of some future effects may be acquired by man. Thus, a physician foreknows future death or good health from the condition of natural strength, which he knows from the pulse, the urine, and signs of this kind. Now, this kind of knowledge of future matters is partly certain, but partly uncertain. In fact, there are some pre-existing causes from which future events follow of necessity; for instance, if there be a pre-existing composition of contraries in an animal, death results necessarily. But, from some pre-existing causes future effects do not follow necessarily, but usually. For instance, in most cases a perfect human being results from the insemination of a mother by a man's semen; sometimes, however, monsters are generated, be-

6. *SCG*, I, ch. 68.
7. *SCG*, I, ch. 67.

cause of some obstruction which overcomes the operation of the natural capacity. So, there is certain foreknowledge of the first kind of effects, but of those mentioned in the second case there is no infallibly certain foreknowledge. However, the foreknowledge that is acquired concerning future events from divine revelation, according to prophetic grace, is altogether certain, just as divine foreknowledge is also certain. Indeed, God does not merely foreknow future events as they are in their causes, but infallibly, as they are in themselves, as we showed earlier.[8] And so, prophetic knowledge of future things is given man in the same way, with perfect certitude. Nor is this certitude opposed to the contingency of future events, any more than the certitude of divine knowledge is, as we showed above.[9]

[12]   However, some future events are at times revealed to prophets, not as they are in themselves, but as they are in their causes. In that case, if the causes are obstructed from achieving their effects, nothing prevents the prophetic forecast from being modified. Thus, Isaias foretold to the ailing Ezechias: "take order with thy house, for thou shalt die, and not live" (Isa. 38:1), but he was restored to health; and Jonas the Prophet foretold that "after forty days, Ninive shall be destroyed" (Jonas 3:4), yet it was not overturned. Hence, Isaias made his prophecy of the coming death of Ezechias according to the order of his bodily condition and of the lower causes in relation to this result, and Jonas prophesied the disruption of Ninive according to the demands of its merits; however, in both cases, it turned out differently, in accord with the working of a free and health-giving God.

[13]   And so, prophetic prediction of future events is an adequate argument for the faith, since, though men do know some things in advance about future matters, their knowledge of future contingencies is not accompanied by certitude, as is the foreknowledge of prophecy. For, though

8. *SCG*, I, ch. 67–68.
9. *Ibid.*

prophetic revelation is sometimes accomplished on the basis of the order of causes to a given effect, yet at the same time, or later, a revelation may be made to the same prophet concerning the outcome of the future event, as to how it is to be modified. For example, the healing of Ezechias was revealed to Isaias (Isa. 38:5), and the saving of the Ninivites to Jonas (Jonas 4:5ff.).

[14] But malign spirits strive to corrupt the truth of the faith. Just as they make bad use of the working of wonders, in order to lead to error and weaken the proof of the true faith, even though they do not perform miracles in the proper sense, but things that appear wonderful to men, as we showed above[10]—so also they abuse prophetic prediction, not, of course, prophesying, but foretelling certain things according to the order of causes hidden to man, so that they seem to know in advance future events in themselves. Now, though contingent effects come from natural causes, these spirits, as a result of the subtlety of their understanding, can know more than men as to when and how the effects of natural causes may be obstructed. So, in foretelling future things, they appear to be more astonishing and more truthful than men, no matter how learned the latter may be. Of course, among natural causes, the highest and farthest removed from our knowledge are the powers of the celestial bodies. That these are known to the spirits under discussion, in accord with what is proper to their nature, is evident from earlier explanations.[11] Therefore, since all lower bodies are controlled through the powers and motions of the higher bodies,[12] these spirits are far more able than any astronomer to foretell future winds and storms, changing conditions of the atmosphere, and other such things which occur in the changing of lower bodies as a result of the motion of the higher bodies. Also, though celestial bodies can make no impression directly on the in-

10. See above, ch. 103.
11. *SCG*, II, ch. 99ff.
12. See above, ch. 82.

tellectual part of the soul, as we showed above,[13] a good many men follow the impulse of their bodily passions and tendencies, on which we have shown that the celestial bodies do have an influence. In fact, it is only possible for wise men, of whom the number is small, to resist this kind of passion by using their reason. So, the result is that many predictions can be made concerning man's acts, although even these spirits fail at times in their predictions because of freedom of choice.

[15] However, they do not make their predictions of what they foreknow by enlightening the mind, as is done in the case of divine revelation. Indeed, it is not their intention that the human mind be perfected in order to know the truth, but, rather, that it be turned away from the truth. Now, they sometimes predict, indeed, by impressing the imagination, either during sleep, as when they show the signs of certain future events through dreams, or while one is awake, as is apparent in the case of people in a trance or frenzy who foretell future events. At other times, too, they do it through external signs, for instance, by the movement and chirping of birds, and by means of the appearances of the inner parts of animals, and by the drawing of certain kinds of mathematical figures, and in other like ways which seem to work by some kind of lot. At still other times, they do it by visual apparitions and by predicting future events in speech that can be heard.

[16] Although the last of these ways is obviously the work of evil spirits, some people have made efforts to explain the other ways in terms of natural causes. They say, in fact, that when a celestial body moves toward definite effects in these things here below, some signs of the result of the influence of the same body appear, because different things receive the celestial influence in different ways. On this basis, then, they say that the change that is produced in a thing by the celestial body can be taken as a sign of the change in another thing. Hence, they say that movements that are apart from rational deliberation, such as visions in people who

13. See above, ch. 84ff.

are dreaming and in those who are out of their mind, and the flight and crying of birds, and the drawing of figures, when a person does not deliberate on how many points he should draw, are all the results of the influence of a celestial body. So, they say that things like these can be the signs of future effects that are caused by the motion of the heavens.

[17] However, since this has little reason, it is better to think that the predictions that are made from signs of this kind take their origin from some intellectual substance, by whose power the aforesaid motions occurring without deliberation are controlled, in accord with what befits the observation of future events. And while these movements are sometimes controlled by the divine will, through the ministry of good spirits, since many things are revealed by God through dreams—as to Pharao (Gen. 41:25), and to Nabuchodonosor (Dan. 2:28), and "lots that are cast into the lap, that are also at times disposed of by the Lord," as Solomon says (Prov. 16:33)—yet most of the time they happen as a result of the working of evil spirits, as the holy Doctors say, and as even the Gentiles themselves agree. For Maximus Valerius says that the practice of auguries and dreams, and that sort of thing, belongs to the religion in which idols were worshiped.[14] And so, in the Old Law, along with idolatry, all these practices were prohibited. Indeed, it is said in Deuteronomy (18:9-11): "beware lest thou have a mind to imitate the abominations of those nations," that is, those that serve idols; "neither let there be found among you anyone that shall expiate his son or daughter, making them to pass through the fire; or that consulteth soothsayers, or observeth dreams and omens; neither let there be any wizard nor charmer, nor anyone that consulteth pythonic spirits, or fortune tellers, or that seeketh the truth from the dead."

[18] Moreover, prophecy attests to the preaching of the faith in another way, namely, in so far as some tenets of the faith are preached which took place in time, such as the

14. Maximus Valerius, *Factorum et dictorum memorabilium libri novem*, I, 1 (Paris: 1841), p. 565.

birth of Christ, His passion and resurrection, and events of that kind. And lest these be thought fictions made by the preachers, or to have come about by chance, they are shown to have been preached long beforehand by the Prophets. Consequently, the Apostle says in Romans (1:1): "Paul, a servant of Jesus Christ, called to be an apostle, separated unto the gospel of God, which He had promised before, by His prophets in the holy scriptures, concerning His Son, Who was made to Him of the seed of David, according to the flesh."

[19]   Following the degree of those who receive revelation directly from God, another degree of grace is necessary. In fact, since men receive revelation from God not only for their own time, but also for the instruction of all men that are to come, it was necessary that the things revealed to them not only be recounted orally to their contemporaries, but also that they be written down for the instruction of men to come. Consequently, there had to be some who would *interpret* this kind of writings. Now, this should be a divine grace, just as revelation was accomplished by the grace of God. Hence, it is said in Genesis (40:8): "Doth not interpretation belong to God."

[20]   Then there follows the last degree: of those, namely, who faithfully believe the things that are revealed to others, and interpreted by still others. But that this is a gift of God was shown earlier.[15]

[21]   But, since some things are done by evil spirits similar to the things whereby the faith is confirmed, both in the working of wonders and in the revelation of future events, as we said above,[16] lest men that have been deceived by such things believe in a lie, it is necessary that they be instructed by the help of divine grace concerning the *discernment of this kind of spirits*, in accord with what is said in I John (4:1): "believe not every spirit, but try the spirits if they be of God."

15. See above, ch. 152.
16. Above, ¶13.

[22]   Now, the Apostle enumerates these effects of grace, that are directed to the instruction and confirmation of the faith, in I Corinthians (12:8–10), saying: "To one indeed, by the Spirit is given the word of wisdom; and to another, the word of knowledge, according to the same Spirit; to another, faith in the same Spirit; to another, the grace of healing in one Spirit; to another, the working of miracles; to another, prophecy; to another, the discerning of spirits; to another, divers kinds of tongues; to another, the interpretation of speeches."

[23]   By this conclusion we set aside the error of certain Manicheans, who say that corporeal miracles are not performed by God. At the same time we exclude the error of those men, in so far as they assert that the Prophets did not speak by the Spirit of God. We also dispose of the error of Prisca and Montanus,[17] who said that the Prophets, like epileptics, did not understand what they spoke about. For this does not agree with divine revelation, whose chief effect is the illumination of the mind.

[24]   Among the effects of grace that have been noted above[18] there is a difference which must be observed. Though the name grace is suitable to all, since it is conferred *gratis*, without preceding merit, only the effect of love is further entitled to the name grace by virtue of the fact that it makes one in the good graces of God. For it is said in Proverbs (8:17): "I love them that love me." Thus, faith and hope, and other things related to faith, can be present in sinners who are not in the good graces of God. But love alone is the special gift of the just, for "he that abideth in charity abideth in God, and God in him," as is said in I John (4:16).

[25]   Moreover, there is still another difference to be considered in the preceding effects of grace. Some of them are necessary during the whole life of man, for without them he cannot be saved: for example, to believe, hope, love, and obey

---

17. See St. Augustine, *De haeresibus*, 26 (*PL*, 42, col. 30).
18. See above, ch. 151ff.

the commandments of God. So, in regard to these effects, there must be certain habitual perfections present in men, so that they may perform these acts when the occasion demands. But other effects are necessary, not for a whole life, but for definite times and places; for example, to work miracles, to foretell future events, and such actions. So, for these actions habitual perfections are not given, but certain impressions are made by God, which cease to exist as soon as the act stops, and these impressions have to be repeated when the act is again to be repeated. Thus, the mind of the Prophet is illumined for each revelation by a new light, and in each case of the working of miracles there must be a new influence of divine power.

Chapter 155.

THAT MAN NEEDS THE HELP OF GRACE
TO PERSEVERE IN THE GOOD

[1]   Man also needs the help of divine grace so that he may persevere in the good.

[2]   Indeed, everything that is variable in itself needs the help of an immovable mover so that it may be fixed on one objective. But man is subject to variation, both from evil to good and from good to evil. So, in order that he may immovably continue in the good, which is to persevere, he needs divine help.

[3]   Again, for that which surpasses the powers of free choice, man needs the help of divine grace. But the power of free choice does not extend to the effect of final perseverance in the good. This is evident as follows. In fact, the power of free choice applies to those things which fall within the scope of election. Now, what is chosen is some particular operation that can be performed. But such a particular operation is what is here and now present. Hence, that which falls under the power of free choice is some-

thing that is to be done now. But to persevere does not mean something as now operable, but the continuation of an operation throughout time. Now, this effect, of persevering in the good, is beyond the power of free choice. Therefore, man needs the help of divine grace to persevere in the good.

[4] Besides, though man is the master of his action through will and free choice, he is not the master of his natural powers. So, while he is free to will or not to will something, he cannot by willing produce such a result that his will, by the very fact of willing, would be immovably fixed on what he wills or chooses. But this is what is required for perseverance; that is, the will must endure immovably in the good. So, perseverance is not within the scope of free choice. Therefore, the help of divine grace must be available to man so that he may persevere.

[5] Moreover, suppose that there are several agents in succession, such that one of them acts after the action of another: the continuation of the action of these agents cannot be caused by any one of them, for no one of them acts forever; nor can it be caused by all of them, since they do not act together. Consequently, the continuity must be caused by some higher agent that always acts, just as the Philosopher proves, in *Physics* VIII, that the continuity of the generative process in animals is caused by some higher, external agent.[1] Now, let us suppose the case of someone who is persevering in the good. There are, then, in his case many movements of free choice tending toward the good, successively following each other up to the end. So, for this continuation in the good, which is perseverance, no one of these movements can be the cause, since none of them lasts forever. Nor can all of them together, for they are not together, and so they cannot cause something together. It remains, then, that this continuation is caused by some higher being. Therefore, man needs the help of higher grace to persevere in the good.

1. Aristotle, *Physics*, VIII, 6 (258b 10–259a 13).

[6]   Furthermore, if many things are ordered to one end, their entire order until they reach the end comes from the first agent directing them to the end. Now, in the case of a man who perseveres in the good there are many movements and many actions reaching to the end. So, the entire order of these movements and actions must be caused by the first agent directing them to the end. But we showed[2] that they are directed by the help of divine grace to the ultimate end. Therefore, the entire order and continuity of good works, in him who perseveres in the good, is due to the help of divine grace.

[7]   Hence, it is said to the Philippians (1:6): "He who hath begun a good work in you will perfect it unto the day of Christ Jesus"; and in I Peter (5:10): "the God of all grace, Who hath called us unto His eternal glory . . . after you have suffered a little, will Himself perfect you and confirm you and establish you."

[8]   There are also found in Sacred Scripture many prayers in which perseverance is sought from God: thus, in the Psalm (16:5): "Perfect Thou my goings in Thy paths, that my footsteps be not moved"; and in II Thessalonians (2:15–16; Douay modified): "May God, our Father, exhort your hearts and confirm you in every work and word." This is also what is asked in the Lord's Prayer, especially when one says, "Thy kingdom come"; indeed, the kingdom of God will not come for us unless we have persevered in the good. Now it would be ridiculous to ask something from God if He were not the giver of it. So, man's perseverance is from God.

[9]   By this we set aside the error of the Pelagians,[3] who said that free choice is sufficient for man to persevere in the good, and that he does not need the help of grace for this purpose.

[10]   However, we should note that even he who possesses grace asks God that he may persevere in the good. Just as

2. See above, ch. 147.
3. Ibid.

free choice is not sufficient without the external help of God, for this effect of persevering in the good, so neither is a habit infused in us enough for this purpose. For habits that are divinely infused in us during the present state of life do not take away entirely from free choice the possibility of being moved toward evil, even though free choice is somewhat fixed in the good by means of them. And so, when we say that man needs the help of grace to persevere unto the end, we do not understand that, in addition to habitual grace previously infused to assure good operation, another must further be infused for persevering; what we do understand is that, once possessed of all the gratuitous habits, a man still needs the help of divine providence externally governing him.

Chapter 156.

THAT HE WHO FALLS FROM GRACE
THROUGH SIN MAY AGAIN BE
RESTORED THROUGH GRACE

[1]   From these considerations it is apparent that man, even if he does not persevere but falls into sin, may be restored to the good by the help of grace.

[2]   Indeed, it pertains to the same power to maintain the continued salvation of a person and to restore it when it has been interrupted, just as health is continually maintained by natural power in the body, and an interruption of health is repaired by that same natural power. Now, man perseveres in the good by means of divine grace, as we showed.[1] Therefore, if one has fallen as a result of sin, he may be restored by means of the same grace.

[3]   Again, an agent that does not require a disposition in its subject can impress its effect on the subject, no matter how the subject be disposed. For this reason, God, Who

1. See above, ch. 155.

does not require a subject that is disposed for His action, can produce a natural form without a disposition of the subject; for example, when He enlightens the blind, revives the dead, and so on for similar cases. But, just as He requires no natural disposition in a corporeal subject, He does not need merit in the will in order to grant grace, for it is given without there being any merits, as we showed.[2] Therefore, God can grant a person sanctifying grace, through which sins are removed, even after he has fallen from grace by sin.

[4] Besides, the only things that man cannot recover when they are lost are those which come to him through generation, such as his natural potencies and organs, and the reason for this is that man cannot be generated a second time.[3] Now, the help of grace is not given man through generation, but after he already exists. Therefore, he can again be restored in order to destroy sin after the loss of grace.

[5] Moreover, grace is a habitual disposition in the soul, as we showed.[4] But habits that are acquired by activity, if lost, can again be acquired through the acts suitable for their acquisition. So, it is much more likely that, if it be lost, grace uniting one to God and freeing one from sin can be restored by divine working.

[6] Furthermore, among the works of God, none is futile, as none is futile among the works of nature, for nature gets this characteristic from God. Now, it would be futile for something to be moved if it could not reach the end of its motion. It must be, then, that what is naturally moved toward an end is able to come to that end. But, after man has fallen into sin, for as long as he continues in the present state of life, there remains in him an aptitude to be moved toward the good. The signs of this are the desire for the good and sorrow for evil which still continue in man after

2. See above, ch. 149.
3. See above, ch. 144.
4. See above, ch. 150.

sin. So, it is possible for man to again return after sin to the good which grace works in man.

[7] Again, no passive potency is found in the nature of things which cannot be reduced to act by some natural active potency. Much less, then, is it possible for there to be a potency in the human soul which is not reducible to act by divine active potency. But there remains in the human soul, even after sin, a potency toward the good; for the natural potencies are not removed by sin, and by means of them the soul is directed toward its good. So, it can be restored to the good by divine potency. Thus, man can obtain the remission of sins by means of grace.

[8] Hence, it is said in Isaias (1:18): "If your sins be as scarlet, they shall be made as white as snow"; and in Proverbs (10:12): "charity covereth all sins." This, too, we ask daily of the Lord, and not in vain, for we say: "Forgive us our trespasses."

[9] By this we set aside the error of the Novatians,[5] who said that man could not obtain pardon for sins which he commits after baptism.

Chapter 157.

THAT MAN CANNOT BE FREED FROM SIN EXCEPT THROUGH GRACE

[1] On the same basis, it can be shown that man cannot revive from mortal sin except through grace.

[2] For by mortal sin man is turned away from his ultimate end. But man is not ordered to his ultimate end except by grace.[1] Therefore, by grace alone can man revive from sin.

5. See St. Augustine, *De haeresibus*, 28 (*PL*, 42, col. 31).
1. See above, ch. 147.

[3]   Again, an offense can be removed only by love. But through mortal sin man offends God, for it is said that "God hateth sinners" (see Wisd. 14:9; Ecclus. 12:3, 7), inasmuch as He wills to deprive them of the ultimate end which He makes ready for those whom He loves. So, man cannot revive from mortal sin except through grace, whereby a certain friendship is developed between God and man.

[4]   For this purpose, also, all the arguments given above[2] for the necessity of grace could be brought forward.

[5]   Hence, it is said in Isaias (43:25): "I am He that blot out thy iniquities for My own sake"; and in the Psalm (84:3): "Thou hast forgiven the iniquity of Thy people; Thou hast covered all their sins."

[6]   By this we set aside the error of the Pelagians,[3] who said that man can rise from sin by his free will.

Chapter 158.

HOW MAN IS FREED FROM SIN

[1]   Since man cannot return to one member of a pair of contraries without moving away from the other extreme, he must, in order to return to the state of rectitude by means of grace, move away from the sin whereby he had swerved from rectitude. And because man is chiefly directed toward the ultimate end, and also turned away from it, through his will, it is not only necessary for man to abandon sin in the external act, but also to renounce it in his will, for the purpose of rising again from sin. Now, man renounces sin in his will provided he repents his past sin and forms the intention of avoiding it in the future. So, it is necessary that a man who is rising again from sin both repent for past sin

2. See above, ch. 147ff.
3. See above, ch. 147.

and intend to avoid future sin. Indeed, if he would not make up his mind to refrain from sin, then sin in itself would not be against his will. But, if he did will to refrain from sin, but was not sorry for past sin, then this sin that he had committed would not be against his will. Now, the movement whereby one moves away from something is contrary to the movement whereby one approaches it; thus, whitening is contrary to blackening. Consequently, the will must abandon sin by moving in a contrary direction from those movements whereby it was inclined toward sin. Now, it was inclined toward sin by appetition and enjoyment in regard to lower things. Therefore, it must move away from sin by means of certain penances whereby it suffers some injury because of the sin that it has committed. For, just as the will was drawn toward consent to the sin by means of pleasure, so is it strengthened in the detestation of sin by means of penances.

[2] Again, we observe that even brute animals may be drawn back from the greatest pleasures by means of painful blows. But he who rises again from sin must not only detest past sin, but also avoid future sin. So, it is fitting that he suffer some affliction for his sin so that in this way he may be strengthened in his resolution to avoid sins.

[3] Besides, the things that we gain as a result of labor and suffering we love more and preserve more carefully. Thus, those who amass wealth by their own labor spend less money than those who get it without work—say, from their parents or in any other way. But for the man who is rising again from sin, it is most necessary that he maintain the state of grace and the love of God carefully, for he lost them by sinning through negligence. Therefore, it is proper for him to endure labor and suffering for the sins that he has committed.

[4] Moreover, the order of justice demands that a punishment be assigned for a sin. Now, the wisdom of the governance of God becomes evident from the fact that order is preserved in things. So, it belongs to the manifestation of

the divine goodness, and of the glory of God, for punishment to be the payment for sin. But the sinner, by sinning, acts against the order that is divinely established, thus trespassing against the laws of God. So, it is fitting that he should pay for this action by punishing himself because he had formerly sinned; indeed, in this way, he dissociates himself entirely from disorder.

[5]   By this, then, it becomes evident that, after a man has secured remission of his sin by grace and has been brought back to the state of grace, he remains under an obligation, as a result of God's justice, to some penalty for the sin that he has committed. Now, if he imposes this penalty on himself by his own will, he is said to *make satisfaction* to God by this: inasmuch as he attains with labor and punishment the divinely established order by punishing himself for the sin, which order he had transgressed by sinning through following his own will. But, if he does not exact this penalty of himself, then, since things subject to divine providence cannot remain disordered, this penalty will be inflicted on him by God. Such a punishment is not called one of satisfaction, since it is not due to the choice of the one who suffers it; but it will be called *purificatory*, because through being punished by another he will be cleansed, as it were, until whatever disorder there was in him is brought back to proper order. Hence, there is this statement of the Apostle in I Corinthians (11:31-32): "if we would judge ourselves, we should not be judged, but whilst we are judged, we are chastised by the Lord, that we be not condemned with this world."

[6]   It should be kept in mind, however, that when the mind is turned away from sin the displeasure with sin can be so forceful, and the attachment of the mind to God so strong, that no obligation to punishment will remain. For, as may be gathered from things said earlier, the punishment that a person suffers after the remission of sin is necessary so that the mind may adhere more firmly to the good; since man is chastised by punishments, these punishments are, then, like remedies. It is also necessary so that

the order of justice may be observed, in the sense that he who has sinned must stand the penalty. But love for God is enough to set the mind of man firmly in the direction of the good, especially if this love be strong; and displeasure for a past fault, when intense, brings great sorrow. Consequently, through the strength of one's love for God, and of one's hatred of past sin, there is removed the need for punishments of satisfaction or of purification. Moreover, if this strength be not great enough to set aside punishments entirely, nevertheless, the stronger it is, the smaller will be the punishment that suffices.

[7] "But the things that we can accomplish through the efforts of our friends we seem to do ourselves,"[1] for friendship makes two persons one in love, and especially in the love of charity. And so, just as a person can make satisfaction to God by himself, so also can he do it through another person, especially in case of necessity. Indeed, the punishment that a friend suffers for oneself one regards as if it were suffered by oneself. Thus, one does not escape punishment provided one suffer along with a suffering friend —and all the more so, the more one is the cause of his suffering. Besides, the love of charity in the person who suffers for a friend makes his satisfaction more acceptable to God than if he suffered for himself, for in the one case it is prompted by charity; in the other, by necessity. It may be taken from this that one person can make satisfaction for another provided both abide in charity. Hence, the Apostle says in Galatians (6:2): "Bear ye one another's burdens, and so you shall fulfill the law of Christ."

1. Aristotle, *Nicomachean Ethics*, III, 3 (1112b 28).

Chapter 159.

THAT IT IS REASONABLE TO HOLD A MAN RESPONSIBLE IF HE DOES NOT TURN TOWARD GOD, EVEN THOUGH HE CANNOT DO THIS WITHOUT GRACE

[1] As we gather from the foregoing,[1] since one cannot be directed to the ultimate end except by means of divine grace, without which no one can possess the things needed to work toward the ultimate end, such as faith, hope, love, and perseverance, it might seem to some person that man should not be held responsible for the lack of such aids. Especially so, since he cannot merit the help of divine grace, nor turn toward God unless God convert him, for no one is held responsible for what depends on another. Now, if this is granted, many inappropriate conclusions appear. In fact, it follows that he who has neither faith, hope, nor love of God, nor perseverance in the good, is not deserving of punishment; whereas, it is clearly stated in John (3:36): "He that believeth not the Son shall not see life, but the wrath of God abideth on him." And since no one reaches final happiness without the aids that we have mentioned, it follows that there are certain men who neither attain happiness nor suffer punishment from God. The contrary of this is shown from the statement in Matthew (25:34, 41) that to all who are present at the divine judgment, it will be said: "Come . . . possess you the kingdom prepared for you" or "Depart . . . into everlasting fire."

[2] To settle this difficulty, we ought to consider that, although one may neither merit in advance nor call forth divine grace by a movement of his free choice, he is able to prevent himself from receiving this grace. Indeed, it is said in Job (21:14): "Who have said to God: Depart from

1. See above, ch. 147ff.

us, we desire not the knowledge of Thy ways"; and in Job (24:13): "They have been rebellious to the light." And since this ability to impede or not to impede the reception of divine grace is within the scope of free choice, not undeservedly is responsibility for the fault imputed to him who offers an impediment to the reception of grace. In fact, as far as He is concerned, God is ready to give grace to all; "indeed He wills all men to be saved, and to come to the knowledge of the truth," as is said in I Timothy (2:4). But those alone are deprived of grace who offer an obstacle within themselves to grace; just as, while the sun is shining on the world, the man who keeps his eyes closed is held responsible for his fault, if as a result some evil follows, even though he could not see unless he were provided in advance with light from the sun.

Chapter 160.

THAT MAN IN THE STATE OF SIN, WITHOUT GRACE, CANNOT AVOID SIN

[1] Now, this statement of ours, that it is within the power of free choice not to offer an impediment to grace,[1] is applicable to those persons in whom natural potency is integrally present. But if, through a preceding disorder, one swerves toward evil, it will not at all be within his power to offer no impediment to grace. For, though at any definite instant he may be able to refrain from a particular act of sin by his own power, however, if long left to himself, he will fall into sin, whereby an impediment is offered to grace.

Indeed, whenever man's mind swerves away from the state of rectitude it is evident that he has departed from the order of his proper end. So, what should be the most important thing in his affection, the ultimate end, becomes a less important object of love than that object to which his mind is inordinately turned, as if to an ultimate end. So,

1. See above, ch. 159.

whenever anything comes up that is in agreement with the
inordinate end but incompatible with his proper end, it
will be chosen, unless he is brought back to his proper end,
so that he favors the proper end above all things, and this is
the effect of grace. However, in so far as he chooses something that is incompatible with his ultimate end, he offers
an impediment to grace, for grace gives the direction to the
end. It is consequently obvious that after sin a man cannot
refrain from all sin during the period preceding his being
brought back to the proper order by grace.

[2]   Besides, when the mind is inclined toward some object it does not stand in a relation of impartiality toward
contrary alternatives, but, instead, is more favorable to the
object to which it is inclined. But, unless it be drawn away
from it by a certain concern arising from rational examina-
tion, the mind chooses the object to which it is more favorable; hence, in sudden actions, an indication of one's inner
state of character may be especially found.[2] But it is not
possible for a man's mind continually to maintain such vigi-
lance that it can make a rational investigation of whatever
he ought to will or do. Thus, it follows that the mind at
times chooses what it is inclined to, provided the inclination be undisturbed. And so, if it be inclined toward sin,
it will not long stay without sinning, thus offering an impediment to grace, unless it is brought back to the state of
rectitude.

[3]   The impulsion of the bodily passions also works
toward this result, as also do the things that are attractive
on the sense level, and most occasions for bad action
whereby man is easily stimulated to sin, unless one be
drawn back by means of a firm attachment to the ultimate
end, which grace produces.

[4]   Consequently, the opinion of the Pelagians is evidently stupid, for they said that man in the state of sin is
able to avoid sin, without grace.[3] The contrary to this is

2. See Aristotle, Nicomachean Ethics, III, 8 (1117a 21).
3. See above, ch. 147.

apparent from the petition in the Psalm (70:9): "When my strength shall fail, do not Thou forsake me." And the Lord teaches us to pray: "And lead us not into temptation, but deliver us from evil."

[5] However, although those who are in sin cannot avoid by their own power putting an impediment in the way of grace, as we showed, unless they be helped in advance by grace, nevertheless, this is regarded as their fault, because this defect is left in them as a result of a previous fault. Thus, for example, an intoxicated man is not excused from homicide committed in the state of intoxication which he got into through his own fault.

[6] Besides, although he who is in sin does not have, of his own power, the ability entirely to avoid sin, he has it in his power at present to avoid this or that sin, as we said. Hence, whatever one he does commit, he does so voluntarily. And so, not undeservedly, he is held responsible for his fault.

Chapter 161.

THAT GOD FREES SOME MEN FROM SIN
AND LEAVES OTHERS IN SIN

[1] Now, although the man who sins puts an impediment in the way of grace, and as far as the order of things requires he ought not to receive grace, yet, since God can act apart from the order implanted in things,[1] as He does when He gives sight to the blind or life to the dead—at times, out of the abundance of His goodness, He offers His help in advance, even to those who put an impediment in the way of grace, turning them away from evil and toward the good. And just as He does not enlighten all the blind, or heal all who are infirm, in order that the working of His power may be evident in the case of those whom He heals, and in

1. See above, ch. 99.

the case of the others the order of nature may be observed, so also, He does not assist with His help all who impede grace, so that they may be turned away from evil and toward the good, but only some, in whom He desires His mercy to appear, so that the order of justice may be manifested in the other cases. Hence, the Apostle says, in Romans (9:22–23): "What if God, willing to show His wrath and to make His power known, endured with much patience vessels of wrath, fitted for destruction, that He might show the riches of His glory on the vessels of mercy which He hath prepared unto glory?"

[2]   However, while God does indeed, in regard to men who are held back by the same sins, come to the assistance of and convert some, while He suffers others or permits them to go ahead in accord with the order of things—there is no reason to ask why He converts the former and not the latter. For this depends on His will alone; just as it resulted from His simple will that, while all things were made from nothing, some were made of higher degree than others; and also, just as it depends on the simple will of the artisan that, from the same material uniformly disposed, he forms some vessels for noble uses and others for ignoble purposes. Hence, the Apostle says, in Romans (9:21): "Or hath not the potter power over the clay, of the same lump to make one vessel unto honor and another unto dishonor?"

[3]   By this we set aside the error of Origen, who said that certain men are converted to God, and not others, because of some works that their souls had done before being united to their bodies. In fact, this view has been carefully disproved in our Book Two.[2]

2. SCG, II, ch. 44 and 83ff. See also Origen, *Peri Archon*, II, 9 (*PG*, 11, col. 229).

Chapter 162.

THAT GOD IS NOT THE CAUSE OF SIN FOR ANY PERSON

[1]   Although God does not convert certain sinners to Himself, but leaves them in their sins according to their merits, He does not lead them into sinful action.

[2]   In fact, men sin because they turn away from Him Who is their ultimate end, as is evident from our earlier statements.[1] But, when every agent acts for an end that is proper and suitable to it, it is impossible by the action of God for any of them to be turned away from the ultimate end, Who is God. So, it is impossible for God to cause any persons to sin.

[3]   Again, good cannot be the cause of evil. But sin is an evil for man, since it is opposed to man's proper good which is to live in accord with reason. Therefore, it is impossible for God to be the cause of sinful action for anyone.

[4]   Besides, all wisdom and goodness in man are derived from the wisdom and goodness of God, as a certain likeness of Him. But it is incompatible with human wisdom and goodness to cause anyone to sin; much more, then, is it incompatible with these divine qualities.

[5]   Moreover, every sin stems from a defect in the proximate agent, and not from the influence of the primary agent: as the defect of limping results from the condition of the leg bone and not from the motor power, for, in fact, whatever perfection of motion is apparent in the act of limping, it is due to this power. But the proximate agent of human sin is the will. Therefore, the defect of sin comes from the will of man and not from God Who is the primary

1. See above, ch. 139 and 143.

agent; from Him, however, comes whatever pertains to perfection of action in the sinful act.

[6]   Hence, it is said in Ecclesiasticus (15:12): "Say not:
He hath caused me to err. For He hath no need of wicked
men." And later: "He hath commanded no man to do
wickedly, and He hath given no man license to sin"
(Ecclus. 15:21). And in James (1:13) it is said: "Let no
man, when he is tempted, say that he is tempted by God:
for God is not a tempter of evils."

[7]   However, some passages are found in Scripture from
which it seems that God is the cause of sinning for certain
men. Indeed, it is said in Exodus (10:1): "I have hardened
Pharao's heart, and the heart of his servants"; and in Isaias
(6:10): "Blind the heart of this people, and make their
ears heavy . . . lest they see with their eyes . . . and be
converted, and I heal them"; and in Isaias (63:17; Douay
modified): "Thou hast made us to err from Thy ways; Thou
hast hardened our heart, lest we fear Thee." Again, in
Romans (1:28) it is said: "God delivered them up to a
reprobate sense, to do those things which are not conven-
ient." All these texts are to be understood in this way: God
does not grant to some people His help in avoiding sin,
while to others He does grant it.

[8]   Moreover, this help is not only the infusing of grace,
but also external guardianship, whereby the occasions of
sinning are taken away from man by divine providence and
whereby provocations to sin are suppressed. God also helps
man in opposing sin by the natural light of reason and by
the other natural goods which He accords man. So, when He
takes away these aids from some, according to the merit of
their action, as His justice demands, He is said to harden or
to blind them, or to do any of the other things mentioned.

Chapter 163.

ON PREDESTINATION, REPROBATION, AND DIVINE ELECTION

[1] So, since we have shown[1] that some men are directed by divine working to their ultimate end as aided by grace, while others who are deprived of the same help of grace fall short of their ultimate end, and since all things that are done by God are foreseen and ordered from eternity by His wisdom, as we showed above,[2] the aforementioned differentiation of men must be ordered by God from eternity. According, then, as He has preordained some men from eternity, so that they are directed to their ultimate end, He is said to have *predestined* them. Hence, the Apostle says, in Ephesians (1:5): "Who hath predestinated us unto the adoption of children . . . according to the purpose of His will." On the other hand, those to whom He has decided from eternity not to give His grace He is said to have *reprobated* or to have *hated*, in accord with what we find in Malachias (1:2–3): "I have loved Jacob, but have hated Esau." By reason of this distinction, according to which He has reprobated some and predestined others, we take note of divine *election*, which is mentioned in Ephesians (1:4): "He chose us in Him, before the foundation of the world."

[2] Thus, it appears that predestination, election, and reprobation constitute a certain section of divine providence, according as men are ordered to their ultimate end by divine providence. Hence, it is possible to show that predestination and election impose no necessity, by the same reasoning whereby we showed above[3] that divine providence does not take away contingency from things.

1. See above, ch. 161.
2. See above, ch. 64.
3. See above, ch. 72.

[3]   Moreover, that predestination and election do not find
their cause in any human merits can be made clear, not only
from the fact that God's grace which is the effect of predestination is not preceded by merits but rather precedes
all human merits, as we showed,[4] but it can also be shown
from this, that the divine will and providence is the first
cause of things that are done, but that there can be no
cause of the divine will and providence,[5] although, among
the effects of providence, and likewise of predestination,
one may be the cause of another.

> "For who," as the Apostle says (Rom. 11:35–
> 36; Douay modified), "hath first given to
> Him, and who shall make recompense to
> Him? For of Him, and in Him, and by Him,
> are all things. To Him be honor and glory
> for ever. Amen."

4. See above, ch. 149.
5. SCG, I, ch. 87; III, ch. 97.

SUBJECT INDEX

Parts 1 and 2

INDEX OF PROPER NAMES

Parts 1 and 2